Accountants' Handbook

Handbook

Eleventh Edition
2008 Supplement

Update Service

BECOME A SUBSCRIBER!

Did you purchase this product from a bookstore?

If you did, it's important for you to become a subscriber. John Wiley & Sons, Inc. may publish, on a periodic basis, supplements and new editions to reflect the latest changes in the subject matter that you **need to know** in order to stay competitive in this ever-changing industry. By contacting the Wiley office nearest you, you'll receive any current update at no additional charge. In addition, you'll receive future updates and revised or related volumes on a 30-day examination review.

If you purchased this product directly from John Wiley & Sons, Inc., we have already recorded your subscription for this update service.

To become a subscriber, please call **1-877-762-2974** or send your name, company name (if applicable), address, and the title of the product to:

mailing address:	**Supplement Department**
	John Wiley & Sons, Inc.
	One Wiley Drive
	Somerset, NJ 08875
e-mail:	**subscriber@wiley.com**
fax:	**1-732-302-2300**

For customers outside the United States, please contact the Wiley office nearest you:

Professional & Reference Division
John Wiley & Sons Canada, Ltd.
22 Worcester Road
Etobicoke, Ontario M9W 1L1
CANADA
Phone: 416-236-4433
Phone: 1-800-567-4797
Fax: 416-236-4447
Email: canada@wiley.com

John Wiley & Sons Australia, Ltd.
33 Park Road
P.O. Box 1226
Milton, Queensland 4064
AUSTRALIA
Phone: 61-7-3859-9755
Fax: 61-7-3859-9715
Email: brisbane@johnwiley.com.au

John Wiley & Sons, Ltd.
The Atrium
Southern Gate, Chichester
West Sussex PO 19 8SQ
ENGLAND
Phone: 44-1243-779777
Fax: 44-1243-775878
Email: customer@wiley.co.uk

John Wiley & Sons (Asia) Pte., Ltd.
2 Clementi Loop #02-01
SINGAPORE 129809
Phone: 65-64632400
Fax: 65-64634604/5/6
Customer Service: 65-64604280
Email: enquiry@wiley.com.sg

ACCOUNTANTS' HANDBOOK

ELEVENTH EDITION

2008 SUPPLEMENT

LYNFORD GRAHAM

WILEY

John Wiley & Sons, Inc.

Library of Congress Cataloging-in-Publication Data:

ISBN 978-0-471-79041-9; ISBN 978-0-470-13577-8 (supplement)

Printed in the United States of America

10 9 8 7 6 5 4 3 2 1

ABOUT THE EDITOR

Lynford Graham, CPA, PhD, CFE is a Certified Public Accountant with more than 25 years of public accounting experience in audit practice and national policy development groups. He was a Partner and the Director of Audit Policy for BDO Seidman, LLP, and was a National Accounting & SEC Consulting Partner for Coopers & Lybrand, responsible for the technical issues research function and database, auditing research, audit automation, and audit sampling techniques. Prior to joining BDO Seidman LLP, Dr. Graham was an Associate Professor of Accounting and Information Systems and a Graduate Faculty Fellow at Rutgers University in Newark, New Jersey, where he taught primarily financial accounting courses. Dr. Graham is a member of the American Institute of Certified Public Accountants and a recent past member of the AICPA Auditing Standards Board. He is a Certified Fraud Examiner and a member of the Association of Certified Fraud Examiners. Throughout his career he has maintained an active profile in the academic as well as the business community. In 2002 he received the Distinguished Service Award of the Auditing Section of the AAA. His numerous academic and business publications span a variety of topical areas including information systems, internal controls, expert systems, audit risk, audit planning, fraud, sampling, analytical procedures, audit judgment, and international accounting and auditing. Dr. Graham holds an MBA in Industrial Management and PhD in Business and Applied Economics from the University of Pennsylvania (Wharton School).

ABOUT THE CONTRIBUTORS

Barry Jay Epstein, PhD, CPA, is a partner at Russell Novak & Company, LLP. With almost forty years' experience in the public accounting profession, as auditor and technical director/partner for several national and local firms, Dr. Epstein's current practice is concentrated on providing technical consultations to CPA firms and corporations on U.S. GAAP and IFRS accounting and financial reporting matters; on U.S. and international auditing standards; financial analysis; forensic accounting investigations; and corporate governance. A widely published authority on accounting and auditing, his current publications include *Wiley GAAP*, now in its 22nd edition, and *Wiley IFRS*, for both of which he is the lead coauthor. He previously chaired the Audit Committee of the AICPA's Board of Examiners, responsible for the Uniform CPA Examination, and has served on other professional panels at state and national levels. Dr. Epstein holds degrees from DePaul University (Chicago—BSC, accounting and finance, 1967) University of Chicago (MBA, economics and industrial relations, 1969), and University of Pittsburgh (PhD, information systems and finance, 1979).

Christopher J. Leisner, CPA, CMC, is founder of Creative IP Solutions, LLC, an intellectual property consulting firm that specializes in managing and monetizing intellectual property for a diverse domestic and international client base, from Fortune 100 companies to privately held companies. A speaker at several IP management and patent securitization conferences, Mr. Leisner has authored several articles and white papers on IP value extraction techniques, and has served as an expert witness on accounting malpractice, fraud, and damages. He was previously Midwest Partner in Charge of Litigation Consulting Services and Regional Business Line Leader for Specialty Consulting Services at BDO Seidman, LLP. A certified management consultant, Mr. Leisner has assisted clients in resolving various business issues relating to strategic planning, equity and debt financing, mergers and acquisitions support, management reporting systems, and internal control procedures.

Cynthia Pon, CPA has over 15 years of professional experience providing auditing, accounting, and consulting services to the private and public sectors. She leads the San Francisco Bay Area public sector assurance practice of Macias Gini & O'Connell LLP (MGO), bringing extensive experience in federal, state, and local financial and compliance auditing. Cindy is experienced in the application of governmental GAAP and has been recognized by the Governmental Accounting Standards Board for her leadership in assisting large California governments with early implementation of its standards. Cindy also serves on the Government Finance Officers Association Special Review Committee for Comprehensive Annual Financial Report awards and has instructed numerous governmental clients on a variety of audit issues and challenges.

Ernie Gini is a Partner with Macias Gini & O'Connell LLP (MGO) with 33 years of experience as a CPA. Recognized in the field of governmental and nonprofit accounting, Ernie was appointed to the 2006–2007 AICPA Virtual Grassroots Panel, formerly known as the Group of 100. Ernie is a Certified Government Financial Manager by the Association of Government Accountants and has conducted seminars for public finance officials on the New Financial Reporting Model (GASB 34), Changes to OMB Circular A-133, Accounting for Redevelopment Agencies, Single Audit Applications, Changes in Government Auditing Standards, GASB Statement Updates, Program-Specific Audits, and other topics. Ernie also served on the GASB Advisory Committee in preparation of the *User Guide to Local Government Financial Statements* and was a contributor to *What You Should Know about Your Local Government's Finances, A Guide to Financial Statements.*

Jae K. Shim, PhD, is a professor of accounting and finance at California State University, Long Beach, and CEO of Delta Consulting Company, a financial consulting and training firm. Dr. Shim received his MBA and PhD degrees from the University of California at Berkeley (Haas School of Business). He has been a consultant to commercial and nonprofit organizations for over 30 years. Dr. Shim has also published numerous articles in professional and academic journals and has over 50 college and professional books to his credit.

Kevin J. O'Connell, CPA is the Managing Partner of Macias Gini & O'Connell LLP (MGO), a leading California certified public accounting and consulting firm. He has over 15 years of experience in federal, state, and local financial compliance auditing at all levels of government including California's largest cities and counties and governmental component organizations in the airport, mass transit, utilities, and health care industries. Kevin has served on the AICPA State and Local Government Expert Panel and contributed to the AICPA guide *Audits of State and Local Governments (GASB 34 Edition).* In 2007, Kevin was recognized by *CPA Technology Advisor* magazine as one of the nation's top 40 tax and accounting professionals under the age of 40 who will help lead the professions of public accounting and professional tax preparation into the future.

CONTENTS

Note to the Reader: Sections not in the main bound volume, *Accountants' Handbook Eleventh Edition* (978-0-471-79041-9), are indicated by "(New)" after the title. Material from the main bound volume that has been updated for *this* supplement is indicated by "(Revised)" after the title.

PREFACE

This is the first supplement to the 11th edition of the Accountant's Handbook. Annual updates to this work provide important revisions and new topics that update the Handbook between editions. In addition, feedback suggests additional topical areas that are of interest to our readers. We are pleased to expand the Handbook to include those topical areas of significant interest. This supplement brings forward two chapters that were scheduled to be included in the published 11th edition. In addition, it introduces a new set of experienced authors for and a revision of the very important chapter on State and Local Government Accounting—Chapter 34.

Chapter 20: Goodwill and Other Intangible Assets includes a comprehensive examination of all current accounting literature bearing on the financial reporting of intangible assets, with a new emphasis on the intellectual property rights that are increasingly the foundation for business operations. Among the complex matters given expanded attention are determinations of useful economic lives, the handling of research and development costs, and accounting for such intangible assets as patents, royalty and license agreements, goodwill, and specialized industry accounting rules. The impact of Sarbanes-Oxley on governance matters pertaining to intangible assets is also addressed.

Chapter 34: State and Local Government Accounting is a revision of the 11th edition chapter. In the last decade there have been significant changes in accounting for State and Local Government entities and this has been a significant period of activity for the Governmental Accounting Standards Board. The further emphasis on accrual accounting and financial reporting that focuses on the stewardship and responsibility aspects of government accounting make this topic both interesting and important and one of potentially fast-breaking change. The new authors of this chapter are particularly well qualified to address the contemporary, fast-moving environment and we welcome them to the Accountants' Handbook.

Chapter 50: Cost-Volume-Revenue Analysis for Nonprofit Organizations. Ideally, breaking even is a potential targeted goal of a nonprofit organization. If you generate a surplus over a number of periods, donors or funding agents may question your need for the funds, and they may be curtailed. On the other hand, operating at a long-term deficit, the nonprofit may become insolvent or unable to perform the desired level of services. It is a delicate balancing act. Cost-volume-revenue (CVR) analysis, together with cost behavior information and budgeting, can assist nonprofit managers in performing many useful planning analyses. By studying the relationships of costs, service volume, and revenue, nonprofit management is better able to understand the implications of many planning decisions. The chapter discusses this useful technique.

ACCOUNTANTS' HANDBOOK

ELEVENTH EDITION

FINANCIAL ACCOUNTING AND GENERAL TOPICS

GOODWILL AND OTHER INTANGIBLE ASSETS: AN UPDATE[1] (NEW)

BARRY JAY EPSTEIN, PHD, CPA
Russell Novak & Company LLP
CHRISTOPHER J. LEISNER, CPA, CMC
Creative IP Solutions LLC

---

1. Portions of this chapter originally appeared in Chapter 20, "Goodwill and Other Intangible Assets," written by Lailani Moody, CPA, MBA, of Grant Thornton LLP. This entire chapter also appeared in the 2006 Cumulative Supplement to the *Accountants' Handbook*, Tenth Edition.

20A.1 CHARACTERIZATION OF INTANGIBLE ASSETS

Intangible assets are assets—other than financial assets—that lack physical substance yet do have utility and value in the hands of the reporting entity. Examples include patents, copyrights, trade names, customer lists, royalty agreements, databases, and computer software. They also include the assets called leasehold improvements, which are frequently but mistakenly viewed as being tangible assets.

The range of intangibles is quite broad, and this fact is perhaps more clearly understood now than during earlier years, since changing business and economic conditions have brought intellectual property and certain other intangible assets to much greater prominence than had formerly been the case. While for many mostly traditional (e.g., manufacturing) businesses the value of intangibles may still be underappreciated, for high-technology and other so-called knowledge-based companies, the primary assets may be intangible ones such as patents and copyrights. Even for professional services firms, the key assets may be "soft" resources such as knowledge bases and client relationships.

There are several possible taxonomies of intangible assets. First, intangible assets can be classified either as *identifiable*—for example, trademarks and most other intangibles—or as *unidentifiable*, which generally implies goodwill. A second way to classify intangible assets is based on how they are acquired. They can be internally developed or acquired from external sources, which include both simple purchases of one or more intangibles (e.g., groups of related patents) or those that are part of business combinations. Intangible assets acquired in a business combination may be recognized as assets separate from goodwill or as part of goodwill, depending on whether the intangible assets satisfy certain criteria. As discussed in this chapter, the applicable accounting pronouncements and accounting requirements differ significantly, depending on whether the intangible asset is identifiable, whether it is internally developed or acquired externally, and, if acquired externally, whether it was acquired in a business combination.

Yet other classification schemes for intangible assets were first offered by the now superseded Accounting Principles Board (APB) Opinion No. 17, which indicated that intangible assets could also be categorized based on either

1. Expected period of benefit—whether limited by law or contract, related to human or economic factors, or indefinite or indeterminate duration; or
2. Separability from an entire enterprise—rights transferable without title, salable, or inseparable from the enterprise or a substantial part of it.

While all of the foregoing taxonomies assist one in thinking about intangibles and are to a greater or lesser extent incorporated into current generally accepted accounting principles (GAAP) (primarily SFAS No. 142), perhaps the most important distinctions are between intangibles acquired in business combinations accounted for under SFAS No. 141 or otherwise; between those having finite lives and those having indefinite lives; and between those that are severable from the reporting entity and those that are not. All of these matters are addressed in this chapter.

20A.2   ACCOUNTING AND FINANCIAL MANAGEMENT OVERVIEW

Numerous pronouncements provide guidance on the accounting for intangibles. This section provides an overview of those pronouncements.

(a) INTANGIBLE ASSETS INCLUDING GOODWILL ACQUIRED IN A BUSINESS COMBINATION   Under SFAS No. 141, "Business Combinations," all business combinations must now be accounted for as purchases; pooling accounting is no longer permitted. This necessitates purchase-price allocation. It provides initial measurement and recognition guidance for intangible assets and goodwill acquired in a business combination, including mandates as to the recognition of intangible assets apart from goodwill.

Subsequent accounting for intangible assets, including goodwill, is provided in SFAS No. 142, "Goodwill and Other Intangible Assets." SFAS No. 142 provides that goodwill should not be amortized; it mandates that impairment tests of goodwill be conducted annually or, in some circumstances, more frequently; and it provides guidance on recognizing impairments. In contrast with earlier GAAP, which required amortization of all intangibles, SFAS No. 142 addresses whether intangible assets other than goodwill have *indefinite* useful lives and therefore should not be amortized but instead tested at least annually for impairment, or *finite* useful lives and therefore should be amortized over their estimated useful lives.

Intangible assets with finite useful lives are tested for impairment under SFAS No. 144, "Accounting for the Impairment or Disposal of Long-Lived Assets." Intangibles that have finite lives and thus are amortized must also be reviewed for recoverability of carrying amounts in a process similar to that under SFAS No. 144, and useful lives must be reassessed and altered when warranted by circumstances (e.g., technological obsolescence making the useful life of a patent much shorter than the legal term).

(b) INTANGIBLE ASSETS ACQUIRED SEPARATELY OR WITH OTHER ASSETS   SFAS No. 142 provides initial recognition and measurement guidance for intangible assets acquired other than in a business combination—that is, intangible assets acquired individually or together with a group of other assets that do not constitute a business. SFAS No. 142 also provides guidance to the subsequent accounting for intangible assets, including determining whether they have finite or indeterminate useful lives and therefore whether they should be amortized or not. Finally, it addresses accounting for impairments of intangible assets with indeterminate lives. A separate standard, SFAS No. 144, provides guidance on impairment of intangible assets with finite useful lives.

(c) INTERNALLY DEVELOPED INTANGIBLE ASSETS SFAS No. 142 addresses the initial and subsequent accounting for internally developed intangible assets. It carries forward the requirement set forth by the predecessor standard, APB No. 17, that the costs of internally developing, maintaining, or restoring intangibles that cannot be identified specifically, have indeterminate lives, or are inherent in an ongoing business and pertain to the entity as a whole cannot be capitalized. Such costs must be expensed currently as incurred.

(d) INTANGIBLE ASSETS RECOGNIZED ON ACQUISITION OF A NONCONTROLLING INTEREST IN A SUBSIDIARY SFAS No. 142 provides guidance on the initial and subsequent accounting for goodwill and other intangible assets recognized on acquisition of noncontrolling interests in a subsidiary. Under current GAAP, goodwill associated with minority (i.e., noncontrolling) interests is not recognized. Note, however, that the Financial Accounting Standards Board (FASB) is currently considering a major change in purchase-business combination accounting that will, if adopted, result in the recognition of goodwill associated with minority interests.

(e) GOODWILL RECOGNIZED WHEN APPLYING THE EQUITY METHOD SFAS No. 142 provides that amounts recognized as corresponding to goodwill in applying the equity method accounting to investments should not be amortized. Equity method goodwill is tested for impairment under APB Opinion No. 18, "The Equity Method of Accounting for Investments in Common Stock."

(f) SPECIFIC GUIDANCE ON CERTAIN INTANGIBLES Accounting pronouncements, such as Statements of Position issued by the Accounting Standards Executive Committee of the American Institute of Certified Public Accountants (AICPA), provide guidance on the accounting for specific intangible assets, such as start-up costs, internally developed software, and advertising. These matters are addressed subsequently.

(g) INTANGIBLE ASSETS IN SPECIALIZED INDUSTRIES Certain FASB Statements and Interpretations provide guidance on accounting for certain intangibles of specialized industries, such as airlines and computer software development. Impairment testing for intangible assets in many specialized industries is performed under the general requirements (SFAS No. 144), but for certain industries or assets, such as broadcasters' program rights, guidance under particular AICPA Industry Audit and Accounting Guides must be followed instead.

(h) THE NEW EMPHASIS ON MANAGEMENT OF INTANGIBLE ASSETS
(i) Sarbanes-Oxley Act of 2002—Implications for the Financial Reporting of Intangible Assets Sound financial and operating management of reporting entities has always been a critical concern, of course, but developments in the early 2000s have caused renewed emphasis on managements' and directors' fiduciary duties, including the duty to maximize the value of all assets under management. The widely reported corporate management and financial

reporting scandals of the late 1990s, in particular, created a groundswell of demand for reforms in corporate governance practices. Among other things, this led to the hurried passage by Congress of the Sarbanes-Oxley Act of 2002 ("Sarbanes" or "the Act"), the ramifications of which are still being comprehended.

Sarbanes has generated a considerable amount of interest in, and focus on, the quality of financial reporting and the reliability of internal control systems. The widely publicized and sometimes controversial Section 404 requirements for reporting on the effectiveness of internal controls, certified by both management and the entity's independent accountants, has been a costly and demanding undertaking for many companies, including some whose quality of controls and financial management were previously unquestioned by investors.

Sarbanes has also highlighted the historically troublesome disparity between corporate managers and shareholders regarding many entities' true financial condition, which is sometimes referred to as the "transparency" issue. GAAP-basis financial reporting is based on a "mixed-attribute" model that combines historical costs and current fair values, with some costs subject to amortization and others only sporadically tested for impairment, making financial statements often unsuited for directly assessing the reporting entity's value. Because intangible assets now account for the majority of many publicly traded companies' stock values (by some estimates, as much as two-thirds), and because accounting for intangibles has been largely overlooked in the accounting pronouncements and literature, this area is now overdue for much greater attention. The demand for greater transparency has increased the pressure on accountants to develop the means to more fully report the value of intangible assets of the companies they manage, report, and/or opine on.

When the 2002 Sarbanes requirements are evaluated in conjunction with the 2001 FASB pronouncements regarding goodwill, intangibles, and business combinations (SFAS Nos. 141 and 142), it is clear that today's accountants (both internal staff and outside auditors) must increase their awareness of the intangible assets a company possesses and the value those assets bring to the company, which may in part be driven by the potential value those assets may hold for other entities. Even the SEC now recognizes that the way in which intangible assets are accounted for, as well as which valuation method is employed, can have a material effect on investors' decisions (see discussion by SEC staff on "market participation" valuation requirements in Section 20A.3(a)(ii)).

For example, when the accountant considers how off–balance-sheet transactions may impact (either negatively or positively) the financial condition of a company, intangible assets will be, in many instances, a likely asset class to inspect and analyze. Section 401(a) of the Act directed the SEC to enact rules so that

> [E]ach annual and quarterly report required to be filed with the Commission shall disclose all material off–balance-sheet transactions, arrangements, obligations (including contingent obligations), and other relationships of the issuer with unconsolidated entities or other persons, that may have a material current or future effect on financial condition, changes in financial condition, results of operations, liquidity, capital expenditures, capital resources, or significant components of revenues or expenses.

In its rules (Final Rule: Disclosure in Management's Discussion and Analysis about Off–Balance-Sheet Arrangements and Aggregate Contractual Obligations, effective April 7, 2003), the SEC mandated that registrants provide explanations of off–balance-sheet arrangements in separately captioned subsections of the so-called Management Discussion and Analysis (MD&A)

section of their periodic filings with the Commission. While certain of these disclosures were already required under MD&A rules, the new requirements are somewhat more comprehensive. These rules do not, however, alter underlying accounting for or disclosures about owned intangible assets, nor do they alter the accounting, under GAAP, for transfers or sales of such assets.

The SEC rule does require that executory contracts, such as purchase obligations for goods or services, be included in a new tabular presentation of off–balance-sheet obligations, which is at variance with GAAP requirements but deemed to be important because of liquidity implications. In the case of a license arrangement (e.g., for patent rights previously sold), disclosure in the MD&A under this rule would be appropriate, even though the obligation is not a liability under GAAP definitions.

(ii) Improved Internal Controls over Intangible Assets under Sarbanes   In Section 404(a), the Act addresses a new requirement for management to prepare an internal control report that shall

(1)   state the responsibility of management for establishing and maintaining an adequate internal control structure and procedures for financial reporting and

(2)   contain an assessment, as of the end of the most recent fiscal year of the issuer, of the effectiveness of the internal control structure and procedures of the issuer for financial reporting.

As discussed previously, SFAS Nos. 141 and 142 require revised accounting for intangibles and goodwill arising from business combinations. Similarly, as a company generates new intellectual property through innovation, invention, or operational insights, it may be necessary to establish new accounting procedures to measure the carrying value and fair value of an acquired reporting unit (and perhaps existing reporting units), including the value of intangibles.

Both the cost to create and the cost to protect intangibles are measured and reported in the financial statements, either as an expense (if properly considered research and development costs under GAAP) or as capital assets. In general, due to SFAS No. 2's strict requirements, most of the cost of patent or other intellectual property development, if internally accomplished, will be expensed—one reason that GAAP-compliant financial reporting sometimes underserves entities that rely on intellectual property for their operations and valuation.

An important concern, then, is that if these assets are largely missing from the financial statements, how can these entities ensure that fiduciary responsibilities relative to these hidden assets are properly discharged? There are at least two aspects to this concern: first, developing and implementing internal controls over these assets such that the requirements of Sarbanes will be met; and second, that the value of these assets is recognized for the benefit of the shareholders.

An axiom in management is that what is not measured is not managed; a corollary to that is that what is not in plain sight is also likely not to be well managed. The relatively trivial carrying values of intellectual property often can result in undermanagement, meaning a failure to manage these assets for the benefit of shareholders, whether by using them more effectively internally or by seeking external sources of income from these intangible assets.

As part of a comprehensive effort to establish meaningful controls over their intangible assets, entities should consider developing metrics that would raise the profile of both the holdings of intangibles and of the productivity derived therefrom. Productivity measures would address (as appropriate) both internal usage and external revenue generation. When such internal control procedures are devised and monitored, compliance with this section of Sarbanes would seem to have been accomplished.

(iii) Practical Approaches to Internal Control Structures for Intangible Assets   The authors propose the following approach to the fabrication of an internal control structure used to capture, measure, and report the presence and value of intangible assets. This can be accomplished by assisting personnel in the legal, research, and/or technology transfer departments to establish the appropriate record-keeping and asset-control procedures. Those procedures would relate to documenting the creation, acquisition, and disposal of intellectual assets. Such documentation could include data about the specific identity of the asset; correspondence with appropriate patent, trademark, or copyright offices; ownership and/or assignments; estimated useful lives; associated costs to acquire or create; and, when appropriate, market values.

It is potentially the case that in-house and/or outside counsel may be aware of existing third-party claims that could be asserted against the company, as well as claims the company may be able to assert against third parties. Such analyses may already be in process by the tech-transfer and/or legal staff as part of their normal process of selecting what technologies to outlicense or protect through an infringement action. They may also be in possession of demand letters from other entities that are asserting claims based on their intellectual assets.

Accounting for such claims may also suggest that a review of the company's various insurance policies, vendor and customer contracts, and licensing agreements might be warranted. Because the accountant is typically required under SFAS No. 5 to assess the likelihood that a loss event will occur and whether the estimated loss amounts can be reasonably determined, this should be a routine procedure. Under SFAS No. 5, however, indemnification and insurance provisions may give rise to a recovery claim, but this cannot be offset.

As part of an assessment of the company's disclosure controls it may be helpful to prepare documentation procedures throughout the life cycle of the intangible asset. If the company is International Organization for Standardization (ISO)-compliant, much of the key information regarding intangibles may already be documented relating to

1. Creation and acquisition identification of the intangible asset
2. Applicable filings and prosecution of applications to obtain a formal or registered intellectual property right for the intangible asset
3. Encumbrances to ownership rights, including licensing and assignments that may narrow or eliminate rights for the intangible asset
4. Maintenance of the asset, such as repair and upkeep or the payment of appropriate registration fees
5. Outlicensing and/or cross-licensing agreements
6. Infringement claims against and/or by third parties regarding the intangible asset
7. Disposal, retirement, or expiration of the asset

An additional reference to assist accountants to structure internal control procedures is the guidance presented in the AICPA toolkit, *The Fair Value Measurement Valuation Toolkit for Financial Accounting Standards Board Statements of Financial Accounting Standards No. 141, Business Combinations, and No. 142, Goodwill and Other Intangible Assets.*

Much of the foregoing is directed toward maintaining a current record of the existence of intangible assets and various agreements, such as licensing arrangements. Another aspect, and one vital to the goal of maximizing shareholder wealth, is to address those actions that are not currently being taken but that could be valuable for the enterprise and its various stakeholders. Doing this requires that external data sources be incorporated into the entity's information system. Without external references, poor performance may be misread as good simply because of an improvement over prior periods.

One cited statistic, for example, is that each patent in existence (circa 2000) was producing an average of $60,000 in licensing revenues per year, or about $1,000,000 over its economic life. Information about the average licensing revenue per patent is an external metric that can be used to evaluate the entity's own licensing portfolio. Over time, such analyses can be used to gauge portfolio trends, to show whether the licensing revenue of the patent portfolio is acceptable versus expected licensing revenues, based on statistical averages. If not, an investigation can be focused to determine why not. This control mechanism is fully consistent with the explicit requirements and implicit objectives of Sarbanes.

This type of information also sets out a framework for an internal metric. The licensing revenue per patent can be determined for a company patent portfolio. An average licensing revenue can be determined and tracked over time. Patents that are underperforming can be reviewed to ascertain whether these should be preserved for commercial purposes other than licensing, or whether they should be sold or abandoned. Trend data can be accumulated over time to report on whether the portfolio is underperforming based on internally set expectations.

Some examples of metrics that can be used to evaluate an intellectual property (IP) program include the number of patents or patent applications owned by type (utility or design), by country, by the royalty income received from each patent, and by an average royalty for each type of patent or type of technology. Patents owned should include all patents to which the company has unimpaired title. (Title would be deemed impaired if the reporting entity is not the sole assignee.) The dollar value of sales for products covered by the patents is another metric that permits such evaluations of a patent portfolio or IP program.

20A.3 INITIAL RECOGNITION AND MEASUREMENT OF INTANGIBLE ASSETS

(a) ACQUIRED INTANGIBLE ASSETS   SFAS No. 142, Goodwill and Other Intangible Assets, issued in June 2001, superseded the former standard, APB Opinion No. 17, Intangible Assets. It uses the term *intangible assets* to refer to intangible assets other than goodwill. While amortization is no longer universally required, as it had been for more than 30 years under APB No. 17, SFAS No. 142 did carry forward certain of the requirements of that former standard.

(i) Cost Allocation and Other Valuation Issues   An intangible asset acquired either individually or with a group of other assets—other than as part of a business combination—is initially recognized and measured based on its fair value. The cost of a group of assets acquired in a transaction other than a business combination is allocated to the individual assets acquired based on their relative fair values and cannot result in the recognition of goodwill.

Intangible assets acquired in a business combination are initially recognized and measured in conformity with SFAS No. 141—that is, via the purchase price allocation process, which is based on fair values or—for goodwill only—represents the residual cost of the acquisition. Goodwill can arise only in connection with purchase accounting for business combinations. So-called *negative goodwill* is not included in the definition of goodwill as discussed in this chapter. (Under SFAS No. 141, any excess of fair value of net assets acquired over the cost of a business combination is recognized in earnings immediately.)

(ii) SEC/PCAOB Valuation Issues for Intangible Assets—More Changes, Greater Confusion on the Horizon   In unofficial remarks before the December 2004 AICPA National Conference on Current SEC and PCAOB Developments, a staff member of the SEC's Office of the Chief Accountant explained why fair value, determined by using the actual amounts negotiated by the buyer and seller (referred to below as "entity specific") would be superseded by an "estimated" fair value based on an analysis from a "marketplace participant" perspective. In these remarks, it was stated that

> An underpinning to the determination of fair value of an acquired intangible asset under SFAS No. 141 is that it is determined from the perspective of a marketplace participant.

This is clear in SFAS No. 141, paragraph B174, which indicates that the fair value estimate

> should incorporate assumptions that marketplace participants would use in making estimates of fair value, such as assumptions about future contract renewals and other benefits such as those that might result from acquisition-related synergies . . ."
> In contrast, the useful life concept in SFAS No. 142 is not necessarily viewed from that of a marketplace participant. Rather the useful life of an intangible asset is inherently related to the expectations of the particular entity and therefore would incorporate entity specific assumptions.
>
> In this context, the entity may believe that the fair value determination should therefore be entirely consistent with the useful life then assigned to the intangible asset as in this case, both were developed based on entity specific assumptions.
>
> I would point out, however, that the utilization of entity specific assumptions to determine fair value in this case is just a proxy for those assumptions that may be developed by a marketplace participant.

Subsequent to these remarks the FASB issued an Exposure Draft of SFAS No. 141(R) (June 2005), which in many particulars is based on an analysis of international accounting standards. At paragraph 20, proposed SFAS No. 141(R) seeks to clarify the definition of fair value for a business combination when it states:

> Business combinations are usually arm's-length exchange transactions in which knowledgeable, unrelated willing parties exchange equal values. Therefore, in the absence of evidence to the contrary, the exchange price (referred to as the consideration transferred in this Statement) paid by the acquirer on the acquisition date is presumed to be the best evidence of the acquisition date fair value of the acquirer's interest in the acquiree.

The SEC remarks and the FASB exposure draft provisions are indicative of a changing landscape of the acceptable valuation methodologies and technical experts to whom the accountant can turn for support when computing an intangible's fair value.

FASB Concept Statement No. 7 was identified in SFAS No. 142, issued in 2002, as guidance for valuation methodologies, principally citing the comparables and income method approaches. However, intangible asset values measured in actual business transactions are often based more on expected and potential benefits rather than on historical and/or actual revenues. Therefore, the application of the income approach requires a stacking or layering of assumptions. As the number of those assumptions increases, compliance with Rule 201 of the AICPA *Code of Professional Conduct* (specifically concerning the reliance on sufficient relevant data in support of any professional opinion) becomes more and more difficult.

There are real-world situations in which technical experts from other disciplines have addressed the situation of determining the fair value of intangibles where historical cash flows do not exist. One of those situations arises during the dispute resolution process, and a second is seen in the technology-transfer industry.

(iii) Valuation Approaches Supported by Court Opinions In the federal courts, a jury is frequently asked to estimate the damages attributable to a violation of intellectual property rights. Several cases, including *Georgia Pacific v. United States Plywood Corp.* and *Panduit Corp. v. Stahlin Bros. Fibre Works, Inc.,* have compiled a technical body of knowledge regarding methodologies to determine the fair value of intangible assets. For example, *Panduit* sets forth these four tests:

1. Is there demand for the patented product?
2. Are there acceptable noninfringing alternatives to the infringing product?
3. Does the patent holder have the manufacturing and marketing capacity to make and sell more of the product?
4. Can the damages consultant quantify the lost profits to a reasonable degree of certainty?

In the earlier *Georgia-Pacific* case, the court considered 15 factors as a means to compute damages arising from a dispute over intangible assets:

1. The royalties received by Georgia-Pacific for licensing the patent, proving or tending to prove an established royalty
2. The rates paid by the licensee for the use of other similar patents
3. The nature and scope of the license, such as whether it is exclusive or nonexclusive, restricted or nonrestricted in terms of territory or customers
4. Georgia-Pacific's policy of maintaining its patent monopoly by licensing the use of the invention only under special conditions designed to preserve the monopoly
5. The commercial relationship between Georgia-Pacific and licensees, such as whether they are competitors in the same territory in the same line of business or whether they are inventor and promoter
6. The effect of selling the patented specialty in promoting sales of other Georgia-Pacific products; the existing value of the invention to Georgia-Pacific as a generator of sales of nonpatented items; and the extent of such derivative or "convoyed" sales
7. The duration of the patent and the term of the license
8. The established profitability of the patented product, its commercial success, and its current popularity
9. The utility and advantages of the patent property over any old modes or devices that had been used
10. The nature of the patented invention, its character in the commercial embodiment owned and produced by the licensor, and the benefits to those who have used it
11. The extent to which the infringer used the invention and any evidence probative of the value of that use
12. The portion of the profit or selling price that is customary in the particular business or in comparable businesses

13. The portion of the realizable profit that should be credited to the invention as distinguished from any nonpatented elements, manufacturing process, business risks, or significant features or improvements added by the infringer

14. The opinion testimony of qualified experts

15. The amount that Georgia-Pacific and a licensee would have agreed upon at the time the infringement began if they had reasonably and voluntarily tried to reach an agreement

In a subsequent case based in part on the *Panduit* findings, the courts have held that damages based on a loss of market share can be used to compute damages (*State Industries, Inc. v. Mor-Flo Industries, Inc.*). In *State Industries,* the Federal Circuit accepted evidence of the patentee's market share to prove that the patentee would have made at least a percentage of the infringer's sales had there been no infringement. Quantifying market share allows the patentee to measure lost profits in the ratio of their original market share to their diluted market share after the infringement.

In these cases and several others, the courts have held that intellectual property owners may be entitled to lost profits that can never be realized (hence the claim for "lost" profits), but were nonetheless measured to "a reasonable degree of accounting certainty."

(iv) Valuation Approaches Used by Tech-Transfer Practitioners   Taking a page from the dispute resolution practitioners, several technology transfer specialists (also referred to as licensing professionals) have adopted market-based measures of value. Here, however, rather than measure the amount of damages, the computation is made for the purpose of measuring the amount of benefits that would be recognized by the adoption of the licensor's technology by the licensee. In 2002 Ted Hagelin analyzed different concepts and methods of valuation, including the cost, market, and income methods.[2] Other valuation methods developed especially for intellectual property law were also examined, including the "25 percent" rule, industry standards, ranking, surrogate measures, disaggregation, Monte Carlo, and option methods. In his article, Professor Hagelin presents a newly devised tech-transfer valuation model labeled "Competitive Advantage Valuation" and suggests that

> The . . . premise of the CAV [Competitive Advantage Valuation] method is that the value of a given intellectual property asset can best be measured by the competitive advantage which that asset contributes.

When one incorporates this tech-transfer CAV approach with the previously cited assertion by SEC staff that "market-participant" value drivers must be considered under SFAS Nos. 141 and 142, it becomes obvious that there are multiple, well-established, fully vetted intangible asset valuation approaches that accounting practitioners can employ when answering the question, "What are the values of these intangible assets?"

(v) Valuation Approaches Seen in Wall Street Transactions   An additional market validation of the alignment of these various intangible asset valuation approaches is found in the

---

2.   Ted Hagelin, "A New Method to Value Intellectual Property,"*American Intellectual Property Law Association Quarterly Journal*, Vol. 30, p. 33.

emergence of numerous intellectual asset-based transactions on Wall Street. One of the most familiar transactions seen in the entertainment and garment industries is the securitization of anticipated intangible asset-based revenues, as reflected in the Bowie Bond (David Bowie) and Bill Blass securitizations.

Another example is the adaptation of the traditional lending structure known as a sale lease-back (used for tangible assets) that has been deployed using intangible assets and has been referred to as a sale/license-back. In a presentation to the National Knowledge and Intellectual Property Management Taskforce's annual executive briefing in September 2002, Mitchell Fillet, of Riderwood Group, Inc., stated that

> We are in the midst of a paradigm shift that is so economically powerful that it ranks with the other two that have defined our economic history. . . .
> I am suggesting that intellectual property, primarily patents and derivative products from those patents, as well as licenses to use that intellectual property is emerging as an important asset class both on corporate balance sheets and off them, as collateral for loans and legally separate securitizations.

As a result of the sale/license-back structure, intangible assets are now being acquired by large investment banking firms, much as mortgage portfolios were acquired starting in the 1970s, thus giving birth to a highly liquid market for what had previously been difficult-to-trade assets. As such, the value drivers associated with intangible assets now reflect several of the financial modeling aspects found in commercial paper and various asset-backed securitizations.

As evidence of the importance such intangible assets have, and the market-based impact they can make, we can review the Federal Reserve Chairman's October 2005 comments on this market built on intangibles, citing the significant economic benefits to the U.S. economy of the secondary market launched in the mid-1970s:

> These increasingly complex financial instruments have contributed to the development of a far more flexible, efficient, and hence resilient financial system than the one that existed just a quarter-century ago. After the bursting of the stock market bubble in 2000, unlike previous periods following large financial shocks, no major financial institution defaulted, and the economy held up far better than many had anticipated.[3]

To gain an understanding about how intangible assets account for such significant market values, the accounting of a sale/license-back transaction can be reviewed; both the buyer and the seller in this transaction recognize distinct benefits.

From the seller's position, the closing would generate significant pretax earnings, as the only significant offset to sales price paid for internally generated intangibles would be the transaction fees (attorneys, financial consultants, valuation experts) and any unamortized capitalized cost of the underlying assets. In the sale/license-back structure, the attributes of the intangible assets permit the transaction to unleash earnings (unlike the sale/lease-back that was treated as a financing), principally because title to the intangible asset is transferred to the buyer.

---

3. Alan Greenspan, speech on economic flexibility, presented before the National Italian American Foundation, Washington, D.C., October 12, 2005.

Additionally, any license-back provision would qualify as a fully deductible expense for tax purposes. Unlike the sale/lease-back of a tangible asset, which is governed by SFAS No. 13, the "license" in a sale/license-back is a period expense and not debt; the license is consumed in the period in which the expense is incurred. Such accounting treatment suggests that the seller's cost of capital would be reduced to the extent that the proceeds from the sale are used to reduce bank or other outstanding debt, thereby deleveraging the balance sheet.

From the buyer's perspective, intangible assets with measurable, market-based value (presumably from outlicensing potential) can be selectively acquired, without incurring all of the fixed and sunk costs attributed to a research and development facility. Generally speaking, the licensing activity of a large corporation enjoys a greater contribution margin than the company taken as a whole. Additionally, the operating costs would be partially offset by the license granted to the seller, and the intangible assets acquired would be treated as an amortizable asset.

(vi) Identifiable Intangibles Distinguishable from Goodwill   SFAS No. 141 provides that intangible assets acquired in a business combination are to be recognized as an asset *apart from goodwill,* but only if they meet the asset recognition criteria in the FASB's Statement of Financial Accounting Concept No. 5 (CON 5), *and* if either (1) control over the future economic benefits of the assets results from contractual or other legal rights (the "legal/ contractual" criterion) or (2) the intangible assets are capable of being separated or divided and sold, transferred, licensed, rented, or exchanged (referred to as the separability criterion). Even if the intangible assets cannot be sold, transferred, licensed, rented, or exchanged individually, the assets would still meet the separability criterion if they could be sold, transferred, licensed, rented, or exchanged along with a related contract, asset, or liability.

Examples of intangible assets that meet the "legal/contractual" criterion include trademarks, newspaper mastheads, Internet domain names, order backlog, books, magazines, musical works, license agreements, construction permits, broadcast rights, mortgage servicing contracts, patented technology, and computer software. Examples of assets that meet the separability criterion include customer lists, noncontractual customer relationships, unpatented technology, and databases such as title plants. Note that it is not necessary for the acquiring entity to actually intend to dispose of, sell, or rent the separable intangible in order to satisfy this criterion.

SFAS No. 141 presents a lengthy listing of intangibles that are to be separately recognized, along with the useful lives relevant for amortization purposes. Certain exceptions are identified, such as for those intangibles having indefinite lives, as is the case for perpetually renewable broadcast licenses, which are maintained at cost (subject to potential impairment write-downs) until a finite life can be ascertained, if ever. These intangibles generally can be categorized as being (i) customer- or market-based assets (e.g., customer lists, newspaper mastheads, and trademarked brand names); (ii) contract-based assets (e.g., covenants not to compete, broadcast rights); (iii) artistic-based assets (e.g., plays, other literary works, musical compositions); and (iv) technology-based assets (e.g., title plant, databases, computer software). With the exception of indefinite-life intangibles, all identifiable intangibles are to be amortized over their estimated useful lives, defined as the period over which the intangible asset is expected to directly or indirectly generate cash flows for the entity.

Appendix A to SFAS No. 141 identifies intangible assets that have characteristics that meet one of the two criteria (legal/contractual or separability). However, depending on the facts and circumstances, a specific acquired intangible asset might not meet the criteria. A good approach would be to first consider whether the acquired intangibles are among those specifically described by the FASB, and then to consider whether other intangibles also meeting the two criteria for separate capitalization might also be present.

Identified intangibles can be aggregated into permits, intellectual property, technology tools, procurement rights, competitor arrangements, and customer arrangements. *Permits* include:

- *Broadcast rights:* a license to transmit over certain bandwidths in the radio frequency spectrum, granted by the operation of communication laws
- *Certification marks:* the right to be able to assert that a product or service meets certain standards of quality or origin, such as "ISO 14000 Certified"
- *Collective marks:* rights to signify membership in an association
- *Construction permits:* rights to build a specified structure at a specified location
- *Franchise rights:* permits to engage in a trade-named business, to sell a trademarked good, or to sell a service-marked service in a particular geographic area
- *Internet domain names:* domain names using alphabetical characters such as www. samplecompany.com in lieu of using numeric addresses provide more memorable internet addresses
- *Operating rights:* permits to operate in a certain manner, such as that granted to a carrier to transport specified commodities
- *Use rights:* permits to use specified land, property, or air space in a particular manner, such as the right to cut timber, expel emissions, or land airplanes

Intellectual property includes, inter alia, the following:

- *Copyrights:* the rights to reproduce, distribute, and so on an original work of literature, music, art, photography, or film
- *Newspaper mastheads:* the rights to use the information that is displayed on the top of the first pages of newspapers
- *Patents:* the rights to make, use, or sell an invention for a specified period
- *Service marks:* the rights to use the name or symbol that distinguishes a service
- *Trade dress:* access to the overall appearance and image (unique color, shape, or package design) of a product
- *Trademarks:* rights to use the word, logo, or symbol that distinguishes a product
- *Trade names:* the right to use the name or symbol that distinguishes a business
- *Trade secrets:* information, such as a formula, process, or recipe, that is kept confidential
- *Unpatented technology:* access to the knowledge about the manner of accomplishing a task

Technology tools may consist of computer software, including programs, procedures, and documentation associated with computer hardware, as well as databases, which are collections of a particular type of information, such as scientific data or credit information.

Procurement rights include the following:

- *Construction contracts:* rights to acquire the subject of the contract in exchange for taking over the remaining obligations (including any payments)
- *Employment contracts:* rights to take the seller's place as the employer under the contract and thus obtain the employee's services in exchange for fulfilling the employer's remaining duties, such as payment of salaries and benefits, under the contract

- *Lease agreements:* if assignable, rights to step into the shoes of the lessee and thus obtain the rights to use assets that are the subject of the agreement, in exchange for making the remaining lease payments
- *License agreements:* rights to access or use properties that are the subjects of licenses in exchange for making any remaining license payments and adhering to other responsibilities as licensee
- *Royalty agreements:* rights to take the place of payors and thus assume the payors' remaining rights and duties under the agreements
- *Service or supply contracts:* rights to become the customer of particular contracts and thus purchase the specified products or services for the prices specified in those contracts

Competitor arrangements may include

- *Noncompete agreements:* rights to assurances that companies or individuals will refrain from conducting similar businesses or selling to specific customers for an agreed-upon period
- *Standstill agreements,* which convey rights to assurances that companies or individuals will refrain from engaging in certain activities for specified periods

Customer arrangements are items such as

- *Customer lists:* information about companies' customers, including names, contact information, and order histories that a third party, such as a competitor or a telemarketing firm, would want to use in its own business
- *Customer relationships:* the relationships between entities and their customers for which
  - o The entities have information about the customers and have regular contacts with the customers and
  - o The customers have the ability to make direct contact with the entity
- *Contracts and related customer relationships:* relationships that arise through contracts and are of value to buyers who can "step into the shoes" of the sellers and assume their remaining rights and duties under the contracts, and that hold the promise that the customers will place future orders with the entity
- *Noncontractual customer relationships:* relationships that arise through means such as regular contacts by sales or service representatives, the value of which are derived from the prospect of the customers placing future orders with the entities
- *Order or production backlogs:* providing buyers rights to step into the shoes of sellers on unfilled sales orders for services and for goods in amounts that exceed the quantity of finished goods and work-in-process on hand for filling the orders

(b) INTERNALLY DEVELOPED INTANGIBLE ASSETS   Costs of internally developing, maintaining, or restoring intangible assets including goodwill that are not specifically identifiable, that have indeterminate lives, or that are inherent in a continuing business and related to a reporting entity as a whole are recognized as an expense when incurred. This rule was grounded, in part, on the traditional aversion to recognition of self-developed goodwill, which is a prohibition nominally still in effect (although the prescribed procedures for the impairment testing of goodwill under SFAS No. 142 implicitly allow for recognition of self-created goodwill, to the extent that it replaces acquired goodwill).

As a practical matter, capitalization of internally developed intangibles is generally obviated by the requirements of SFAS No. 2, which requires that all research and development costs be expensed as incurred. This rule, which is controversial (e.g., the corresponding international financial reporting standard requires expensing of research costs but capitalization of development expenditures) and likely to become more so (as general awareness of the importance of intangibles increases and as the move toward the "knowledge-based economy" continues and even accelerates), would probably preclude most costs incurred in connection with internal generation of intangibles from being recognized as assets in any event.

20A.4 ACCOUNTING FOR INTANGIBLE ASSETS

(a) DETERMINING THE USEFUL LIFE OF AN INTANGIBLE ASSET The accounting for recognized intangible assets is based on their useful lives *to the reporting entity*. Note that these may well differ from the legal or contractual lives, and could also easily diverge from the useful lives in the hands of *other* reporting entities holding similar or even identical assets. The amounts of intangible assets with finite useful lives are amortized, whereas the amounts assigned to intangible assets with indefinite useful lives are not amortized. The useful lives of intangible assets to a reporting entity are the respective periods over which the assets are expected to contribute directly or indirectly to the future cash flows of the reporting entity. The estimates of the useful lives of intangible assets to the reporting entity are based on analyses of all pertinent factors. Particular attention is to be given to the following:

- Expected use of the assets by the reporting entity
- Expected useful lives of other assets or groups of assets to which the useful lives of the intangible assets may relate, such as mineral rights to depleting assets
- Any legal, regulatory, or contractual provisions that may limit the useful lives
- Any legal, regulatory, or contractual provisions that enable renewals or extensions of the assets' legal or contractual lives without substantial cost, provided that there is evidence to support renewals or extensions, and renewals or extensions can be accomplished without material modifications of the respective existing terms and conditions
- Effects of obsolescence, demand, competition, and other economic factors, such as the stability of the industry, known technological advances, legislative action that results in an uncertain or changing regulatory environment, and expected changes in distribution channels
- Levels of maintenance expenditures required to obtain the expected future cash flows from the assets—for example, a material level of required maintenance in relation to the carrying amount of an asset may suggest a very limited useful life

If no legal, regulatory, contractual, competitive, economic, or other factors limit the useful lives of the intangible assets to the reporting entity, those useful lives are considered to be indefinite, which does not mean *infinite.*

(b) INTANGIBLE ASSETS SUBJECT TO AMORTIZATION The amounts of recognized intangible assets recognized are to be amortized over the useful lives of the respective assets to the reporting entity, unless those lives are determined to be indefinite. SFAS No. 142 requires that the recorded amounts of intangible assets with finite lives, but without precisely known lives, be amortized over the best estimates of the useful lives. The methods of amortization should reflect the patterns by which the economic benefits of the intangible assets are consumed or otherwise used up. If the patterns cannot be reliably determined, the straight-line amortization method is to be used. Intangible assets are not written down or off in the period of acquisition unless impairments occur during that initial period, which is unlikely but not impossible.

Under SFAS No. 142, the amount of an intangible asset subject to amortization is the value initially assigned to the asset less any residual value. However, the residual value of an intangible asset must be presumed to be zero unless at the end of the useful life to the reporting entity the asset is expected to continue to have a useful life to another entity *and* either (a) the reporting entity has a commitment from a third party to purchase the asset at the end of its useful life to the reporting entity or (b) the residual value can be determined by reference to an exchange transaction in an existing market for that asset and that market is expected to exist at the end of the asset's useful life. In practice, residual values are rarely justified for intangibles subject to amortization.

Reporting entities must evaluate the remaining useful lives of intangible assets that are being amortized each reporting period to determine whether events and circumstances warrant a revision to the remaining periods of amortization. If estimates of intangible assets' useful lives are changed, the remaining carrying amounts of the intangible assets are to be amortized prospectively over their revised remaining useful lives.

If any of the intangible assets being amortized are subsequently determined to have indefinite useful lives, these assets are to be tested for impairment, as is discussed subsequently. These intangible assets are then no longer amortized and are instead accounted for the same way as other intangible assets not subject to amortization.

Intangible assets subject to amortization are to be reviewed for impairments in conformity with SFAS No. 144. After an impairment loss is recognized, the adjusted carrying amount of that intangible asset is its new accounting basis. A previously recognized impairment loss is not subsequently reversed, despite evidence of value recovery.

(c) INTANGIBLE ASSETS NOT SUBJECT TO AMORTIZATION   Intangible assets that were determined to have indefinite useful lives are not amortized until their respective useful lives are determined no longer to be indefinite. The reporting entity is required to evaluate the remaining useful lives of intangible assets not being amortized each reporting period, in order to determine whether events and circumstances continue to support indefinite useful lives. Intangible assets not being amortized, but subsequently determined to have finite useful lives, are tested for impairment, as discussed next. The assets are then amortized prospectively over their estimated remaining useful lives and accounted for the same way as other intangible assets subject to amortization.

Intangible assets not subject to amortization are to be tested for impairments annually, or more frequently if events or changes in circumstances indicate that the assets might have become impaired. The impairment tests consist of making comparisons of the fair values of the assets with their respective carrying amounts. If the carrying amount for a given intangible asset exceeds its fair value, an impairment loss is recognized in an amount equal to the excess. After an impairment loss is recognized, the asset's adjusted carrying amount is the intangible asset's new accounting basis. A previously recognized impairment loss cannot be reversed.

In EITF Issue No. 02-7, "Unit of Accounting for Testing Impairment of Indefinite-Lived Intangible Assets," there was a consensus that separately recorded indefinite-lived intangible assets should be combined into a single unit of accounting for impairment testing purposes if they are operated as a single asset and are therefore essentially inseparable. EITF Issue No. 02-7 includes indicators and illustrations of when intangible assets should be—and when they should not be—combined.

Indicators that suggest that indefinite-lived intangibles should be combined as a single unit of accounting include the following:

1. The intangibles will be used together to construct or enhance a single asset.
2. If the intangibles had been part of the same acquisition, they would have been recorded as a single asset.
3. The intangibles, as a group, represent "the highest and best use of the assets" (e.g., they could probably realize a higher sales price if sold together than if they were sold separately). Indicators pointing to this situation are
   a. The degree to which it is unlikely that a substantial portion of the assets would be sold separately, or
   b. The fact that should a substantial portion of the intangibles be sold individually, there would be a significant reduction in the fair value of the remaining assets in the group.
4. The marketing or branding strategy of the entity treats the assets as being complementary (e.g., a trademark and its related trade name, formulas, recipes, and patented or unpatented technology can all be complementary to an entity's brand name).

Indicators that imply that indefinite-lived intangibles should not be combined as a single unit of accounting include the following:

1. Each separate intangible generates independent cash flows.
2. In a sale, it would be likely that the intangibles would be sold separately. If the entity had previously sold similar assets separately, this would constitute evidence that combining the assets would not be appropriate.
3. The entity is either considering or has already adopted a plan to dispose of one or more of the intangibles separately.
4. The intangibles are used exclusively by different asset groups (as defined in SFAS No. 144).
5. The assets have different useful economic lives.

EITF 02-7 provided additional guidance regarding the "unit of accounting" determination that must be made for impairment testing purposes.

1. Goodwill and finite-lived intangibles may not be combined in the "unit of accounting" since they are subject to different impairment testing rules (set forth by SFAS Nos. 142 and 144, respectively).
2. If the intangibles collectively constitute a business, they may not be combined into a unit of accounting.
3. If the unit of accounting includes intangibles recorded in the separate financial statements of consolidated subsidiaries, it is possible that the sum of impairment losses recognized in the separate financial statements of the subsidiaries will not equal the consolidated impairment loss.
4. Should a unit of accounting be included in a single reporting unit, that same unit of accounting and associated fair value are to be used in computing the implied fair value of goodwill for measuring any goodwill impairment loss.

Identifiable intangible assets, such as franchise rights, customer lists, trademarks, patents and copyrights, and licenses, are to be amortized over their expected useful economic lives, even if they exceed the former 40-year ceiling. However, if longer amortization periods (useful lives) are elected, impairment reviews of the assets' recoverability are required when necessitated by changes in facts and circumstances in the same manner as set forth in SFAS No. 144 for tangible long-lived assets. SFAS No. 144 also requires consideration of the intangible assets' residual values (which are analogous to salvage values for tangible assets) in determining the amounts of the intangibles to amortize. Residual value is defined as the value of the intangible to the entity at the end of its (entity-specific) useful life reduced by any estimated disposition costs. The residual value of an amortizable intangible is assumed to be zero unless the intangible will continue to have a useful life to another party after the end of its useful life to its current holder, and one or both of the following criteria are met:

1. The current holder has received a third-party commitment to purchase the intangible at the end of its useful life, *or*
2. A market for the intangible exists and is expected to continue to exist at the end of the asset's useful life as a means of determining the residual value of the intangible by reference to marketplace transactions.

A broadcast license is nominally subject to expiration in five years, but might be indefinitely renewable at little additional cost to the broadcaster. If cash flows can be projected indefinitely, and assuming a market exists for the license, no amortization is to be recorded until such time as a finite life is predicted. However, it is required that the asset be tested for impairment at least annually, to ensure that it is carried at no greater than its fair value.

20A.5   CERTAIN IDENTIFIABLE INTANGIBLE ASSETS

(a) PATENTS   Accounting for patents is affected by the laws governing the legal rights of a patent holder. A U.S. patent is a nonrenewable right granted by the federal government that enables the recipient to exclude others from the manufacture, sale, or other use of an invention for a period of 17 years from the date of grant. Enforceability of a patent begins only on its grant, and the exclusive right of use is not retroactive. However, the filing of a patent application provides protection from the claims of a later inventor for the same item so that the period of partial protection may be considered to extend from the date of the original application. While the legal term of the patent is 17 years, the effective period of competitive advantage may extend beyond the original 17-year patent term if additional patents are obtained as improvements are made. Many patent holders do endeavor to create various modifications and improvements that can be patented in their own right, to accomplish this de facto extension of protection for many years. The rights to a patent may be assigned in whole or in part, as can the right to use the patent (i.e., licenses under the patent) on a royalty or other basis.

(i) *Capitalizable Amounts for Patents*   Patents may be purchased from others or developed internally as a result of research and development activities. The cost of a purchased patent includes the purchase price and any related expenditures, such as attorneys' fees. If a patent is developed internally, its cost includes legal fees in connection with patent applications, patent fees, litigation fees, litigation costs, costs of sale or licensing, and filing fees. Any related research, experimental, and developmental expenditures, including the cost of models and drawings not specifically required for a patent application, are research and development costs and should be expensed as incurred in accordance with SFAS No. 2.

The grant of a patent through the U.S. Patent Office is no guarantee of protection. It is often necessary to defend the patent's validity in court tests and also to refute allegations of infringement of other patents and to prosecute infringement of the patent by others. The costs of successful court tests may be capitalized as additional costs of the patent, and then amortized over the remaining useful life of the underlying patent. However, if the litigation is unsuccessful, the costs of the litigation should be written off immediately, as should any carrying value of the patent that has been stripped of its economic value.

(ii) Amortization of Patents   A U.S. patent has a specified legal life. It provides protection for 17 years, and that is the maximum amortization period. The period used in practice is often less because of technological or market obsolescence factors, such as the issuance of new patents to competitors, improved models, substitutes, or general technological progress. These factors must be taken into account in determining the original useful life and during the subsequent reviews of remaining economic life. The amortization period should not extend beyond the market life of the product with which the patent is associated, unless it is demonstrable that the patent can also be used in other applications. However, if it is possible to extend a patent's economic life by obtaining additional patents, it is permissible to amortize the remaining balance of the costs of the old patent over the estimated economic lives of the new ones. (For example, if a patent is half amortized when a successor patent is issued and the estimated life of the successor is 10 years, the unamortized carrying value of the original patent should be added to the cost of the new one, with the entire sum then amortized over 10 years.)

The impairment accounting guidance in SFAS No. 144 is applicable to patents. Once it is determined that the monopolistic advantage offered by use and ownership of the patent no longer exists, the remaining unamortized balance should be written off. Also, any increases in separately identified deferred costs, due to such factors as an additional lawsuit establishing the validity of the patent, should be written off over the remaining estimated economic life of the patent.

(b) COPYRIGHTS   A copyright is the exclusive right to reproduce, publish, and sell a literary product or artistic work. The term of the copyright in the United States is now the life of the author plus 50 years (formerly 28 years with a single renewal option). As in the case of a patent, the rights to a copyright may be assigned, licensed, or sold.

(i) Capitalizable Amounts for Copyrights   The costs of developing copyrights and the costs of purchased copyrights may be substantial and should be deferred. For a copyright developed internally, costs include expenditures for government filing fees and attorneys' fees and expenses, along with outlays for wages and materials in the preparation of the material to be copyrighted and expenditures incurred to establish the right. If a copyright is purchased, the initial valuation includes the acquisition price plus any costs incurred in establishing the right.

(ii) Amortization of Copyrights   Copyrighted materials, for various reasons, often do not have an active market past the first few years after the issuance of the copyright. It is rare that copyrighted materials will have lengthy economic lives, although there are exceptions. The capitalized amounts are to be amortized over the number of years in which sales or royalties related to the copyright can be expected to occur.

SFAS No. 144, "Accounting for the Impairment or Disposal of Long-Lived Assets," provides guidance on the impairment of intangible assets with finite lives, such as copyrights. Continuing review of the status of copyrights is essential to determine whether they have continuing value. If the copyrighted material will no longer be used, it should be written off.

(c) CUSTOMER AND SUPPLIER LISTS   Customer and supplier lists can be particularly valuable to a business, as they represent groups of customers or suppliers with whom business relations have been established. The value of such lists is based on the assumption of continuing business relationships, as well as possibly reducing the marketing costs that would otherwise be necessary (e.g., to develop customer lists).

(i) Capitalizable Amounts for Customer and Supplier Lists   Customer or supplier lists often are developed internally, and the cost specifically identified with development generally is impossible to determine. These costs are often analogous to research and development expenditures; accordingly, such costs are not deferred. However, when lists are purchased from others, the acquisition cost should be deferred. While generally these are identifiable assets and thus separately recognizable, a customer or supplier list acquired in a business combination would not meet the criteria for recognition apart from goodwill if there are terms of confidentiality or other agreements that prohibit the selling, leasing, or otherwise exchanging of the acquired customer or supplier information.

(ii) Amortization of Customer and Supplier Lists   The value of customer or supplier lists decreases as customers or suppliers are lost or cease to exist. Ideally, the cost of a list should be written off based on these factors—that is, on a units-lost basis. However, since it is often difficult to track lost customers or suppliers precisely, straight-line amortization over a reasonable average customer or supplier retention period is commonly used. The estimate of the useful life should consider all available information and should be reevaluated each reporting period. To the extent that there is a rapid turnover of customers or suppliers, this suggests that little or even no value should have been attributed to the acquired lists.

(d) FRANCHISES   Franchises may be granted by governmental units, individuals, or corporate entities. Public utilities are granted franchises by the communities they serve. These franchises establish the right to operate and specify the conditions under which utilities must function. Such franchises may place certain restrictions on the enterprise concerning rates and operating conditions, but they also confer certain privileges, ranging from minor ones to the granting of a full monopoly.

Private franchises are contracts for the exclusive right to perform certain functions or to sell certain (usually branded) products or services. Such agreements involve the use by the franchisee of a trademark, trade name, patent, process, or know-how of the franchisor for the term of the franchise. For example, a manufacturer may grant a dealer a franchise to market a product within a given territory and agree not to allow other dealers to market the same product in that area.

Costs of obtaining a franchise include any fees paid to the franchisor along with legal and other expenditures incurred in obtaining the franchise. If a franchise agreement covers a specified period of time, the cost of the franchise should be written off over that period unless the economic life is anticipated to be less. If the franchise is perpetual, the franchisee should evaluate the expected useful life of the franchise, considering the effect of obsolescence, demand, competition, and other relevant economic factors. Additional periodic payments based on revenues or other factors may be required in addition to initial fees. These period costs should be expensed as incurred, because they pertain to only the current period and represent no future benefit. The franchise agreement may also require certain property improvements that should be capitalized and included in property, plant, and equipment.

(e) LEASES AND LEASEHOLD RIGHTS   A favorable lease is one in which the property rights obtained under the lease could presently be obtained only at a higher rental. This concept is not to be mistaken for the issue of capitalized leases or capital additions classified as leasehold improvements. Favorable leases may be recognized when a business is purchased or when a payment is made to an existing lessee for the right to sublease, if indeed there is sufficient evidence to demonstrate a below-market rate of rental payments.

(i) Capitalizable Amounts for Favorable Leases and Leasehold Rights   The favorable lease usually is measured by the present value of the cost differential between the terms of the lease and the amount that could be obtained currently in an arm's-length transaction. This corresponds to the economic or fair value of the favorable terms.

(ii) Amortization of Favorable Leases   The cost assigned to a favorable lease is amortized over the lease term. A lump-sum payment at the inception of the lease should be amortized to rent expense over the life of the lease.

(f) ORGANIZATION COSTS   Organization costs are expenditures made to promote and organize a concern, including costs (i.e., legal and state filing fees) of establishing the entity's existence. Under Statement of Position (SOP) 98-5, "Reporting on the Costs of Start-Up Activities," start-up activities include organization costs. This SOP concludes that costs of start-up activities, including organization costs, should be expensed as incurred.

(g) REGISTRATION COSTS   The Securities and Exchange Commission staff in Staff Accounting Bulletin (SAB) Topic 5A stated that specific incremental costs directly attributable to a proposed or actual offering of securities may properly be deferred and charged against the gross proceeds of the offering. Management salaries or other general and administrative expenses may not be allocated as costs of the offering. Costs of an aborted offering may not be deferred and charged against a subsequent offering. According to SEC staff, a short postponement of up to 90 days does not represent an aborted offering.

(h) RESEARCH AND DEVELOPMENT COSTS   So-called R&D expenses have long been a controversial accounting topic. Prior to the imposition of current GAAP, it had been common to defer such costs, and investors often were dismayed at sporadic "big baths" when the hoped-for developments failed to be consummated or proved to have less economic value than expected. In reaction to the formerly liberal practices of deferring R&D costs, therefore, one of the FASB's first acts was to impose SFAS No. 2, "Accounting for Research and Development Costs," which requires that all R&D costs be charged to expense as incurred.

SFAS No. 142 did not change the stringent accounting requirements of SFAS No. 2. It includes the following definitions of research and development:

> Research is planned search or critical investigation aimed at discovery of new knowledge with the hope that such knowledge will be useful in developing a new product or service . . . or a new process or technique . . . or in bringing about a significant improvement to an existing product or process.

> Development is the translation of research findings or other knowledge into a plan or design for a new product or process or for a significant improvement to an existing product or process whether intended for sale or use. It includes the conceptual formulation, design, and testing of product alternatives, construction

of prototypes, and operation of pilot plants. It does not include routine or periodic alterations to existing products, production lines, manufacturing processes, and other on-going operations even though those alterations may represent improvements, and it does not include market research or market testing activities. (SFAS No. 2, para. 8.)

The distinction between "research" and "development" is more than semantic. For example, under International Financial Reporting Standards, while research costs must be expensed at once, as under U.S. GAAP, development costs are to be deferred and amortized over the economic lives of the resultant products or processes. Even under U.S. GAAP the distinction between "research" and "development" is germane, albeit not as a general principle. However, for certain categories of software development costs, costs incurred before technological feasibility has been demonstrated (i.e., those that are analogous to research costs) are expensed, whereas those incurred after feasibility has been demonstrated (which are, arguably, more suggestive of development costs) are capitalized and amortized.

Given the huge economic significance of R&D expenditures and the growing recognition that substantial amounts of assets are being omitted from many reporting entities' balance sheets (with an equivalent understatement of net stockholders' equity), this is likely to receive renewed attention. Particularly given the FASB's commitment to "converge" U.S. GAAP and International Financial Reporting Standards (IFRS), there would appear to be some possibility that future GAAP will permit or require deferral of development-type expenses, subject to amortization and, perhaps, impairment assessments.

Research and development costs, according to SFAS No. 2, include the following elements:

Materials, Equipment and Facilities. The cost of materials . . . and equipment or facilities that are acquired or constructed for research and development activities and that have alternative future uses . . . shall be capitalized as tangible assets when acquired or constructed. The cost of such materials consumed in research and development activities and the depreciation of such equipment or facilities used in those activities are research and development costs. However, the costs of materials, equipment, or facilities that are acquired or constructed for a particular research and development project and that have no alternative future uses . . . are research and development costs at the time the costs are incurred.

Personnel. Salaries, wages, and other related costs of personnel engaged in research and development activities shall be included in research and development costs.

Intangibles Purchased from Others. The costs of intangibles that are purchased from others for use in research and development activities and that have alternative future uses ... shall be accounted for in accordance with FASB Statement No. 142, "Goodwill and Other Intangible Assets." . . . The amortization of those intangible assets used in research and development activities is a research and development cost. However, the costs of intangibles that are purchased from others for a particular research and development project and that have no alternative future uses . . . are research and development costs at the time the costs are incurred.

Contract Services. The costs of services performed by others in connection with the research and development activities of an enterprise, including research and development conducted by others in behalf of the enterprise, shall be included in research and development costs.

Indirect Costs. Research and development costs shall include a reasonable allocation of indirect costs. However, general and administrative costs that are not clearly related to research and development activities shall not be included as research and development costs. SFAS No. 2 requires that all costs of activities identified as R&D be charged to expense as incurred. The only exception is that government-regulated enterprises may be required to defer certain costs for rate-making purposes. This occurs when the rate regulator reasonably assures the recovery of R&D costs by permitting the inclusion of the costs in allowable costs for rate-making purposes. SFAS No. 2 also requires disclosure of total R&D costs charged to expense in each period. [SFAS No. 2, paras. 11–13.]

There are three ways in which R&D costs may be incurred by a reporting entity:

1. Conducting R&D activities for the benefit of the reporting entity itself
2. Conducting R&D for others under a contractual arrangement
3. Purchasing R&D from other entities

As noted, under SFAS No. 2 all research and development expenditures must be expensed as incurred. Examples of such R&D costs include

1. Laboratory research to discover new knowledge
2. Formulation and design of product alternatives:
   a. Testing for product alternatives
   b. Modification of products or processes
3. Preproduction prototypes and models:
   a. Tools, dies, and so on, for new technology
   b. Pilot plants not capable of commercial production
4. Engineering activity performed until the product is ready for manufacture

Not all costs that appear related to research and development are to be accounted for as such, however. Examples of costs that are *not* considered R&D include

1. Engineering during an early phase of commercial production
2. Quality control for commercial production
3. Troubleshooting during a commercial production breakdown
4. Routine, ongoing efforts to improve products
5. Adaptation of existing capacity for a specific customer or other requirements
6. Seasonal design changes to products
7. Routine design of tools, dies, and so on
8. Design, construction, start-up, and so on, of equipment except that used solely for R&D

In many cases, entities will pay other parties to perform R&D activities on their behalf. In some instances, these are simply rational business decisions and are not undertaken with any financial reporting motive ("earnings management") in mind. In some instances, however, the intent of "outsourcing" certain R&D activities is to try to avoid the immediate expensing requirement of SFAS No. 2, and to instead disguise these expenditures as capital asset purchases.

In applying substance over form in evaluating these arrangements, a financial reporting result cannot be obtained indirectly if it would not have been permitted if accomplished directly. Thus, if costs incurred to engage others to perform R&D activities that, in substance, could have been performed by the reporting entity itself, those costs must be expensed as incurred. On the other hand, if the payment is to acquire intangibles for use in R&D activities, and these assets have other uses, then the expenditure is capitalized and accounted for in accordance with SFAS No. 142.

When R&D costs are incurred as a result of contractual arrangements, the nature of the agreement dictates the accounting treatment of the costs involved. The key determinant is the transfer of the risk associated with the R&D expenditures. If the business receives funds from another party to perform R&D and is obligated to repay those funds regardless of the outcome, a liability must be recorded and the R&D costs must be expensed as incurred. In order to conclude that a liability does not exist, the transfer of the financial risk must be substantive and genuine.

The SEC staff has stated that if a significant portion of the purchase price in a business combination is expensed as purchased R&D, the SEC staff may raise issues such as the following:

- Purchased R&D must be valued based on appropriate assumptions and valuation techniques; it may not be determined as a residual amount similar to goodwill.
- Allocation of purchase price to purchased R&D will be questioned if it differs significantly from the estimated replacement cost for the acquiring enterprise.
- Policies used for internally developed products should be used to determine whether R&D is in process or complete and whether alternative future uses exist.
- If substantially all of the purchase price is allocated to purchase R&D, the staff will challenge whether some should be allocated to other identifiable intangible assets and goodwill and would object to useful lives of those intangible assets and goodwill exceeding five to seven years.

The AICPA has issued the following Practice Aid on accounting for R&D projects acquired in a business combination: "Assets Acquired in a Business Combination to Be Used in Research and Development Activities: A Focus in Software, Electronic Devices, and Pharmaceutical Industries."

(i) RESEARCH AND DEVELOPMENT ARRANGEMENTS   Research and development arrangements may take a variety of forms, but a central feature of each of these is to conduct R&D that is to be financed by another entity. According to SFAS No. 68, certain of these arrangements are actually financing transactions, and funds to be repaid, irrespective of the outcome of the research, must be reported as liabilities, with actual research or development costs expensed as incurred by the reporting entity. Only if there is a substantive risk transfer to the entity providing financing will it be appropriate not to record such a liability.

The actual obligation can take various forms, including an outright unconditional commitment to repay the funds advanced; an option giving the other entity the right to require that the reporting entity purchase the other party's interest in the outcome of the R&D efforts; and a firm obligation to issue debt or equity instruments to the funding party at completion. In all such instances, the payment for R&D is actually a loan, not a purchase of R&D services. Accordingly, the reporting entity (the party conducting R&D) must currently expense all R&D expenditures.

On the other hand, to the extent that the financial risk associated with the research and development has been transferred because repayment of any of the funds provided is conditioned on the results of the R&D having future economic benefit, the reporting entity is to account for its obligation as a contract to perform research and development for others, not as debt.

(j) ACQUIRED IN-PROCESS RESEARCH AND DEVELOPMENT So-called in-process research and development (IPRD) has long been a difficult financial reporting issue. On one hand, purchase business combination accounting suggests that the purchase cost be allocated to the fair value of all assets acquired; on the other hand, to allow capitalization of IPRD would result in deferral of costs that would have to be immediately expensed under SFAS No. 2 if incurred directly by the reporting entity.

In many business combinations, a part of the premium (i.e., the amounts in excess of the fair value of tangible net assets) paid is in recognition of the value of the acquiree's previously expensed research and development efforts. Since what is banned under GAAP (e.g., capitalization of R&D costs) if accomplished directly cannot be attained indirectly (e.g., via a business combination), it was logical to prohibit the creation of an intangible asset in purchase business combinations to reflect the value of research and development already completed by the acquiree entity.

IPRD is virtually the only asset acquired in a purchase business combination transaction that is expensed rather than being capitalized. This includes not only the amount paid for actual in-process work (which was, per SFAS No. 2, already expensed as incurred by the acquiree entity), but also certain tangible assets used in research and development. As stated in FASB Interpretation No. 4, "Applicability of FASB Statement No. 2 to Business Combinations Accounted for by the Purchase Method," any identifiable assets of the acquiree to be used in research and development (R&D) projects that do not also have an alternative future use should be first valued as part of the purchase price allocation, and then charged to expense of the combined companies simultaneous with consummation of acquisition. This matter was considered by the EITF (in Issue 86-14, "Purchased Research and Development Projects in a Business Combination"), but no changes to the requirement were made.

In the mid- to late 1990s, overly aggressive use of the mandate that "in-process research and development" costs be immediately expensed upon consummation of a purchase business combination became something of a concern. In many acquisitions a disproportionately large part of the premium paid was assigned to in-process R&D, on the assumption that immediate charge-offs as part of purchase accounting were less of a concern to stockholders and other stakeholding parties than would be regular periodic charges against earnings lasting many years. There were even some instances, in fact, where more than 99 percent of the entire purchase cost was allocated to in-process R&D cost, and then immediately written off. This phenomenon drew the attention of the SEC as well as of accounting standard setters. The elimination of goodwill amortization by SFAS No. 142 reduced the motivation for exaggerated allocations to IPRD, but this remains a concern.

In response to this perceived problem, the FASB at first indicated an intent to develop a new requirement that, it was widely presumed, would have imposed a requirement that purchased in-process R&D costs be capitalized and amortized. However, upon further reflection, it became clear that to have a diametrically opposite rule for in-process R&D costs, as distinguished from internally generated R&D, would be neither logical nor defensible. Consequently, no action was taken by the FASB, and the requirement that purchased in-process R&D be immediately expensed, after purchase cost is first allocated to it, remained.

Clearly, the last chapter has not yet been written regarding proper accounting for research and/or development costs in general, or regarding in-process R&D acquired in purchase transactions in particular.

(k) ROYALTY AND LICENSE AGREEMENTS Royalty and license agreements are contracts allowing the use of patented, copyrighted, or proprietary (trade secrets) material in return for royalty payments. An example is the licensing of a patented chemical process for use in a customer's operating system.

The costs to be assigned to royalty and license agreements include any initial payments required plus legal costs incurred in establishing the agreements. Royalty or usage fees are expensed as incurred, because they relate to services of products and not to future benefits.

The capitalized costs of royalty and license agreements should be amortized over the lesser of the life of the agreement or the expected economic life, with the useful life reassessed each reporting period. Unamortized costs of royalty and license agreements should be written off when it is determined that they have become worthless.

(l) SECRET FORMULAS AND PROCESSES A formula or process known only to a particular producer may be a valuable asset, even if not patented. As in the case of a patent, the value of a trade secret is derived from the exclusive control that it gives. Trade secrets, like patents and copyrights, are recognized legal property and are transferable. Costs that can be directly identified with secret formulas and processes are properly capitalized, except that costs of activities constituting R&D as defined by SFAS No. 2 must be expensed. Costs are normally assigned only to acquired secret formulas and processes. Because secret formulas and secret processes have unlimited lives in a legal sense, costs capitalized are amortized over the useful life of the secret formula or are not amortized if the secret formula is determined to have an indefinite useful life. Whether the value of the formula or process is impaired because of lack of demand for the related product, development of a substitute product or process, loss of exclusivity, or other factors should be determined as discussed in Section 20A,4(b) or 4(c), as appropriate.

(m) START-UP ACTIVITIES Under SOP 98-5, "Reporting on the Costs of Start-Up Activities," costs of start-up activities, including organization costs, should be expensed as incurred. For purposes of the SOP, start-up activities are defined broadly as those one-time activities related to opening a new facility, introducing a new product or service, conducting business in a new territory, conducting business with a new class of customer or beneficiary, initiating a new process in an existing facility, or commencing some new operation. Start-up activities include activities related to organizing a new entity (commonly referred to as organization costs). The SOP applies to all nongovernmental entities and would apply to development-stage entities as well as established operating entities.

(n) TOOLING COSTS Initial tooling costs are sometimes treated as an intangible asset, but they are more often considered an element of property, plant, and equipment or, in the case of certain long-term contracts, inventory. SFAS No. 2 states that the design of tools, jigs, molds, and dies involving new technology is a R&D cost, which must be expensed as incurred. However, routine design of those items is not R&D, and the cost may be deferred and amortized over the periods expected to benefit. Deferred tooling may be written off over a period of time (generally less than five years, with shorter periods used when tooling relates to products with frequent style or design obsolescence) or anticipated production (using the unit-of-production method). Replacements of parts of tooling for reasons other than changes in the product are usually expensed.

If deferred initial tooling costs are material, the accounting policy regarding those costs should be disclosed. SEC registrants are required to state, if practicable, the amount of unamortized deferred tooling costs applicable to long-term contracts or programs (Regulation S-X, Rule 5.02-6(d)(i)).

EITF Issue No. 99-5, "Accounting for Pre-Production Costs Related to Long-Term Supply Arrangements," provides guidance on design and development and tooling costs related to new long-term supply arrangements. The Task Force concluded that

- Design and development costs for products to be sold under long-term supply arrangements should be expensed as incurred.
- Design and development costs for molds, dies, and other tools that a supplier will own and that will be used in producing the products under the long-term supply arrangements should, in general, be capitalized as part of the cost of the molds, dies, and other tools. However, if the molds, dies, and tools involve new technology, their costs should be expensed as incurred.
- If the supplier will not own the molds, dies, and other tools, the design and development costs should be capitalized only if the supply arrangement provides the supplier the noncancelable right to use them during the supply arrangement. Otherwise, the design and development costs should be expensed as incurred, including costs incurred before the supplier receives a noncancelable right to use the molds, dies, and other tools during the supply arrangement.
- Design and development costs that would otherwise be expensed should be capitalized if the supplier has a contractual guarantee for reimbursement of those costs. A contractual guarantee means a legally enforceable agreement under which the amount of the reimbursement can be objectively measured and verified.

SEC registrants are expected to disclose their accounting policy for preproduction design and development costs and the aggregate amount of the following:

- Assets recognized pursuant to agreements that provide for contractual reimbursement of preproduction design and development costs
- Assets recognized for molds, dies, and other tools that the supplier owns
- Assets recognized for molds, dies, and other tools that the supplier does not own

Design and development costs for molds, dies, and other tools that are capitalized are subject to impairment assessment under SFAS No. 144.

(o) TRADEMARKS AND TRADE NAMES   Broadly defined, a trademark is any distinguishing label, symbol, or design used by a concern in connection with a product or service. A trade name identifies the entity.

Trademarks can be registered with the U.S. Patent Office to provide access to the federal courts for litigation and to serve as notice of ownership. Proof of prior and continuing use of the trademark is required to obtain and retain the right to use the registered item. Protection of trademarks and trade names that cannot be registered or are not registered can also be sought through common law. These assets have an unlimited life as long as they are used continuously, although technically the term of registration at the U.S. Patent Office is 20 years with indefinite renewal for additional 20-year periods.

They may also be registered under the laws of most states. It is customary to consider trademarks and trade names as being of value only as long as they are used. The value of a trademark or trade name consists of the product differentiation and identification that it provides, which theoretically contributes to revenue by enabling a business to sell such products at a higher price than unbranded products. Although closely related to goodwill, trademarks and trade names are property rights that are separately identifiable and, as such, can be assigned or sold.

(i) Capitalizable Amounts for Trademarks and Trade Names Costs   The cost of a trademark or trade name developed internally consists of legal fees associated with successful litigation involving the trademark or trade name, registration fees, and all developmental expenditures that can be reasonably associated with trademarks, such as payments to design firms. The cost of a purchased trademark or trade name is its purchase price, along with any other costs required to maintain exclusive use of the mark or name. Obviously, much of the value of a trademark or trade name is established by continuing operations that create a reputation with customers. Some of that reputation, however, may have been gained through the use of advertising and other marketing techniques.

The costs should be amortized over the trademark's or trade name's useful life to the entity, unless the trademark or trade name is determined to have an indefinite useful life, in which case it is not amortized, as discussed in Section 20A.4(c). The expected useful life should be reassessed each reporting period. These expenditures should be accounted for under SOP 93-7, which is discussed next.

(ii) Amortization of Trademarks and Trade Names   Because of the legal status of trademarks and trade names, established trademarks and trade names have unlimited legal lives as long as they are used. There is no specified statutory life that restricts the amortization period.

(p) ADVERTISING   While many, if not most, businesses engage in some forms of advertising, it has long been held that demonstrating the actual effectiveness of such efforts is too speculative to warrant deferral of costs to future periods. Put another way, advertising has been held to be a "sunk cost," and thus must be expensed as incurred. However, SOP 93-7, "Reporting on Advertising Costs," did provide a limited exception to this general principle.

Under this SOP, the costs of advertising should be expensed either as incurred or the first time the advertising takes place, unless the advertising is direct-response advertising that meets specific, rather rigorous criteria, in which case deferral and amortization is prescribed. Examples of first-time advertising include the first public showing of a television commercial for its intended purpose or the first appearance of a magazine advertisement for its intended purpose. The cost of direct-response advertising is deferred and reported as an asset, subject to amortization, if the primary purpose of the advertising is to elicit sales to customers who can be shown to have responded specifically to the advertising, *and* if the advertising results in *probable* future benefits. Showing that a customer responded to specifically identifiable direct-response advertising requires documentation, including a record that can identify the name of the customer and the advertising that elicited the direct response. Such documentation could include, for example, files listing the customer names and the related direct-response advertisement, a coded order form, coupon, or response card included with the advertisement that would indicate the customer's name, or a log of customers who made phone calls responding to a number appearing in an advertisement.

Probable future benefits are highly likely future primary revenues resulting from the direct-response advertising, net of future costs to realize the revenues. Probable future primary revenues are limited to revenues from sales to customers receiving and responding to the direct-response advertising. To demonstrate that direct-response advertising will result in probable future benefits, an entity is required to provide persuasive evidence that the results of the advertising will be similar to the results of its past direct-response advertising activities that had future benefits. The evidence should include verifiable historical patterns of results specific to the entity. To determine if results will be similar, attributes to consider include the demographics of the audience, the method of advertising, the product, and economic conditions. Industry statistics would not provide objective evidence of probable future benefits in the absence of the entity's own operating history.

Other requirements of the SOP include the following:

- Costs of direct-response advertising should include only incremental direct costs incurred in transactions with independent third parties plus payroll and payroll-related costs for the activities of employees that are directly associated with the direct-response advertising project. Allocated administrative costs, rent, depreciation, and other occupancy costs are not costs of direct-response advertising activities.
- The costs of the direct-response advertising directed to all prospective customers, not just the cost related to the portion of the potential customers that is expected to respond to the advertising, should be deferred.
- Deferred direct-response advertising costs should be amortized using a cost-pool method over the period during which the future benefits are expected to be received. The amortization should be the ratio that current period revenues for a cost pool bear to the total current and estimated future period revenues for that cost pool. The amount of estimated future revenues should not be discounted, but it may be adjusted in subsequent periods. The ratio should be recalculated at each reporting date.
- The realizability of the deferred advertising should be evaluated, at each balance sheet date, by comparing, on a cost-pool by cost-pool basis, the carrying amount of the deferred advertising with the probable remaining future net revenues expected to result directly from such advertising. Only probable future primary revenues should be used to determine the probable remaining future net revenues.
- There are certain disclosures required, such as the accounting policy selected for advertising, the total amount charged to advertising, a description of the direct-response advertising reported as assets (if any), the accounting policy and amortization period of direct-response advertising, the total amount of advertising reported as assets, and the amounts, if any, written down to net realizable income.

The SEC staff considers the requirements for deferral of direct-response advertising costs to be met only if the advertising results in a direct revenue-generating response—for example, if the respondent orders the product when placing the call to the advertised number. The staff believes capitalization is not appropriate for advertising that results not in sales but only in sales opportunities, even if these are likely to produce results. For example, an advertisement for aluminum siding that includes a phone number to call to schedule a visit from a sales representative would not qualify for capitalization as direct-response advertising because the advertisement leads only indirectly to the revenue-generating transaction. The SEC staff also would object to the classification of deferred advertising costs as current assets, because such costs do not meet the definition of a current asset in ARB No. 43.

(q) WEB SITE DEVELOPMENT COSTS   With the rapid growth in so-called e-commerce in the late 1990s, many reporting entities incurred costs to develop and maintain Web sites.

EITF Issue No. 00-2 provided the following guidance for accounting for Web site development costs:

- During the planning phase, an entity develops a project plan, determines the desired functionalities of the Web site, identifies the needed hardware and software applications, and determines whether suitable technology exists. All costs incurred in the planning stage should be expensed as incurred.
- During the Web site development phase, the entity acquires or develops hardware and software to operate its Web site and develops appropriate graphics. Costs related to software and graphics should be accounted for under SOP 98-1 as software for internal use unless the entity has or is developing a plan to market the software. Software, including graphics, to be marketed should be accounted for under SFAS No. 86, "Computer Software to Be Sold, Leased, or Otherwise Marketed." See Section 20A.6(f) for a discussion of SOP 98-1 and SFAS No. 86. Costs incurred for Web site hosting should generally be expensed over the period of benefit.

20A.6   INTANGIBLE ASSETS IN SPECIALIZED INDUSTRIES

Intangible assets are particularly significant or receive unique accounting treatment in certain industries. These requirements are generally to be found in AICPA Industry Audit and Accounting Guides or in Statements of Position.

(a) AIRLINES   Under the AICPA Industry Audit Guide, *Audits of Airlines,* as amended by SOP 88-1, "Accounting for Developmental and Pre-operating Costs, Purchases and Exchanges of Take-off and Landing Slots, and Airframe Modifications," and SOP 98-5, "Reporting on the Costs of Start-Up Activities," the capitalization of preoperating costs related only to the integration of new types of aircraft. The costs of acquiring take-off and landing slots, whether by exchange of stock or through purchase, are identifiable intangible assets. Developmental costs related to preparation of new routes should not be capitalized.

(b) BANKING AND THRIFTS   During the thrift and banking crises of the late 1980s and early 1990s, precipitated in part by the high interest rate environment and negative interest rate spreads of those years, many insured financial institutions, when evaluated on a fair value basis, were threatened with insolvency or already were insolvent. The federal insurers (FDIC and FSLIC) were themselves facing insolvency, and would likely have been unable to repay all depositors of closed institutions from available reserves. It was hoped that, with an anticipated return to a normal interest rate environment, many of these banks and thrifts would regain solvency and survive, sparing the insurers (and ultimately the taxpayers) these losses.

Given this situation, there was a concerted political effort to postpone bank and thrift closings, and one perhaps ill-conceived solution was to encourage the takeovers of failing banks and thrifts by offering the acquirers the ability to treat the net liabilities acquired (measured at fair value) as so-called supervisory goodwill. Although this did not comport with the traditional GAAP concept of goodwill, the profession accommodated this regulatory mandate. Under SFAS No. 72, "Accounting for Certain Acquisitions of Banking or Thrift Institutions," this goodwill was to be amortized over the terms set forth in the assisted, supervisory mergers (often 20 or more years), even though the so-called core deposit intangible (related to the expected holding term of deposits acquired) would have a much shorter expected life.

The elimination of goodwill amortization by SFAS No. 142 necessitated a change to many of the SFAS No. 72 provisions. SFAS No. 147, "Acquisitions of Certain Financial Institutions," eliminates the special accounting imposed by SFAS No. 72, with the exception that mergers between mutual enterprises continue to be governed by that standard. Thus, as amended, SFAS No. 72 applies only to acquisitions of financial institutions that are mutual enterprises by other financial institutions that are also mutual enterprises. For those acquisitions, goodwill that is created by an excess of the fair value of liabilities assumed over the fair value of tangible and identified intangible assets acquired is to be amortized by the interest method over a period no greater than the estimated remaining life of the long-term, interest-bearing assets acquired. If the assets acquired do not include a significant amount of long-term, interest-bearing assets, such goodwill is to be amortized over a period not exceeding the estimated average life of the existing customer (deposit) base acquired.

At the effective date of SFAS No. 147, any remaining unidentified intangible other than that arising from a business combination continued to be amortized, while that arising from business combinations (the assisted supervisory mergers, for example) was to be reclassified as goodwill and thereafter tested for impairment per SFAS No. 142. Transitional impairment testing procedures were also specified.

(c) MORTGAGE BANKING Under SFAS No. 140, "Accounting for Transfers and Servicing of Financial Assets and Extinguishments of Liabilities," servicing of mortgage loans becomes a distinct asset or liability only when contractually separated from the underlying amounts by sale or securitization of the assets with servicing retained, or through the separate purchase or assumption of the servicing rights.

An entity that undertakes a contract to service financial assets shall recognize either a servicing asset or a servicing liability, unless the transferor transfers the assets in a guaranteed mortgage securitization, retains all of the resulting securities, and classifies them as debt securities held to maturity in accordance with SFAS No. 115, in which case the servicing asset or liability may be reported together with the asset being serviced. Each sale or securitization with servicing retained or separate purchase or assumption of servicing results in a servicing contract. Each servicing contract results in a servicing asset (when the benefits of servicing are expected to be more than adequate compensation to the servicer for performing the servicing) or a servicing liability (when the benefits of servicing are not expected to compensate the servicer adequately for performing the servicing). If the servicer is more than adequately compensated and if the servicing was retained in a sale or securitization, the servicer shall account for the contracts to service the mortgage loans separately from the loans by initially measuring the servicing assets at their allocated previous carrying amounts based on relative fair value at the date of sale or securitization. If the servicing asset is purchased or servicing liability assumed, it is measured at fair value. If the servicer is not adequately compensated, a servicing liability undertaken in a sale or securitization is measured at fair value.

Servicing assets are amortized in proportion to and over the period of estimated net servicing income—the excess of service revenues over servicing costs. Servicing liabilities are amortized in proportion to and over the period of estimated net servicing loss—the excess of servicing costs over servicing revenues, if practicable.

Impairment of servicing assets should be measured as follows:

1. Stratify servicing assets based on one or more of the predominant risk characteristics of the underlying assets.

2. Recognize impairment through a valuation allowance for an individual stratum for the amount by which the carrying amount of the servicing assets for the stratum exceeds their fair value.
3. Adjust the valuation allowance to reflect changes in the measurement of impairment subsequent to the initial measurement of impairment.

Rights for future income from the serviced assets that exceed contractually specified servicing fees should be accounted for separately. Those rights are not servicing assets; they are financial assets, effectively interest-only strips to be accounted for in accordance with paragraph 14 of SFAS No. 140.

In EITF No. 95-5, "Determination of What Risks and Rewards, If Any, Can Be Retained and Whether Any Unresolved Contingencies May Exist in a Sale of Mortgage Loan Servicing Rights," the issue addressed was whether the inclusion of any provision that results in the seller's retention of specified risk (1) precludes recognition of a sale at the date title passes or (2) allows recognition of the sale at that date if (a) the seller can reasonably estimate, and record a liability for, the costs related to protection provisions, or (b) the sale agreement provides for substantially all risks and rewards to irrevocably pass to the buyer, and the seller can reasonably estimate, and record a liability for, the minor protection provisions.

The EITF consensus was that sales of rights to service mortgage loans should be recognized when the following conditions are met: (1) title has passed, (2) substantially all risks and rewards of ownership have irrevocably passed to the buyer, and (3) any protection provisions retained by the seller are minor and can be reasonably estimated. If a sale is recognized and minor protection provisions exist, a liability should be accrued for the estimated obligation associated with those provisions. The seller retains only minor protection provisions if (a) the obligation associated with those provisions is estimated to be no more than 10 percent of the sales price and (b) risk of prepayment is retained for no longer than 120 days. Mortgage banking is covered in more detail in Chapter 29.

(d) BROADCASTING INDUSTRY   The principal intangible assets in the broadcasting industry are Federal Communications Commission (FCC) licenses, broadcast rights (license agreement to program material), and network affiliation agreements. Television and radio stations may not operate without a FCC license, which specifies, for example, the frequency to be used. A broadcasting license is granted for a 10-year period and is renewable for additional 10-year periods if the entity provides at least an average level of service to its customers and complies with applicable FCC rules and policies. Licenses thus may be renewed indefinitely at little cost.

If the entity intends to renew the license indefinitely and has the ability to do so, a broadcast license would be deemed to have an indefinite useful life. It would not be amortized until its useful life was no longer deemed to be indefinite. Impairment would be tested as provided in Section 20A.4(c). On the other hand, if the entity does not intend to renew a broadcast license indefinitely, if would amortize the license over its remaining useful life and follow the impairment guidance in SFAS No. 144.

(i) Broadcast Rights   SFAS No. 63, "Financial Reporting by Broadcasters," contains industry-specific GAAP. Its primary mandate is that broadcasters must account for license agreements for program materials as purchases of rights, thus necessitating the presentation of assets and liabilities on the entities' balance sheets. Broadcast rights result from a contract or license to exhibit films, programs, or other works and permit one or more exhibitions during a specified license period. Compensation is ordinarily payable in installments over a period shorter than the period of the licensing contract, but it may also take the form of a lump-sum payment at the beginning of the period. The license expires at the end of the contract period.

Amounts recorded for broadcasting rights are to be segregated on the balance sheet as current and noncurrent assets based on estimated usage within one year. Rights should be amortized based on the estimated number of future showings. Items that may be used on an unlimited basis, rather than a limited number of showings, may be amortized over the period covered by the agreement. An accelerated method of amortization is required when the first showing is more valuable than reruns, as is usually the case. Straight-line amortization is allowable only when each telecast or broadcast is expected to generate approximately the same revenue.

Feature programs are to be amortized on a program-by-program basis; however, amortization as a package may be appropriate if it approximates the amortization that would have been provided on a program-by-program basis. The capitalized costs of rights to program material should be reported in the balance sheet at the lower of unamortized cost or estimated net realizable value on a program-by-program, series, package, or "daypart" basis, as appropriate. If management's expectations of the programming usefulness of a program, series, package, or daypart are revised downward, it may be necessary to write down unamortized cost to estimated net realizable value. *Daypart* is defined in SFAS No. 63 as an aggregation of programs broadcast during a particular time of day (e.g., daytime, evening, late night) or programs of a similar type (e.g., sports, news, children's shows). A write-down from unamortized cost to a lower estimated net realizable value establishes a new cost basis.

(ii) Revoked or Nonrenewed Broadcast Licenses When broadcasting licenses are not renewed or are revoked, unamortized balances should be written off. If a network affiliation is terminated and is not immediately replaced or under agreement to be replaced, the unamortized balance of the amount originally allocated to the network affiliation agreement should be charged to expense. If a network affiliation is terminated and immediately replaced or is under agreement to be replaced, a loss is recognized to the extent that the unamortized cost of the terminated affiliation exceeds the fair value of the new affiliation. Gain is not to be recognized if the fair value of the new network affiliation exceeds the unamortized cost of the terminated affiliation.

(e) CABLE TELEVISION Cable television companies experience a long preoperating and development period. SFAS No. 51, "Financial Reporting by Cable Television Companies," defines the "pre-maturity period" as that during which a cable television system is partially under construction and partially in service. Costs incurred during this period that relate to both current and future operations are partially expensed and partially capitalized. In a cable system, portions or segments that are in the pre-maturity period and can be clearly distinguished from the remainder of the system should be accounted for separately. Costs incurred to obtain and retain subscribers and general and administrative expenses incurred during the pre-maturity period are to be expensed as period costs. Programming costs and other system costs that will not vary significantly regardless of the number of subscribers are allocated between current and future operations. The amount currently expensed is based on a relationship of subscribers during the current month (as prescribed in the SFAS) and the total number of subscribers expected at the end of the pre-maturity period. The capitalized portions decrease each month as the cable company progresses toward the end of the pre-maturity period. Prior to the pre-maturity period, system-related costs are capitalized; subsequent thereto, none of these costs is deferred. Capitalized costs should be amortized over the same period used to depreciate the main cable television plant. Costs of successful franchise applications are capitalized and amortized in accordance with SFAS No. 142. Costs of unsuccessful applications and abandoned franchises are charged to expense.

(f) COMPUTER SOFTWARE   SFAS No. 86, "Computer Software to Be Sold, Leased, or Otherwise Marketed," prescribes the accounting for the costs of computer software purchased or internally developed as a marketable product by itself. Costs incurred to establish the technological feasibility are charged to expense when incurred. Technological feasibility is established on completion of all planning design, coding, and testing activities necessary to establish that the product can be produced. The completion of a detailed program design or completion of a working model provides evidence of the establishment of technological feasibility.

Costs incurred subsequent to the establishment of technological feasibility are capitalized. Software used as an integral part of product or process is not capitalized until both technological feasibility has been established and all R&D activities for the other components have been completed. When the product is available for release to customers, capitalization ceases. Costs of maintenance and customer support are expensed when the related revenue is recognized or when the costs are incurred, whichever occurs first. Purchased software that has alternative future uses should be capitalized but subsequently accounted for according to its use.

Amortization of capitalized software costs is based on the ratio that current gross revenues bear to the total current and anticipated revenues with a minimum amortization equivalent to straight-line over the remaining estimated economic life of the product. The excess of unamortized capitalized costs over a product's net realizable value is written off (and not subsequently restored).

The unamortized computer costs included in the balance sheet, the total amortization charged to expense in each income statement presented, and amounts written down to net realizable value should be disclosed.

FIN (FASB Interpretations) No. 6 (par. 4) states that to the extent the acquisition, development, or improvement of a process for use in selling and administrative activities includes costs for computer software, these costs are not R&D costs. Examples given of excluded costs are the development by an airline of a computerized reservation system or the development of a general management information system. SFAS No. 86 does not cover accounting for costs of software used internally. For that subject, see the discussion of SOP 98-1 in this subsection.

In Issue No. 96-6, "Accounting for the Film and Software Cost Associated with Developing Entertainment and Educational Software Products," the EITF considered the issue of how companies should account for the film and software costs associated with developing entertainment and educational software (EE) products such as computer games, interactive videos, and other multimedia products. The SEC staff announced that EE products that are sold, leased, or otherwise marketed are subject to the accounting requirements of SFAS No. 86. The SEC staff believes that the film costs incurred in development of an EE product should be accounted for under the provisions of SFAS No. 86. In addition, exploitation costs should be expensed as incurred unless those costs include advertising costs that qualify for capitalization in accordance with SOP 93-7. Because of the SEC staff's position, the EITF was not asked to reach a consensus on this issue.

In EITF No. 97-13, "Accounting for Costs Incurred in Connection with a Consulting Contract or an Internal Project That Combines Business Process Reengineering and Information

Technology Transformation," the EITF addressed the accounting for business process reengineering costs. These costs may be included in a contract that combines business process reengineering and a project to acquire, develop, or implement internal-use software. The Issue does not address the accounting for internal-use software development costs (which was, however, dealt with subsequently by SOP 98-1). The EITF reached a consensus that costs of business process reengineering, whether done internally or by third parties, should be expensed as incurred. If the project is carried out by a third party and some of the costs are capitalizable, such as fixed asset costs, the EITF concluded that the total contract cost should be allocated to various activities based on the relative fair value of the separate activities. The allocation should be based on the objective evidence of the fair value of the elements in the contract, not separate prices stated within the contract. The consensus opinion identified the following as third-party or internally generated costs typically associated with business process reengineering activities that should be expensed as incurred:

- Preparation of request for proposal
- Current state assessment
- Process reengineering
- Restructuring the workforce

The cost of software used internally is accounted for under SOP 98-1, "Accounting for the Costs of Computer Software for Internal Use." The SOP divides the process of computer software development into three stages: (1) preliminary project stage (conceptual formulation and evaluation of alternatives, determination of existence of needed technology, and final selection of alternatives); (2) application development stage (design of chosen path, coding, installation to hardware, and testing); and (3) postimplementation/operation stage (training and application maintenance). Computer software costs that are incurred in the preliminary project stage should be expensed as incurred.

Once the capitalization criteria of the SOP have been met, external direct costs of materials and services consumed in developing or obtaining internal-use computer software, payroll costs for employees who are directly associated with and who devote time to the project, and interest costs incurred in developing the software should be capitalized. Capitalization should cease no later than the point at which a computer software project is substantially complete and ready for its intended use.

Internal and external training costs and maintenance costs incurred in the postimplementation/ operation stage should be expensed as incurred. General and administrative costs and overhead costs should not be capitalized as costs of internal-use software.

(g) EXTRACTIVE INDUSTRIES   Intangible assets in the extractive industries include leased or purchased rights to exploit mineral and other natural resources based on lump-sum, periodic, or production-based payments. The rights are usually included in the property section of the balance sheet.

A comprehensive discussion of the accounting for these and other assets in the extractive industries is given in Chapter 27.

(h) PRODUCERS OR DISTRIBUTORS OF FILMS   SOP 00-2, "Accounting by Producers or Distributors of Films," provides guidance on the accounting for costs related to all types of films and is applicable to both producers and distributors of films. The costs of producing a film include film costs, participation costs, exploitation costs, and manufacturing costs.

Marketing and other exploitation costs, other than advertising, should be expensed as incurred. Advertising costs should be accounted for under SOP 93-7, "Reporting on Advertising Costs." Entities are required to amortize film costs using the individual-film-forecast-computation method. That method provides for amortization of costs in the same ratio that current-period actual revenue bears to estimated remaining unrecognized ultimate revenue as of the beginning of the current fiscal year. Amortization begins when a film is released and the entity begins to recognize revenue from the film.

Certain events or changes in circumstances, such as an adverse change in the expected performance of a film or a substantial delay in completion of the film, indicate that the fair value of the film may be less than the related unamortized film costs. If such an event occurs, an entity should assess whether the fair value of the film is less than its unamortized film costs. If the unamortized capitalized film costs exceed the film's fair value, the excess should be written off and may not be subsequently restored. See Chapter 30 for more on this topic.

(i) PUBLIC UTILITIES   The general provisions of accounting for intangible assets of various types apply to public utilities. However, since public utilities are required by regulatory agencies to maintain their accounts in accordance with accounting practices that may vary from GAAP, certain differences in treatment may result. An example is R&D costs, which certain regulatory agencies allow to be deferred.

The rate regulator may reasonably assure the existence of an asset by permitting the inclusion of a cost in allowable costs for rate-making purposes. SFAS No. 71, "Accounting for the Effects of Certain Types of Regulation," sets forth two criteria that must both be met in order for a utility to capitalize a cost that would otherwise be required, under GAAP, to be expensed currently:

1. It is probable that future revenue in an amount at least equal to the capitalized cost will result from inclusion of that cost in allowable costs for rate-making purposes.
2. Based on available evidence, the future revenue will be provided to permit recovery of the previously incurred cost rather than to provide for expected levels of similar future costs. If the revenue will be provided through an automatic rate-adjustment clause, this criterion requires that the regulator's intent clearly be to permit recovery of the previously incurred cost.

If at any time the capitalized cost no longer meets those two criteria, it is to be expensed. The value of an asset may be impaired by a regulator's rate actions. If a rate regulator excludes all or part of a capitalized cost from allowable costs and the cost was capitalized based on the foregoing criteria, the asset should be reduced to the extent of the excluded cost. Whether other assets have been impaired is determined under the general rules for impairment, which are described in Sections 20A.4(b) and 20A.4 (c).

If an enterprise discontinues application of SFAS No. 71 because, for example, its operations have been deregulated, it would eliminate from its GAAP balance sheet assets consisting of costs capitalized that would not have been capitalized by unregulated entities. Numerous state legislatures and/or regulatory commissions have approved or are considering deregulating utilities' generation (production) cost of electricity, although the portion of the kilowatt charge attributable to transmission of the electricity to the local area and the distribution cost to the customer are not being deregulated. If some, but not all, of a utility's operations are regulated, SFAS No. 71 should be applied to the portion of the operations that continue to meet the requirements of SFAS No. 71 for regulatory accounting. SFAS No. 101, "Regulated

Enterprises—Accounting for the Discontinuation of Application of FASB Statement No. 71," addresses how an entity that ceases to meet the criteria for application of SFAS No. 71 to all or part of its operations should report that event in its financial statements.

An issue related to the current deregulation environment is when an entity should cease to apply the regulated enterprise accounting model prescribed by SFAS No. 71 to the generation portion of its operations if deregulation is under consideration. In Issue No. 97-4, "Deregulation of the Price of Electricity—Issues Related to the Application of FASB Statements No. 71 and 101," the EITF reached a consensus that when deregulatory legislation or a rate order is issued that contains sufficient detail to determine how the deregulatory plan will affect the portion of the business being deregulated, the entity should stop applying SFAS No. 71 to that separable portion of its business. The Task Force considered the following fact situation: If legislation is passed requiring deregulation of generation charges at the end of five years, the date the legislation is passed is the latest date that the entity can discontinue application of the SFAS No. 71 accounting model to the generation portion of its operations. The consensus does not address whether an entity should stop applying SFAS No. 71 at an earlier time. The Task Force also observed that the financial statements should segregate, either on their face or in the notes, the amounts that pertain to the separable portion.

With regard to goodwill, a regulator may permit a utility to amortize purchased goodwill over a specified period, may direct a utility not to amortize goodwill, or may direct the utility to write off goodwill. SFAS No. 71 requires the goodwill to be amortized for financial reporting purposes over the period during which it will be allowed for rate-making purposes. If the regulator either excludes amortization from allowable costs for rate-making purposes or directs the utility to write off goodwill, goodwill should not be amortized, and it should be accounted for under SFAS No. 142.

(j) RECORD AND MUSIC INDUSTRY   Significant intangible assets in the record and music industry include record masters, recording artist contracts, and copyrights. Accounting for copyrights generally follows that used in other industries, but the accounting for record masters and recording artist contracts is unique.

SFAS No. 50, "Financial Reporting in the Record and Music Industry," is the primary source of accounting principles in this area. Costs of producing a record master include the costs of musical talent; technical talent for engineering, directing, and mixing; equipment to record and produce the master; and studio facility charges. When past performance of an artist provides a reasonable basis for estimating that the cost of a record master borne by the record company will be recovered from future sales, that cost should be recorded as an asset and, when material, should be separately disclosed. The cost of record masters should be amortized by a method that reasonably relates the cost to the net revenue expected to be realized. Ordinarily, amortization occurs over a very short period. Unamortized amounts should be written off when it becomes apparent that they will not be recovered through future sales. The cost of the record master recoverable from the artist's royalties is to be accounted for as an advance royalty.

A recording artist contract is an agreement for personal services. A major portion of the artist's compensation consists of participation in earnings (measured by sales and license fee income, commonly referred to as a "royalty") or of a nonrefundable advance against royalties. Advances should be recorded as an asset (as a prepaid royalty, classified as current or noncurrent depending on when amounts are expected to be realized) if it is anticipated that they will be recovered against royalties otherwise payable to the artist. When it is determined that a prepayment will not be recovered, the balance should be written off.

(k) TIMBER INDUSTRY   Companies in the forest products industry may make lump-sum payments for timber-cutting rights, which allow them to remove trees for a specified period or in specified quantities. Lump-sum payments made at the inception of an agreement are properly deferred and amortized over the period of the agreement or on the basis of estimates of recoverable timber. Periodic or production-based payments are expensed as they do not represent future benefits. Cutting rights are ordinarily included in the Property section of the balance sheet and are stated at cost less amortization. The amortization policy should be disclosed.

20A.7   ACCOUNTING FOR GOODWILL

(a) INITIAL VALUATION   SFAS Nos. 141, "Business Combinations," and 142, "Goodwill and Other Intangible Assets," were both issued in June 2001 and replaced Accounting Principles Board (APB) Opinions Nos. 16 and 17. In these standards, goodwill is defined as

> The excess of the cost of an acquired entity over the net of the amounts assigned to assets acquired and liabilities assumed. The amount recognized as goodwill includes acquired intangible assets that do not meet the criteria in SFAS No. 141, "Business Combinations," for recognition as an asset apart from goodwill.

The previously referenced criteria for separate recognition of intangibles are discussed in Section 20A.3(a). For accounting purposes, the cost of purchased goodwill is the residual cost remaining after all other identifiable assets and liabilities have been valued.

(b) SUBSEQUENT ACCOUNTING   Goodwill is not amortized. It is tested for impairment at a level of reporting referred to as a reporting unit (see Section 20A.7(b)(iv) for a definition of a reporting unit). Impairment is the condition that exists when the carrying amount of goodwill is greater than its implied fair value. A two-step impairment test, discussed next, is used to identify potential goodwill impairment and measure the amount of a goodwill impairment loss to be recognized, if any.

(i) Recognition and Measurement of an Impairment Loss   The first step of a goodwill impairment test compares the fair value of a reporting unit with its carrying amount, including goodwill, applying the guidance provided in Section 20A.7(b)(ii). If the fair value of the reporting unit is more than its carrying amount, goodwill of the reporting unit is considered not impaired, and the second step of the impairment test is not performed. If the carrying amount of the reporting unit is more than its fair value, the second step of the goodwill impairment test, discussed next, is performed to measure the amount of impairment, if any.

The second step of the goodwill impairment test compares the implied fair value of reporting unit goodwill (explained in the next paragraph) with the carrying amount of the goodwill. If the carrying amount of reporting unit goodwill is more than the implied fair value of the goodwill, an impairment loss is recognized in an amount equal to the excess. The loss recognized cannot exceed the carrying amount of goodwill. When a goodwill impairment loss is recognized, the adjusted carrying amount of goodwill is its new accounting basis. Subsequent to the measurement and recognition of the goodwill impairment loss, a later recovery in value cannot be recognized. Thus, goodwill impairments cannot be reversed.

The implied fair value of goodwill is determined in the same way as is the amount of goodwill to be recognized in a business combination. The reporting entity allocates the fair value of the reporting unit to all of the assets and liabilities of the unit, including any unrecognized intangible assets, the same way it would be allocated had the reporting unit been acquired in a business combination and had the fair value of the reporting unit been the price paid to acquire the reporting unit. The excess of the fair value of the reporting unit over the amounts assigned to its assets and liabilities is the *implied fair value of goodwill.*

The allocation process just described is performed only for the purpose of testing goodwill for impairment. A reporting entity does not write up or down a recognized asset or liability, and it does not recognize a previously unrecognized intangible asset as a result of the allocation process exercise.

If the second step of the goodwill impairment test is not complete before the financial statements are issued and a goodwill impairment loss is probable and can be reasonably estimated, the best estimate of the loss is recognized in those financial statements. Any adjustment to the estimated loss based on completion of the measurement of the impairment loss is recognized in the next reporting period.

(ii) Fair Value Measurements SFAS No. 142 defines *fair value* the same way FASB Statement of Concepts No. 7 does:

> The amount at which that asset (or liability) could be bought (or incurred) or sold (settled) in a current transaction between willing parties, that is, other than in a forced or liquidation sale.

According to that definition, the fair value of a reporting unit is the amount at which the unit as a whole could be bought or sold in a current transaction between willing parties. Quoted market prices in active markets are the best evidence of fair value and are used as the basis for measurement, if available. However, the market price of an individual equity security and thus the market capitalization of a reporting unit with publicly traded equity securities may not be representative of the fair value of the reporting unit as a whole, because of a control premium. The quoted market price of an individual equity security, therefore, need not be the sole measurement basis of the fair value of a reporting unit. SEC registrants should be aware that the SEC staff has sometimes questioned valuations not based on the market price of the equity security.

If quoted market prices are not available, the estimate of fair value is based on the best information available, including prices for similar assets and liabilities and the results of using other valuation techniques. A present value technique is often the best available technique with which to estimate the fair value of a group of net assets (i.e., a reporting unit). If a present value technique is used to measure fair value, estimates of future cash flows used in the technique are to be consistent with the objective of measuring fair value. The cash flow estimates should incorporate assumptions that marketplace participants would use in their estimates of fair value. If that information is not available without undue cost and effort, a reporting entity may use its own assumptions.

An entity should base the cash flow estimates on reasonable and supportable assumptions after consideration of all available evidence. The weight given to the evidence should be commensurate with the extent to which the evidence can be verified objectively. If the entity estimates a range for the amount or timing of possible cash flows, it should consider the likelihood of possible outcomes. FASB Concepts Statement No. 7 gives guidance. It states that an "expected present value technique" which uses the sum of probability-weighted present values in a range of estimated cash flows adjusted for risk, all discounted using the same interest rate convention, is the preferred—but not required—approach. The FASB has indicated that such a technique is a more effective measurement tool than was the traditional present value approach, especially in situations in which the timing or the amount of estimated cash flows is uncertain, as is the case in measuring nonfinancial assets and liabilities.

In estimating the fair value of a reporting unit, a valuation technique based on multiples of earnings or revenue or a similar performance measure may be used if that technique is consistent with the objective of measuring fair value. Use of such multiples may be appropriate, for example, when the fair value of an entity that has comparable operations and economic characteristics is observable and the relevant multiples of the comparable entity are known. Conversely, such multiples are not used in situations in which the operations or activities of an entity whose multiples are known are not of a comparable nature, scope, or size as the reporting unit for which fair value is being estimated.

(iii) When to Test Goodwill for Impairment   Goodwill of a reporting unit is tested for impairment annually and between annual tests in certain circumstances, as discussed subsequently. The annual goodwill impairment test may be performed any time during the fiscal year provided the timing of the test is consistent from year to year. Different reporting units may be tested for impairment at different times.

A detailed determination of the fair value of a reporting unit may be carried forward from one year to the next if all of the following criteria have been met:

- The assets and liabilities that make up the reporting unit have not changed significantly since the most recent fair value determination.
- The most recent fair value determination resulted in an amount that exceeded the carrying amount of the reporting unit by a substantial margin.
- Based on an analysis of events that have occurred and circumstances that have changed since the most recent fair value determination, the likelihood that a current fair value determination would be less than the current carrying amount of the reporting unit is remote.

Goodwill of a reporting unit is tested for impairment between annual tests if an event occurs or circumstances change that would more likely than not reduce the fair value of a reporting unit below its carrying amount.

Examples of such events or circumstances include the following:

- A significant adverse change in legal factors or in the business climate
- An adverse action or assessment by a regulator
- Unanticipated competition
- A loss of key personnel
- A more-likely-than-not expectation that a reporting unit or a significant portion of a reporting unit will be sold or otherwise disposed of
- Testing for recoverability under SFAS No. 144 of a significant asset group within a reporting unit
- Recognition of a goodwill impairment loss in the financial statements of a subsidiary that is a component of a reporting unit

Also see Section 20A.7(b)(vii) for the need to test goodwill for impairment after a portion of goodwill has been allocated to a business to be disposed of.

If goodwill and another asset or asset group of a reporting unit are tested for impairment at the same time, the other asset or asset group is tested before goodwill. If the asset or asset group is found to be impaired, the impairment loss is recognized before goodwill is tested for impairment.

(iv) Reporting Unit   A reporting unit is an operating segment or one level below an operating segment, referred to as a component. An operating segment is defined by SFAS No. 131, "Disclosures about Segments of an Enterprise and Related Information." A component of an operating segment is a reporting unit if the component constitutes a business, as discussed in EITF Issue No. 98-3, for which discrete financial information is available and segment management, as defined by SFAS No. 131, regularly reviews the operating results of that component.

Segment management may consist of one or more segment managers. Two or more components of an operating segment are aggregated and deemed a single reporting unit if the components have similar economic characteristics, as discussed in SFAS No. 131. An operating segment is deemed a reporting unit if all of its components are similar, if none of its components is a reporting unit, or if it comprises only a single component.

Because considerable judgment is required for entities to determine their reporting units and the guidance in SFAS No. 142 is quite limited, the FASB staff provided further clarification of that guidance in EITF Topic No. D-101. The basic guidance is that a component of an operating segment is a reporting unit if (1) it constitutes a business, (2) discrete financial information on the component is available, and (3) segment management regularly reviews the results of the reporting unit. A fourth requirement provides that components with similar economic characteristics should be combined into one reporting unit. Topic No. D-101 provides that the first three factors are required for a component to be a reporting unit, but no one factor is individually determinative.

The determinative factors are how an entity manages its operations and how an acquired entity is integrated with the acquiring entity. Topic No. D-101 provides the following clarification of each factor:

- *Component constitutes a business.* Judgment is required to determine whether a component constitutes a business, and entities are required to consider the guidance in EITF Issue No. 98-3 in determining that. To be a business under the guidance in EITF Issue No. 98-3, the activities and assets should include "all the inputs and processes necessary" to conduct normal operations. The fact that operating information may be available does not mean the operations constitute a business. They may be just a part of a business, such as one product line.
- *Discrete financial information.* For purposes of both SFAS No. 131 and SFAS No. 142, discrete financial information can consist of just operating information, with no balance sheet information prepared for the component. However, if the component is a reporting unit, the entity would be required to identify and allocate assets and liabilities applicable to the component to test goodwill for impairment.
- *Reviewed by segment management.* Under SFAS No. 131, segment management may be one level below the chief operating decision maker, and there may be one or more segment managers. The focus of SFAS No. 142 is on how operating segments are managed rather than on how the entity as a whole is managed.
- *Similar economic characteristics.* The evaluation of whether two components have similar economic characteristics requires consideration of the factors in paragraph 17 of SFAS No. 131: similar economic characteristics, such as similar long-term average gross margins; the nature of the products and/or services; the nature of production processes; the type or class of customers; the methods used to distribute products and provide services; and the nature of any regulatory environment. Topic No. D-101 provides

that not all factors have to be met for economic similarity to exist, and the evaluation should be more qualitative than quantitative.

Topic No. D-101 also provides additional factors to consider when evaluating whether components should be combined in a reporting unit because they are economically similar:

- How an entity operates its business and the nature of the operations
- Whether goodwill is recoverable from the separate operations of each component business or from the components working together because, for example, the components are economically interdependent
- The extent to which the component businesses share assets and other resources
- Whether the components provide support and receive benefits from the same R&D projects

Components of different operating segments for purposes of SFAS No. 131 cannot be combined into the same reporting unit, even if they have similar economic characteristics. This might occur, for example, if the entity organized its operating segments on a geographic basis.

Questions have arisen about whether one or more components of operating units aggregated into one reporting unit under SFAS No. 131 could be economically dissimilar and therefore be in separate reporting units under SFAS No. 142. Topic No. D-101 provides two explanations of why that could happen:

1. The determination of reportable segments under SFAS No. 131 requires identification of operating segments and subsequent determination of whether economically similar operating segments should be aggregated. However, the determination of reporting units under SFAS No. 142 begins with operating segments and then requires an analysis of whether economically dissimilar components of an operating segment should be disaggregated.
2. For a component of an operating segment to be an operating segment under SFAS No. 131, its operating performance must be regularly reviewed by the chief operating decision maker. That same component, however, could be a reporting unit if a segment manager regularly reviews its operating performance.

For the purpose of testing goodwill for impairment, acquired assets and assumed liabilities are assigned to a reporting unit as of the acquisition date if both of the following criteria are met:

1. The asset will be employed in or the liability relates to the operations of a reporting unit.
2. The asset or liability will be considered in determining the fair value of the reporting unit.

Assets or liabilities that an entity considers part of its corporate assets or liabilities are also assigned to a reporting unit if both of the preceding criteria are met. Examples are environmental liabilities that relate to an existing operating facility of the reporting unit and a pension obligation that would be included in the determination of the fair value of the reporting unit. Some assets or liabilities may be employed in or relate to the operations of multiple reporting units. The methodology used to determine the amount of those assets or liabilities to assign to a reporting unit is on a reasonable and supportable basis and applied in a consistent manner. For example, this would include assets and liabilities not directly related to a specific reporting unit but from which the reporting unit benefits could be allocated according to the benefit received by the different reporting units or based on the relative fair values of the different reporting units. A pro rata allocation based on payroll expense might be used for pension items.

For the purpose of testing goodwill for impairment, all goodwill acquired in a business combination is assigned to one or more reporting units as of the acquisition date. Goodwill is assigned to reporting units of the acquiring entity expected to benefit from the synergies of the combination even though other assets or liabilities of the acquired entity may not be assigned to that reporting unit. The total amount of acquired goodwill may be divided among a number of reporting units. The methodology used to determine the amount of goodwill to assign to a reporting unit should be reasonable and supportable and applied in a consistent manner. Also, the methodology has to be consistent with the objectives of the process of assigning goodwill to reporting units, described next. In concept, the amount of goodwill assigned to a reporting unit would be determined in a manner similar to how the amount of goodwill recognized in a business combination is determined.

The fair value of the acquired business or portion of the acquired business that will be included in a particular reporting unit is, in essence, the purchase price of that business. The entity allocates that purchase price to the assets acquired and liabilities incurred related to (the portion of) the acquired business assigned to the reporting unit. Any excess purchase price is the amount of goodwill assigned to that reporting unit. However, if the goodwill is to be assigned to a reporting unit that has not been assigned any of the assets acquired or liabilities assumed in that acquisition, the amount of goodwill to be assigned to that unit might be determined by applying a "with and without" computation. That is, the difference between the fair value of that reporting unit before the acquisition and its fair value after the acquisition represents the amount of goodwill to be assigned to that reporting unit.

When an entity reorganizes its reporting structure in a manner that changes the composition of one or more of its reporting units, the guidance given earlier in this section for assigning acquired assets and assumed liabilities to reporting units is used to reassign assets and liabilities to the reporting units affected. However, goodwill is reassigned to the reporting units affected using a relative fair value allocation approach similar to that used when a portion of a reporting unit is to be disposed of, which is discussed in Section 20A.7(b)(vii). For example, if existing reporting unit A is to be integrated with reporting units B, C, and D, goodwill of reporting unit A would be assigned to units B, C, and D based on the relative fair values of the three portions of reporting unit A before those portions are integrated with reporting units B, C, and D.

(v) Goodwill Impairment Testing by a Subsidiary All goodwill recognized by a public or nonpublic subsidiary in its separate financial statements prepared in conformity with GAAP, known as subsidiary goodwill, is accounted for in conformity with SFAS No. 142. It is tested for impairment at the subsidiary level using the subsidiary's reporting units. If a goodwill impairment loss is recognized at the subsidiary level, goodwill of the reporting unit or units at the consolidated level in which the subsidiary's reporting unit with impaired goodwill resides is tested for impairment if the event that gave rise to the loss at the subsidiary level more likely than not would reduce the fair value of the reporting unit at the consolidated level below its carrying amount. A goodwill impairment loss is recognized at the consolidated level only if goodwill at the consolidated level is impaired.

(vi) Goodwill Impairment Testing When a Noncontrolling Interest Exists Goodwill from a business combination with a continuing noncontrolling (minority) interest is tested for impairment using an approach consistent with the approach used to measure the noncontrolling

interest at the acquisition date. For example, if goodwill is first recognized based on only the controlling interest of the parent, the fair value of the reporting unit used in the impairment test is based on the controlling interest and does not reflect the portion of fair value attributable to the noncontrolling interest. Similarly, the implied fair value of goodwill determined in the second step of the impairment test used to measure the impairment loss reflects only the parent's interest in the goodwill.

(vii) Disposal of All or a Portion of a Reporting Unit   When a reporting unit is to be disposed of in its entirety, the carrying amount of goodwill of the reporting unit is included in the carrying amount of the reporting unit in determining the gain or loss on disposal. When a portion of a reporting unit that constitutes a business is to be disposed of, the carrying amount of goodwill associated with the business is included in the carrying amount of the business in determining the gain or loss on disposal. The portion of the carrying amount of goodwill to be included in that carrying amount is based on the relative fair values of the business to be disposed of and the portion of the reporting unit to be retained. However, if the business to be disposed of was never integrated into the reporting unit after its acquisition and thus the benefits of the acquired goodwill were never realized by the rest of the reporting unit, the current carrying amount of the acquired goodwill is included in the carrying amount of business to be disposed of. When only a portion of goodwill is allocated to a business to be disposed of, the goodwill remaining in the portion of the reporting unit to be retained is tested for impairment.

(viii) Equity Method Investments   The portion of the difference between the cost of an investment and the amount of underlying equity in net assets of an equity method investee recognized as goodwill in conformity with paragraph 19(b) of APB Opinion No. 18, "The Equity Method of Accounting for Investments in Common Stock," known as equity method goodwill, is not amortized. However, equity method goodwill is not tested for impairment in conformity with SFAS No. 142.

Equity method investments continue to be reviewed for impairment in conformity with paragraph 19(h) of APB Opinion No. 18.

(ix) Entities Emerging from Bankruptcy   SOP 90-7, "Financial Reporting by Entities in Reorganization Under the Bankruptcy Code," provides that when an entity applies fresh-start accounting on emerging from bankruptcy, the reorganization value should be allocated to all tangible and intangible assets following the procedures in APB Opinion No. 16, "Business Combinations." SFAS No. 142 stipulates that entities should report the excess reorganization value as goodwill and account for it in the same manner as other elements of goodwill.

20A.8   DEFERRED INCOME TAXES

SFAS No. 142 does not change the requirements in SFAS No. 109, "Accounting for Income Taxes," paragraphs 30, 261, and 262, for recognition of deferred income taxes related to goodwill and intangible assets.

20A.9   FINANCIAL STATEMENT PRESENTATION

(a) INTANGIBLE ASSETS   All intangible assets are aggregated and presented as a separate line item in the statement of financial position. In addition, individual intangible assets or classes of intangible assets may be presented as separate line items. Amortization expense and impairment losses for intangible assets are presented in income statement line items within continuing operations as deemed appropriate for each entity. An impairment loss resulting from such an impairment test should not be recognized as a change in accounting principle.

(b) GOODWILL   The aggregate amount of goodwill is presented as a separate line item in the statement of financial position. The aggregate amount of goodwill impairment losses are presented as a separate line item in the income statement before the subtotal *income from continuing operations,* or a similar caption, unless a goodwill impairment loss is associated with a discontinued operation. A goodwill impairment loss associated with a discontinued operation is included net of tax within the results of discontinued operations.

20A.10 DISCLOSURES

The following information is disclosed in the notes to the financial statements in the period of acquisition of intangible assets acquired either individually or with a group of assets:

A. For intangible assets subject to amortization:
1. The total amount assigned and the amount assigned to any major intangible asset class
2. The amount of any significant residual value, in total and by major intangible asset class
3. The weighted-average amortization period, in total and by major intangible asset class

B. For intangible assets not subject to amortization, the total amount assigned and the amount assigned to any major intangible asset class

C. The amount of R&D assets acquired and written off in the period and the line item in the income statement in which the amounts written off are aggregated

The following information is disclosed in the financial statements or the notes to the financial statements for each period for which a statement of financial position is presented:

A. For intangible assets subject to amortization:
1. The gross carrying amount and accumulated amortization, in total and by major intangible asset class
2. The aggregate amortization expense for the period
3. The estimated aggregate amortization expense for each of the five succeeding fiscal years

B. For intangible assets not subject to amortization, the total carrying amount and the carrying amount for each major intangible asset class

C. The changes in the carrying amount of goodwill during the period, including:
1. The aggregate amount of goodwill acquired
2. The aggregate amount of impairment losses recognized on goodwill
3. The amount of goodwill included in the gain or loss on disposal of all or a portion of a reporting unit

Reporting entities that report segment information in conformity with SFAS No. 131 should provide the preceding information about goodwill in total and for each reportable segment and should disclose any significant changes in the allocation of goodwill by reportable segment. If any portion of goodwill has not yet been allocated to a reporting unit at the date the financial statements are issued, that unallocated amount and the reasons for not allocating the amount are disclosed. For each impairment loss recognized related to an intangible asset, the following information is disclosed in the notes to the financial statements that include the period in which the impairment loss is recognized:

- Description of the impaired intangible asset and the facts and circumstances leading to the impairment
- Amount of the impairment loss and the method for determining fair value
- Caption in the income statement or the statement of activities in which the impairment loss is aggregated
- If applicable, the segment in which the impaired intangible asset is reported under SFAS No. 131

For each goodwill impairment loss recognized, the following information is disclosed in the notes to the financial statements that include the period in which the impairment loss is recognized:

- A description of the facts and circumstances leading to the impairment
- The amount of the impairment loss and the method of determining the fair value of the associated reporting unit
- If a recognized impairment loss is an estimate that has not yet been finalized, that fact and the reasons for it and, in subsequent periods, the nature and amount of any significant adjustments made to the initial estimate of the impairment loss

20A.11   EFFECTIVE DATE AND TRANSITION PROVISIONS OF SFAS NO. 142

The provisions of SFAS No. 142 were initially applied in fiscal years beginning after December 15, 2001, to all goodwill and other intangible assets recognized in a reporting entity's statement of financial position at the beginning of that fiscal year, regardless of when those previously recognized assets were first recognized. Early application was permitted for entities with fiscal years beginning after March 15, 2001, provided that the first interim financial statements had not been issued previously. The provisions of the statement were to be first applied at the beginning of a fiscal year. They were not to be applied retroactively.

SFAS No. 142's provisions are not to be applied to previously recognized goodwill and intangible assets acquired in a combination between two or more mutual enterprises, acquired in a combination between not-for-profit organizations, or from the acquisition of a for-profit business entity by a not-for-profit organization until interpretive guidance related to the application of the purchase method to those transactions is issued. As of late 2005, this guidance has yet to be promulgated, although this is anticipated to occur in the near future.

See Section 10.3(o) for transition provisions related to goodwill and intangible assets acquired in business combination for which the acquisition date was before July 1, 2001, that were accounted for by the purchase method.

(a) GOODWILL AND INTANGIBLE ASSETS ACQUIRED AFTER JUNE 30, 2001

Goodwill acquired in a business combination for which the acquisition date is after June 30, 2001 is not amortized. Intangible assets other than goodwill acquired in a business combination or other transaction for which the date of acquisition is after June 30, 2001 are amortized or not amortized in conformity with the discussion in Sections 20A.4(b) and 20A.4(c). Goodwill and intangible assets acquired in a transaction for which the acquisition date is after June 30, 2001 but before the date that SFAS No. 142 was first applied in its entirety were to be reviewed for impairment in conformity with APB Opinion No. 17 or SFAS No. 121 (as appropriate) until the date SFAS No. 142 was applied in its entirety. The financial statement presentation and disclosure provisions of SFAS No. 142 were not to be applied to those assets until SFAS No. 142 was applied in its entirety.

Goodwill and intangible assets acquired in a combination between two or more mutual enterprises, acquired in a combination between not-for-profit organizations, or from the acquisition of a for-profit business entity by a not-for-profit organization for which the acquisition date is after June 30, 2001, continue to be accounted for in conformity with APB Opinion No. 17 until the FASB provides guidance on issues related to the application of the purchase method to such transactions.

(b) PREVIOUSLY RECOGNIZED INTANGIBLE ASSETS   To apply SFAS No. 142 to previously recognized intangible assets (those acquired in a transaction for which the acquisition date is on or before June 30, 2001), the useful lives of those assets are reassessed using the guidance in Section 20A.4(a) and the remaining amortization periods are adjusted accordingly. For example, the amortization period for a previously recognized intangible asset might be increased if its original useful life was estimated to be longer than the 40-year maximum amortization period allowed by APB Opinion No. 17. The reassessment was to be completed before the end of the first interim period of the fiscal year in which SFAS No. 142 was first applied.

Previously recognized intangible assets deemed to have indefinite useful lives were to be tested for impairment as of the beginning of the fiscal year in which SFAS No. 142 was first applied. The transitional intangible asset impairment test was to be completed in the first interim period in which SFAS No. 142 was first applied, and any resulting impairment loss was to be recognized as the effect of a change in accounting principle. The effect of the accounting change and related income tax effects were to be presented in the income statement between the captions extraordinary items and net income. The per-share information presented in the income statement included the per-share effect of the accounting change.

(c) PREVIOUSLY RECOGNIZED GOODWILL   At the date SFAS No. 142 was first applied, the reporting entity was required to establish its reporting units based on its reporting structure at that date and the guidance described in Section 20A.7(b)(iv). Recognized net assets and liabilities that did not relate to a reporting unit, such as an environmental liability for an operation previously disposed of, did not need to be assigned to a reporting unit. All goodwill recognized in a reporting entity's statement of financial position at the date that SFAS No. 142 was first applied was to be assigned to one or more reporting units. Goodwill was to be assigned in a reasonable and supportable manner. The sources of previously recognized goodwill were to be considered in making that initial assignment as well as the reporting units to which the related acquired net assets were assigned. Section 20A.7(b)(iv) provides guidance on assigning goodwill to reporting units on initial application of SFAS No. 142.

Goodwill in each reporting unit was tested for impairment as of the beginning of the fiscal year in which SFAS No. 142 was first applied in its entirety. The first step of the test was to be completed within six months from the date the reporting entity first applied SFAS No. 142. The amounts used in the transitional goodwill impairment test were measured as of the beginning of the year of first application. If the carrying amount of the net assets of a reporting unit (including goodwill) exceeded the fair value of the reporting unit, the second step of the transitional goodwill impairment test was completed as soon as possible, but no later than the end of the year of first application.

An impairment loss as a result of a transitional goodwill impairment test was recognized as the effect of a change in accounting principle. The effect of the accounting change and related income tax effects were to be presented in the income statement between the captions extraordinary items and net income. The per-share information presented in the income statement included the per-share effect of the accounting change. Though a transitional impairment loss for goodwill could be measured in other than the first interim reporting period, it was to be recognized in the first interim period regardless of the period in which it was measured, consistent with paragraph 10 of SFAS No. 3, "Reporting Accounting Changes in Interim Financial Statements."

The financial information for the interim periods of the fiscal year that preceded the period in which the transitional goodwill impairment loss was measured was to be restated to reflect the accounting change in those periods. The aggregate amount of the accounting change is included in restated net income of the first interim period of the year of first application (and in any year-to-date or last-12-months-to-date financial reports that included the first interim period). Whenever financial information is presented that includes the periods that precede the period in which the transitional goodwill impairment loss was measured, that financial information should be presented on the restated basis.

A reporting entity was required to perform the required annual goodwill impairment test in the year that SFAS No. 142 was first applied in its entirety, in addition to the transitional goodwill impairment test, unless the reporting entity designated the beginning of its fiscal year as the date for its annual goodwill impairment test.

(d) EQUITY METHOD GOODWILL   When SFAS No. 142 was first applied, the portion of the excess of cost over the underlying equity in net assets of an investee accounted for using the equity method that had been recognized as goodwill was no longer to be amortized. However, equity method goodwill is not to be tested for impairment under SFAS No. 142. Rather, the guidance under APB No. 18 continues to be applicable in assessing impairment of equity method investments.

(e) TRANSITIONAL DISCLOSURES   Expanded disclosures were mandated during the initial implementation period for SFAS No. 142. Since all entities have now fully adopted this standard, and since comparative disclosures including pre-implementation periods are now unlikely to be encountered in practice, this will not be described in detail.

20A.12   SOURCES AND SUGGESTED REFERENCES

Accounting Principles Board, "Restatement of Revision of Accounting Research Bulletins," Accounting Research Bulletin No. 43. New York: AICPA, 1968.

Accounting Principles Board, "Disclosure of Accounting Policies," APB Opinion No. 22. New York: AICPA, 1973.

Accounting Principles Board, "Reporting the Results of Operations," APB Opinion No. 30. New York: AICPA, 1973.

American Accounting Association Financial Accounting Standards Committee, "Equity Valuation Models and Measuring Goodwill Impairment,"*Accounting Horizons,* June 2001.

American Institute of Certified Public Accountants, "Push Down Accounting," Issues Paper. New York: AICPA, 1979.

American Institute of Certified Public Accountants, "Accounting for Developmental and Preoperating Costs, Purchases and Exchanges of Take-off and Landing Slots, and Airframe Modifications," Statement of Position 88-1. New York: AICPA, 1988.

American Institute of Certified Public Accountants, "Financial Reporting by Entities in Reorganization Under the Bankruptcy Code," Statement of Position 90-7. New York: AICPA, November 19, 1990.

American Institute of Certified Public Accountants, "Reporting on Advertising Costs," Statement of Position 93-7. New York: AICPA, December 29, 1993.

American Institute of Certified Public Accountants, "Accounting for the Costs of Computer Software Developed or Obtained for Internal Use," Statement of Position 98-1. New York: AICPA, 1998.

American Institute of Certified Public Accountants, "Reporting on the Cost of Start-Up Activities," Statement of Position 98-5. New York: AICPA, 1998.

American Institute of Certified Public Accountants, "Accounting by Producers or Distributors of Films," Statement of Position 00-2. New York: AICPA, 2000.

American Institute of Certified Public Accountants, "Assets Acquired in a Business Combination to Be Used in R&D Activities: A Focus on Software, Electronic Devices, and Pharmaceutical Industries," AICPA Practice Aid Series. New York: AICPA, 2001.

American Institute of Certified Public Accountants: "The Fair Value Measurement Valuation Toolkit for Financial Accounting Standards Board Statements of Financial Accounting Standards No. 141, Business Combinations, and No. 142, Goodwill and Other Intangible Assets. New York: AICPA, 2002.

Financial Accounting Standards Board, "Accounting for Research and Development Costs," Statement of Financial Accounting Standards No. 2. Norwalk, CT: FASB, 1974.

Financial Accounting Standards Board, "Applicability of FASB Statement No. 2 to Computer Software (An Interpretation of FASB Statement No. 2)," FASB Interpretation No. 6. Norwalk, CT: FASB, 1975.

Financial Accounting Standards Board, "Accounting for Franchise Fee Revenue," Statement of Financial Accounting Standards No. 45. Norwalk, CT: FASB, 1981.

Financial Accounting Standards Board, "Financial Reporting in the Record and Music Industry," Statement of Financial Accounting Standards No. 50. Norwalk, CT: FASB, 1981.

Financial Accounting Standards Board, "Financial Reporting by Cable Television Companies," Statement of Financial Accounting Standards No. 51. Norwalk, CT: FASB, 1981.

Financial Accounting Standards Board, "Financial Reporting by Broadcasters," Statement of Financial Accounting Standards No. 63. Norwalk, CT: FASB, 1982.

Financial Accounting Standards Board, "Accounting for the Effects of Certain Types of Regulation," Statement of Financial Accounting Standards No. 71. Norwalk, CT: FASB, 1982.

Financial Accounting Standards Board, "Accounting for Certain Acquisitions of Banking or Thrift Institutions," Statement of Financial Accounting Standards No. 72. Norwalk, CT: FASB, 1983.

Financial Accounting Standards Board, "Accounting for the Costs of Computer Software to Be Sold, Leased, or Otherwise Marketed," Statement of Financial Accounting Standards No. 86. Norwalk, CT: FASB, 1985.

Financial Accounting Standards Board, "Statement of Cash Flows," Statement of Financial Accounting Standards No. 95. Norwalk, CT: FASB, 1987.

Financial Accounting Standards Board, "Issues Relating to Accounting for Leases," FASB Technical Bulletin No. 88-1. Norwalk, CT: FASB, 1988.

Financial Accounting Standards Board, "Accounting for Income Taxes," Statement of Financial Accounting Standards No. 109. Norwalk, CT: FASB, February, 1992.

Financial Accounting Standards Board, "Recognition of Liabilities in Connection with a Purchase Business Combination," EITF Issue No. 95-3. Norwalk, CT: FASB, 1995.

Financial Accounting Standards Board, "Determination of What Risks and Rewards, If Any, Can Be Retained and Whether Any Unresolved Contingencies May Exist in a Sale of Mortgage Loan Servicing Rights," EITF Issue No. 95-5. Norwalk, CT: FASB, 1995.

Financial Accounting Standards Board, "Accounting for Contingent Consideration Paid to the Shareholders of an Acquired Enterprise in a Purchase Business Combination," EITF Issue No. 95-8. Norwalk, CT: FASB, 1995.

Financial Accounting Standards Board, "Accounting for the Film and Software Costs Associated with Developing Entertainment and Educational Software Products," EITF Issue No. 96-6. Norwalk, CT: FASB, 1996.

Financial Accounting Standards Board, "Disclosures about Segments of an Enterprise and Related Information," Statement of Financial Accounting Standards No. 131. Norwalk, CT: FASB, 1997.

Financial Accounting Standards Board, "Deregulation of the Price of Electricity—Issues Related to the Application of FASB Statements 71 and 101," EITF Issue No. 97-4. Norwalk, CT: FASB, 1997.

Financial Accounting Standards Board, "Accounting for Contingent Consideration Issued in a Purchase Business Combination," EITF Issue No. 97-8. Norwalk, CT: FASB, 1997.

Financial Accounting Standards Board, "Accounting for Costs Incurred in Connection with a Consulting Contract or an Internal Project That Combines Business Process Reengineering and Information Technology Transformation," EITF Issue No. 97-13. Norwalk, CT: FASB, 1997.

Financial Accounting Standards Board, "Accounting for Transfers and Servicing of Financial Assets and Extinguishments of Liabilities—A Replacement of FASB Statement No. 125," Statement of Financial Accounting Standards No. 140. Norwalk, CT: FASB, 2000.

Financial Accounting Standards Board, "Business Combinations," Statement of Financial Accounting Standards No. 141. Norwalk, CT: FASB, June 2001.

Financial Accounting Standards Board, "Goodwill and Other Intangible Assets," Statement of Financial Accounting Standards No. 142. Norwalk, CT: FASB, June 2001.

Financial Accounting Standards Board, "Accounting for the Impairment or Disposal of Long-Lived Assets," Statement of Financial Accounting Standards No. 144. Norwalk, CT: FASB, June 2001.

Financial Accounting Standards Board, "Accounting for Costs Associated with Exit or Disposal Activities," Statement of Financial Accounting Standards No. 146. Norwalk, CT: FASB, June 2002.

Financial Accounting Standards Board, "Acquisitions of Certain Financial Institutions," Statement of Financial Accounting Standards No. 147. Norwalk, CT: FASB, October 2002.

Financial Accounting Standards Board, "Unit of Accounting for Testing Impairment of Indefinite-Lived Assets," EITF Issue No. 02-7. Norwalk, CT: FASB, 2002.

Financial Accounting Standards Board, "Deferred Income Tax Considerations in Applying the Goodwill Impairment Test in FASB Statement No. 142," EITF Issue No. 02-13. Norwalk, CT: FASB, 2002.

Financial Accounting Standards Board, "Recognition of Customer Relationship Intangible Assets Acquired in a Business Combination," EITF Issue No. 02-17. Norwalk, CT: FASB, 2002.

Financial Accounting Standards Board, "Interaction of Paragraphs 11 and 12 of FASB Statement No. 142 Regarding Determination of the Useful Life and Amortization of Intangible Assets," EITF Issue No. 03-9. Norwalk, CT: FASB, 2003.

Financial Accounting Standards Board, "Interaction of FASB Statements No. 141, *Business Combinations,* and No. 142, *Goodwill and Other Intangible Assets,* and EITF Issue No. 04-2, *Whether Mineral Rights Are Tangible or Intangible Assets,*" FASB Staff Positions 141-1 and 142-1. Norwalk, CT: FASB, 2003.

Financial Accounting Standards Board, "Accounting for Pre-Existing Contractual Relationships Between the Parties to a Business Combination," EITF Issue No. 04-1. Norwalk, CT: FASB, 2004.

Financial Accounting Standards Board, "Whether Mineral Rights Are Tangible or Intangible Assets and Related Issues," EITF Issue No. 04-2. Norwalk, CT: FASB, 2004.

Financial Accounting Standards Board, "Fair Value Measurements," Exposure Draft. Norwalk, CT: FASB, June 2004.

Financial Accounting Standards Board, "Business Combinations (a Replacement of FASB Statement No. 141," Exposure Draft SFAS No. 141(R). Norwalk, CT: FASB, June 2005.

Financial Accounting Standards Board, "Selected Issues Relating to Assets and Liabilities with Uncertainties," Invitation to Comment. Norwalk, CT: FASB, September 2005.

Securities and Exchange Commission, "Expenses of Offering," Staff Accounting Bulletin Topic 5A. Washington, DC: SEC: 1975.

Securities and Exchange Commission, "Acquisitions Involving Financial Institutions," Staff Accounting Bulletin Topic 2-A3. Washington, DC: SEC: 1981.

Securities and Exchange Commission, "Push Down Basic of Accounting Required in Certain Limited Circumstances," Staff Accounting Bulletin Topic 5J. Washington, DC: SEC: 1983.

ACCOUNTANTS' HANDBOOK

ELEVENTH EDITION

SPECIAL INDUSTRIES AND SPECIAL TOPICS

CHAPTER 34

STATE AND LOCAL GOVERNMENT ACCOUNTING[1] (REVISED)

Cynthia Pon, CPA
Macias Gini O'Connell LLP
Kevin J. O'Connell, CPA
Macias Gini O'Connell LLP
Ernest J. Gini, CPA, CGFM
Macias Gini O'Connell LLP

1.   We would like to acknowledge the efforts of the contributors of the previous edition—Andrew J. Blossom, KPMG LLP; Andrew Gottschalk, KPMG LLP; John R. Miller, KPMG LLP; and Warren Ruppel, DiTomasso & Ruppel—and thank them for their undertaking. We also are indebted to Lynford Graham whose thoughtful feedback helped raise our own understanding of governmental accounting.

34.1 INTRODUCTION

Governmental accounting has changed dramatically in recent years in response to changes in the state and local government environment. Subject to greater scrutiny by federal and state agencies and faced with budgetary challenges, governments must also negotiate an ever-increasing level of sophistication required to manage their operations—operations which are on par with the largest and most complex business organizations and are as diverse as airports, hospitals, schools, and fire protection. Add to that concerns involving deteriorating infrastructure, an aging workforce, public health care, and the spread of terrorism, and it is no surprise that governments are finding themselves addressing increasing demands for public accountability and transparency.

Before discussing the specifics of governmental accounting principles and practices, it is important to have an overall sense of the nature and organization of state and local government activities. The goal of this chapter is to provide insight on the current governmental accounting landscape and to shed light on future trends to explore. Continued examination is critical in light of the fact that governments are no longer able to be slow adopters, following behind business-related trends and regulations; they must be innovative and proactive in order to secure the quality of their service delivery, now and in the future.

34.2 THE NATURE AND ORGANIZATION OF STATE AND LOCAL GOVERNMENT ACTIVITIES

(a) STRUCTURE OF GOVERNMENT   For the most part, government is structured on three levels: federal, state, and local. This chapter deals only with state and local governments.

States are specific identifiable entities in their own right, but accounting at the state level is associated more often than not with the individual state functions, such as departments of revenue, retirement systems, turnpike authorities, and housing finance agencies.

Local governments exist as political subdivisions of states, and the rules governing their types and operation are different in each of the 50 states. There are, however, three basic types of local governmental units: general-purpose local governments (counties, cities, towns, villages, and townships), special-purpose local governments, and authorities.

The distinguishing characteristics of general purpose local governments are that they

- Have broad powers in providing a variety of government services—for example, public safety, fire prevention, and public works
- Have general taxing and bonding authority
- Are headed by elected officials

Special-purpose local governments are established to provide specific services or construction. They may or may not be contiguous with one or more general-purpose local governments.

Authorities and agencies are similar to special-purpose governments except that they have no taxing power and are expected to operate with their own revenues. They typically can issue only revenue bonds, not general obligations bonds.

(b) OBJECTIVES OF GOVERNMENT   The purpose of government is to provide the citizenry with the highest level of services possible given the available financial resources and the legal requirements under which it operates. The services are provided as a result of decisions made during a budgeting process that considers the desired level and quality of services. Resources are then made available through property taxes, sales taxes, income taxes, general and categorical grants from the federal and state governments, charges for services, fines, licenses, and other sources. However, there is generally no direct relationship between the cost of the services rendered to an individual and the amount that the individual pays in taxes, fines, fees, and so on.

Governmental units also conduct operations that are financed and operated in a manner similar to private business enterprises, where the intent is that the costs of providing the goods or services be financed or recovered primarily through charges to the users. In such situations, governments have many of the features of ordinary business operations.

(c) ORGANIZATION OF GOVERNMENT   A government's organization depends on its constitution (state level) or charter (local level) and on general and special statutes of state and local legislatures. When governments were simpler and did not provide as many services as they do today, there was less of a tendency toward centralization. The commission and weak-mayor forms of governments were common. The financial function was typically divided among several individuals.

As government has become more complex, however, the need for strong professional management and for centralization of authority and responsibility has grown. There has been a trend toward the strong-mayor and council-manager forms of government. In these forms, a chief financial officer, usually called the *director of finance* or *controller*, is responsible for maintaining the financial records and preparing financial reports; assisting the chief executive officer (CEO) in the preparation of the budget; performing treasury functions such as collecting revenues, managing cash, managing investments, and managing debt; and overseeing the tax-assessment function. Other functions that may report to the director of finance are purchasing, data processing, and personnel administration.

Local governments are also making greater use of the internal audit process. In the past, the emphasis by governmental internal auditors was on preaudit—that is, reviewing invoices and other documents during processing for propriety and accuracy. The internal auditors reported to the director of finance. Today, however, governmental internal auditors have been removing themselves from the preaudit function by transferring this responsibility to the department responsible for processing the transactions. They have started to provide the more traditional internal audit function—that is, conducting reviews to ensure the reliability of data and the safeguarding of assets and to become involved in performance auditing (i.e., reviewing the efficiency and effectiveness of the government's operations). They have also started to report, for professional (as opposed to administrative) purposes, to the CEO or directly to the governing board. Finally, internal auditors are becoming more actively involved in the financial statement audit and single audit of their government.

(d) SPECIAL CHARACTERISTICS OF GOVERNMENT   Several characteristics associated with governments have influenced the development of governmental accounting principles and practices:

- Governments do not have any owners or proprietors in the commercial sense. Accordingly, measurement of earnings attributable or accruing to the direct benefit of an owner is not a relevant accounting concept for governments.
- Governments frequently receive substantial financial inflows for both operating and capital purposes from sources other than revenues and investment earnings, such as taxes and grants.
- Governments frequently obtain financial inflows subject to legally binding restrictions that prohibit or seriously limit the use of these resources for other than the intended purpose.
- A government's authority to raise and expend money results from the adoption of a budget that, by law, usually must balance (e.g., the estimated revenues plus any prior years' surpluses need to be sufficient to cover the projected expenditures).
- The power to raise revenues through taxes, licenses, fees, and fines is generally defined by law.
- There are usually restrictions related to the tax base that govern the purpose, amount, and type of indebtedness that can be issued.
- Expenditures are usually regulated less than revenues and debt, but they can be made only within approved budget categories and must comply with specified purchasing procedures when applicable.
- State laws may dictate the local government accounting policies and systems.
- State laws commonly specify the type and frequency of financial statements to be submitted to the state and to the government's constituency.
- Federal law, the Single Audit Act of 1984 and as amended in 1996, defines the audit requirements for state and local governments.

In short, the environment in which governments operate is complex and legal requirements have a significant influence on their accounting and financial reporting practices.

34.3   SOURCE OF ACCOUNTING PRINCIPLES FOR STATE AND LOCAL GOVERNMENT ACCOUNTING

Governmental accounting principles are not a complete and separate body of accounting principles, but rather are part of the whole body of generally accepted accounting principles (GAAP). Since the accounting profession's standard-setting bodies have been concerned primarily with the accounting needs of profit-seeking organizations, these principles have been defined primarily by groups formed by the state and local governments. In 1934, the National Committee on Municipal Accounting published "A Tentative Outline—Principles of Municipal Accounting." In 1968, the National Committee on Governmental Accounting (the successor organization) published *Governmental Accounting, Auditing, and Financial Reporting* (GAAFR), which was widely used as a source of governmental accounting principles. The American Institute of Certified Public Accountants (AICPA) Industry Audit Guide, "Audits of State and Local Governmental Units," published in 1974, stated that the accounting principles outlined in the 1968 GAAFR constituted GAAP for government entities.

The financial difficulties experienced by many governments in the mid-1970s led to a call for a review and modification of the accounting and financial reporting practices used by governments. Laws were introduced in Congress, but never enacted, that would have given the federal government the authority to establish governmental accounting principles. The Financial Accounting Standards Board (FASB), responding to pressures, commissioned a research study to define and explain the issues associated with accounting for all nonbusiness enterprises, including governments. This study was completed in 1978, and the Board developed Statement of Financial Accounting Concepts (SFAC) No. 4 for nonbusiness organizations. The Statement defined nonbusiness organizations, the users of the statements, the financial information needs of these users, and the information that is necessary to meet these needs.

(a) NATIONAL COUNCIL ON GOVERNMENT ACCOUNTING　The National Council on Governmental Accounting (NCGA) was the successor of the National Committee on Municipal Accounting reconstituted as a permanent organization. One of its first projects was to "restate," that is, update, clarify, amplify, and reorder the GAAFR to incorporate pertinent aspects of "Audits of State and Local Governmental Units." The restatement was published in March 1979 as NCGA Statement No. 1, "Governmental Accounting and Financial Reporting Principles." Shortly thereafter, the AICPA Committee on State and Local Government Accounting recognized NCGA Statement No. 1 as authoritative and agreed to amend the Industry Audit Guide accordingly. This restatement was completed, and a new guide was published in 1986. Thus NCGA Statement No. 1 became the primary reference source for the accounting principles unique to governmental accounting. However, in areas not unique to governmental accounting, the complete body of GAAP still needed to be considered.

(b) GOVERNMENTAL ACCOUNTING STANDARDS BOARD　In 1984, the Financial Accounting Foundation (FAF) established the Governmental Accounting Standards Board (GASB) as the primary standard setter for GAAP for governmental entities. Under the jurisdictional agreement, the GASB has the primary responsibility for establishing accounting and reporting principles for government entities. The GASB's first action was to issue Statement No. 1, "Authoritative Status of NCGA Pronouncements and AICPA Industry Audit Guide," which recognized the NCGA's statements and interpretations and the AICPA's audit guide as authoritative. The Statement also recognized the pronouncements of the FASB issued prior to the date of the agreement as applicable to governments. FASB pronouncements issued after the organization of GASB do not become effective unless the GASB specifically adopts them.

The GASB has operated under this jurisdictional arrangement since 1984. However, the arrangement came under scrutiny during the GASB's mandatory five-year review conducted in 1988. In January 1989 the Committee to Review Structure of Governmental Accounting Standards released its widely read report on the results of its review and proposed to the FAF, among other recommendations, a new jurisdictional arrangement and GAAP hierarchy for governments. These two recommendations prompted a great deal of controversy within the industry. The issue revolved around the Committee's recommended jurisdictional arrangement for the separately issued financial statements of certain "special entities." (Special entities are organizations that can either be privately or governmentally owned and include colleges and universities, hospitals, and utilities.) The Committee recommended that the FASB be the primary accounting standard setter for these special entities when they issue separate, stand-alone financial statements and that the GASB be allowed to require the presentation of "additional data" in these stand-alone statements. This arrangement would allow for greater comparability between entities in the same industry (e.g., utilities) regardless of whether the entities were privately or governmentally owned and still allow government-owned entities to meet their "public accountability" reporting objective.

This recommendation and a subsequent compromise recommendation were unacceptable to many and especially to the various public interest groups such as the Government Finance Officers Association (GFOA) who, 10 months after the Committee's report, began discussions to establish a new body to set standards for state and local government. These actions prompted the FAF to consider whether a standard-setting schism was in the interest of the public and the users of financial statements. Based on this consideration, the FAF decided that the jurisdictional arrangement established in 1984 should remain intact.

In response to the jurisdictional arrangement just described, the AICPA issued Statement on Auditing Standards No. 69, "The Meaning of Present Fairly in Conformity with Generally Accepted Accounting Principles in the Independent Auditor's Report," which creates a hierarchy of GAAP specifically for state and local governments. SAS No. 69 raises AICPA Statement of Positions (SOPs) and audit and accounting guides to a level of authority above that of industry practice. As a result, FASB pronouncements will not apply to state and local governments unless the GASB issues a standard incorporating them into GAAP for state and local government. In September 1993, the GASB issued Statement No. 20, "Accounting and Financial Reporting for Proprietary Funds and Other Governmental Entities That Use Proprietary Fund Accounting."

Statement No. 20 requires proprietary activities to apply all applicable GASB Statements as well as FASB pronouncements, Accounting Principles Board (APB) Opinions, and Accounting Research Bulletins issued on or before November 30, 1989, unless those pronouncements conflict or contradict with a GASB pronouncement. A proprietary activity may also apply, at its option, all FASB pronouncements issued after November 30, 1989, except those that conflict or contradict with a GASB pronouncement.

The GASB subsequently issued Statement No. 29, "The Use of Not-for-Profit Accounting and Financial Reporting Principles by Governmental Entities," which amended Statement No. 20 to indicate that proprietary activities could apply only those FASB statements that were developed for business enterprises. The FASB statements and interpretations whose provisions are limited to not-for-profit organizations or address issues primarily of concern to those organizations may not be applied. These actions, along with the increased activity of the FASB in setting standards for not-for-profit organizations, have resulted in increasing differences in GAAP between nongovernmental entities and state and local governments.

These differences also highlight the importance of determining whether a particular entity is a state or local government. While it is obvious that states, cities, and counties are governments, other units of government are less clear. Is a university considered a government if it is supported 70 percent by taxes allocated by the state? What if the percentage is only 15 percent? If a hospital is created by a county but the county has no continuing involvement with the hospital, is the hospital a government? The GASB acknowledged these concerns in the Basis for Conclusions of Statement No. 29 in stating

> Some respondents believe that the fundamental issue underlying this Statement— identifying those entities that should apply the GAAP hierarchy applicable to state and local governmental entities—will continue to be troublesome until there is an authoritative definition of such "governmental entities." The Board agrees—but does not have the authority to unilaterally establish a definition—and intends to continue to explore alternatives for resolving the issue.

The decision as to whether a particular entity should follow the hierarchy for state and local governments or nongovernmental entities is a matter of professional judgment based on the individual facts and circumstances for the entity in question. The AICPA audit and accounting guide for not-for-profit organizations provides guidance to distinguish between governmental and nongovernmental organizations. It defines governmental organizations as

> Public corporations and bodies corporate and politic. . . . Other organizations are governmental organizations if they have one or more of the following characteristics:
>
> **a.** Popular election of officers or appointment (or approval) of a controlling majority of the members of the organization's governing body by officials of one or more state or local governments;
> **b.** The potential for unilateral dissolution by a government with the net assets reverting to a government; or
> **c.** The power to enact and enforce a tax levy.

Furthermore, organizations are presumed to be governmental if they have the ability to issue directly (rather than through a state or municipal authority) debt that pays interest exempt from federal taxation. However, organizations possessing only that ability (to issue tax-exempt debt) and none of the other governmental characteristics may rebut the presumption that they are governmental if their determination is supported by compelling, relevant evidence.

In 2006, the GFOA questioned the continued role of the GASB in response to its project on Service Efforts and Accomplishments (SEA) Reporting (see Section 34.4(b) Users and Uses of Financial Reports). However, in 2006 FAF reaffirmed that the GASB has the jurisdictional authority to include "service efforts and accomplishments" in its financial accounting and reporting standard-setting activities.

Recently Texas passed legislation that would give the state and any of its public entities permission to ignore GASB Statement 45, an accounting standard requiring state and local governments to disclose their liability for "other post-employment benefits," which include retiree health, dental, and vision benefits as well as some forms of life insurance. Texas CPAs are worried that this is a first step down a road where all 50 states will start developing their own set of accounting standards.

34.4   GOVERNMENTAL ACCOUNTING PRINCIPLES AND PRACTICES

(a) SIMILARITIES TO PRIVATE SECTOR ACCOUNTING   Since the accounting principles and practices of governments are part of the whole body of GAAP, certain accounting concepts and conventions are as applicable to governmental entities as they are to accounting in other industries:

- *Consistency.* Identical transactions should be recorded in the same manner both during a period and from period to period.
- *Conservatism.* The uncertainties that surround the preparation of financial statements are reflected in a general tendency toward early recognition of unfavorable events and minimization of the amount of net assets and net income.
- *Historical cost.* Amounts should be recognized in the financial statements at the historical cost to the reporting entity. Changes in the general purchasing power should not be recognized in the basic financial statements.
- *Matching.* The financial statements should provide for a matching, but in government it is a matching of revenues and expenditures with a time period to ensure that revenues and the expenditures they finance are reported in the same period.
- *Reporting entity.* The focus of the financial report is the economic activities of a discrete individual entity for which there is a reporting responsibility.
- *Materiality.* Financial reporting is concerned only with significant information.
- *Full disclosure.* Financial statements must contain all information necessary to understand the presentation of financial position and results of operations and to prevent them from being misleading.

(b) USERS AND USES OF FINANCIAL REPORTS Users of the financial statements of a governmental unit are not identical to users of a business entity's financial statements. The GASB Concepts Statement No. 1 identifies three groups of primary users of external governmental financial reports:

1. *Those to whom government is primarily accountable—the citizenry.* The citizenry group includes citizens (whether they are classified as taxpayers, voters, or service recipients), the media, advocate groups, and public finance researchers. This user group is concerned with obtaining the maximum amount of service with a minimum amount of taxes and wants to know where the government obtains its resources and how those resources are used.
2. *Those who directly represent the citizens—legislative and oversight bodies.* The legislative and oversight officials group includes members of state legislatures, county commissions, city councils, boards of trustees, and school boards, along with those executive branch officials with oversight responsibility over other levels of government. These groups need timely warning of the development of situations that require corrective action, financial information that can serve as a basis for judging management performance, and financial information on which to base future plans and policies.
3. *Those who lend or participate in the lending process—investors and creditors.* Investors and creditors include individual and institutional investors and creditors, municipal security underwriters, bond-rating agencies (Moody's Investors Service, Standard & Poor's, etc.), bond insurers, and financial institutions.

The uses of a government's financial reports are also different. GASB Concepts Statement No. 1 also indicates that governmental financial reporting should provide information to assist users in (1) assessing accountability and (2) making economic, social, and political decisions by

- *Comparing actual financial results with the legally adopted budget.* All three user groups are interested in comparing original or modified budgets with actual results to get some assurance that spending mandates have been complied with and that resources have been used for the intended purposes.

- *Assisting in determining compliance with finance-related laws, rules, and regulations.* In addition to the legally mandated budgetary and fund controls, other legal restrictions may control governmental actions. Some examples are bond covenants, grant restrictions, and taxing and debt limits. Financial reports help demonstrate compliance with these laws, rules, and regulations.
    - ○ Citizens are concerned that governments adhere to these regulations because noncompliance may indicate fiscal irresponsibility and could have severe financial consequences such as acceleration of debt payments, disallowance of questioned costs, or loss of grants.
    - ○ Legislative and oversight officials are also concerned with compliance as a follow-up to the budget formulation process.
    - ○ Investors and creditors are interested in the government's compliance with debt covenants and restrictions designed to protect their investment.
- *Assisting in evaluating efficiency and effectiveness.* Citizen groups and legislators, in particular, want information about service efforts, costs, and accomplishments of a governmental entity. This information, when combined with information from other sources, helps users assess the economy, efficiency, and effectiveness of government and may help form a basis for voting on funding decisions.
- *Assessing financial condition and results of operations.* Financial reports are commonly used to assess a state or local government's financial condition—that is, its financial position and its ability to continue to provide services and meet its obligations as they come due.
    - ○ Investors and creditors need information about available and likely future financial resources, actual and contingent liabilities, and the overall debt position of a government to evaluate the government's ability to continue to provide resources for long-term debt service.
    - ○ Citizens' groups are concerned with financial condition when evaluating the likelihood of tax or service fee increases.
    - ○ Legislative and oversight officials need to assess the overall financial condition, including debt structure and funds available for appropriation, when developing both capital and operating budget and program recommendations.

With the users and the uses of financial reports clearly defined, the GASB developed the following three overall objectives of governmental financial reporting:

1. Financial reporting should assist in fulfilling a government's duty to be publicly accountable and should enable users to assess that accountability by
    a. Providing information to determine whether current-year revenues were sufficient to pay for current-year services.
    b. Demonstrating whether resources were obtained and used in accordance with the entity's legally adopted budget and in compliance with other finance-related legal or contractual requirements.
    c. Providing information to assist users in assessing the service efforts, costs, and accomplishments of the governmental entity.
2. Financial reporting should assist users in evaluating the operating results of the governmental entity for the year by providing information

    a. About sources and uses of financial resources.

    b. About how the governmental entity financed its activities and met its cash requirements.

    c. Necessary to determine whether the entity's financial position improved or deteriorated as a result of the year's operations.

3. Financial reporting should assist users in assessing the level of services that can be provided by the governmental entity and its ability to meet its obligations as they become due by

    a. Providing information about the financial position and condition of a governmental entity. Financial reporting should provide information about resources and obligations, both actual and contingent, current and noncurrent, and about tax sources, tax limitations, tax burdens, and debt limitations.

    b. Providing information about a governmental entity's physical and other nonfinancial resources having useful lives that extend beyond the current year, including information that can be used to assess the service potential of those resources.

    c. Disclosing legal or contractual restrictions on resources and risks of potential loss of resources.

In April 1994, the GASB issued Concepts Statement No. 2, "Service Efforts and Accomplishments Reporting," which expands on the consideration of service efforts and accomplishments (SEA) reporting included in Concepts Statement No. 1. The GASB believes that the government's duty to be publicly accountable requires the presentation of SEA information. Concepts Statement No. 2 identifies the objective of SEA reporting as providing "more complete information about a governmental entity's performance that can be provided by the operating statement, balance sheet, and budgetary comparison statements and schedules to assist users in assessing the economy, efficiency, and effectiveness of services provided." The Concepts Statement also indicates that SEA information should meet the characteristics of relevance, understandability, comparability, timeliness, consistency, and reliability. In April 2007, the GASB started work on the SEA project, which will include future guidelines for SEA performance reporting issues and measures.

In April 2005, the GASB issued Concepts Statement No. 3, "Communication Methods in General Purpose External Financial Reports That Contain Basic Financial Statements," which provides a conceptual basis for selecting communication methods to present items of information within general-purpose external financial reports that contain basic financial statements. Preparers should select an appropriate communication method to convey information that enhances the consistency, comparability, and understandability of general-purpose external financial reports. The hierarchy for selecting communications methods is as follows:

    a. Recognition in the basic financial statements

    b. Disclosure in notes to basic financial statements

    c. Presentation as required supplementary information

    d. Presentation as supplementary information

In June 2007, the GASB issued Concepts Statement No. 4, "Elements of Financial Statements," which establishes definitions for the seven elements of historically based financial statements of state and local governments. These elements are the fundamental components of financial statements. The five statements of financial position elements are defined as follows:

- *Assets* are resources with present service capacity that the government presently controls.
- *Liabilities* are present obligations to sacrifice resources that the government has little or no discretion to avoid.
- A *deferred outflow* of resources is a consumption of net assets by the government that is applicable to a future reporting period.
- A *deferred inflow* of resources is an acquisition of net assets by the government that is applicable to a future reporting period.
- *Net position* is the residual of all other elements presented in a statement of financial position.

The two resource flows elements are defined as follows:

- An *outflow of resources* is a consumption of net assets by the government that is applicable to the reporting period.
- An *inflow of resources* is an acquisition of net assets by the government that is applicable to the reporting period.

Each element's inherent characteristics provides the primarily basis for these definitions. Central to these definitions is a resource, which in the governmental context is an item that can be drawn on to provide services to the citizenry. These definitions apply to an entity that is a governmental unit (i.e., a legal entity) and are applicable to any measurement focus under which financial statements may be prepared.

(c) SUMMARY STATEMENT OF PRINCIPLES   Because governments operate under different conditions and have different reporting objectives than commercial entities, basic principles applicable to government accounting and reporting have been developed. These principles are generally recognized as being essential to effective management control and financial reporting. In other words, understanding these principles and how they operate is extremely important to the understanding of governments.

(i) Accounting and Reporting Capabilities   A governmental accounting system must make it possible to both (1) present fairly the basic financial statements in conformity with GAAP, which include both government-wide and fund financial statements with full disclosure, and to provide adequately the required supplementary information, including the management's discussion and analysis (MD&A) and required budgetary comparison information; and (2) determine and demonstrate compliance with finance-related legal and contractual provisions.

(ii) Government-Wide and Fund Accounting Systems   Governmental accounting systems should provide information that permits reporting on a fund basis and provide conversion information that facilities reporting on a government-wide basis. A "fund" is defined as a fiscal and accounting entity with a self-balancing set of accounts recording cash and other financial resources, together with all related liabilities and residual equities or balances, and changes therein, which are segregated for the purpose of carrying on specific activities or attaining certain objectives in accordance with special regulations, restrictions, or limitations.

Under GASB Statement No. 34, government-wide financial statements should be presented in addition to fund financial statements. They should report information about the reporting government as a whole, except for its fiduciary activities. The statements should include separate columns for governmental activities, business-type activities, total activities, and component units, which are legally separate organizations for which the elected officials of the primary government (PG) are financially accountable, or other organizations for which the nature and significance of its relationship with a PG are such that exclusion from the financial statements of the PG would cause them to be misleading or incomplete. The government-wide financial statements should be prepared using the economic resources measurement focus and the accrual basis of accounting.

(iii) Types of Funds   The following three types of funds should be used by state and local governments.

(A) Governmental Funds (emphasizing major funds)

1. *The general fund.* To account for all financial resources except those required to be accounted for in another fund.
2. *Special revenue funds.* To account for the proceeds for specific revenue sources (other than expendable trusts, or major capital projects) that are legally restricted to expenditures for specified purposes.
3. *Capital projects funds.* To account for financial resources to be used for the acquisition or construction of major capital facilities (other than those financed by proprietary funds and trust funds).
4. *Debt service funds.* To account for the accumulation of resources for, and the payment of, general long-term debt principal and interest.
5. *Permanent funds.* To account for the resources used to make earnings, of which only the earnings may be used for the benefit of the government or its citizenry, such as a cemetery perpetual-care fund.

(B) Proprietary Funds

1. *Enterprise funds (emphasizing major funds).* To account for operations (a) that are financed and operated in a manner similar to private business enterprises, where the intent of the governing body is that the cost (expenses, including depreciation) of providing goods or services to the general public, on a continuing basis, be financed or recovered primarily through user charges; or (b) where the governing body has decided that periodic determination of revenues earned, expenses incurred, and/or net income is appropriate for capital maintenance, public policy, management control, accountability, or other purposes.
2. *Internal service funds.* To account for the financing of goods or services provided by one department or agency to other departments or agencies of the governmental unit, or to other governmental units, on a cost-reimbursement basis.

(C) Fiduciary Funds (and similar component units)

1. *Pension and other employee benefit trust funds.* To account for resources that are required to be held in trust for the members and beneficiaries of defined-benefit pension plans, defined contribution plans, other postemployment benefit (OPEB) plans, or other employee benefit plans.
2. *Investment trust funds.* To account for the external portion of external investment pools that the government sponsors.

3. *Private-purpose trust funds.* To account for all other trust arrangements under which the principal and income benefit individuals, private organizations, or other governments.

4. *Agency funds.* To account for resources held in a custodial capacity for individuals, private organizations, or other governments.

(iv) Number of Funds   Governmental units should establish and maintain those funds required by law and sound financial administration. Only the minimum number of funds consistent with legal and operating requirements should be established, since unnecessary funds result in inflexibility, undue complexity, and inefficient financial administration.

(v) Accounting for Capital Assets   A clear distinction should be made between proprietary capital assets and general capital assets. Capital assets related to specific proprietary funds should be accounted for through both the government-wide and proprietary funds statements. All other capital assets of a governmental unit should be accounted for only in the government-wide capital assets account, except for fiduciary fund capital assets that should be accounted for only in the fiduciary funds' statements.

(vi) Valuation of Capital Assets   Capital assets should be accounted for at cost or, if the cost is not practicably determinable, at estimated cost. Donated capital assets should be recorded at their estimated fair value at the time received.

(vii) Depreciation and Impairment of Capital Assets   While some assets are not depreciated, such as land, most assets are depreciated over their useful lives. An exception is also those assets accounted for using the modified approach, as outlined in GASB 34. Depreciation of capital assets should be recorded in the government-wide statement of activities; the proprietary fund statement of revenues, expense, and changes in fund net assets; and the statement of changes in fiduciary net assets. Capital assets should be evaluated for impairment when events or changes in circumstances suggest that the service utility of a capital asset may have significantly and unexpected declined.

(viii) Accounting for Long-Term Liabilities   Similar to reporting capital assets, a clear distinction should be made between proprietary fund and fiduciary long-term liabilities and general long-term liabilities. Long-term liabilities of proprietary funds should be accounted both in those funds and in the government-wide statement of net assets. All other outstanding general long-term liabilities should be accounted for in the government activities column in the government-wide statement of net assets, except for fiduciary funds long-term liabilities that should be accounted for only in the fiduciary funds' statements.

(ix) Measurement Focus and Basis of Accounting   The modified accrual or accrual basis of accounting, as appropriate, should be used in measuring financial position and operating results.

- Governmental fund revenues and expenditures should be recognized on the modified accrual basis using the current financial resources measurement focus. Revenues should be recognized in the accounting period in which they become available and measurable. Expenditures should be recognized in the accounting period in which the fund liability is incurred, if measurable, except for unmatured long-term indebtedness and other obligations not due for payment in the current period, which should be recognized when mature or due.

- Proprietary fund revenues and expenses should be recognized using the economic resources measurement focus and the accrual basis. Revenues should be recognized in the accounting period in which they are earned and become measurable; expenses should be recognized in the period incurred, if measurable.
- Fiduciary fund revenues/additions and expenses/reductions should be recognized using the economic resources measurement focus and the accrual basis.
- Transfers should be recognized in the period in which the inter-fund receivable and payable arise.

(x) Budgeting, Budgetary Control, and Budgetary Reporting   An annual budget should be adopted by every governmental unit. The accounting system should provide the basis for appropriate budgetary control. Budgetary comparisons should be presented for the general fund and for each major special revenue fund that has a legally adopted annual budget.

(xi) Transfer, Revenue, Expenditure, and Expense Account Classification   The statement of activities should present activities accounted for in governmental funds by function and activities accounted for in enterprise funds by different identifiable activities.

Governmental fund revenues should be classified by fund and source. Expenditures should be classified by fund, function (or program), organization unit, activity, character, and principal classes of objects.

Proprietary fund revenues and expenses should be classified in essentially the same manner as those of similar business organizations, functions, or activities.

Contributions to term and permanent endowments, contributions to permanent fund principal, other capital contributions, special and extraordinary items, and transfers should each be reported separately.

(xii) Common Terminology and Classification   A common terminology and classification should be used consistently throughout the budget, the accounts, and the financial reports of each fund or activity.

(xiii) Interim and Annual Financial Reports   Appropriate interim financial statements and reports of financial position, operating results, and other pertinent information should be prepared to facilitate management control of financial operations, legislative oversight, and, where necessary or desired, external reporting.

A comprehensive annual financial report (CAFR) covering all funds of the governmental unit may be prepared and published, including appropriate government-wide financial statements; combined, combining, and individual fund statements; notes to the financial statements; required supplementary information; schedules; narrative explanations; and statistical tables.

Basic financial statements may be issued separately from the CAFR. Such statements should include the financial statements, notes to the financial statements, and any required supplementary information essential to a fair presentation of financial position and operating results and cash flows of proprietary funds.

(d) DISCUSSION OF THE PRINCIPLES   To enable readers to more fully understand the principles, a discussion follows.

(e) ACCOUNTING AND REPORTING CAPABILITIES

(i) Legal Compliance   *Principle 1* of governmental accounting (GASB Codification Section 1100.101) states

> A governmental accounting system must make it possible both: (a) to present fairly and with full disclosure the funds of the governmental unit in conformity with GAAPs; and (b) to determine and demonstrate compliance with finance-related legal and contractual provisions.

Several state and local governments have accounting requirements that differ from GAAP—for example, cash basis accounting is required, and capital projects must be accounted for in the general fund. Because of this situation, the legal compliance principle used to be interpreted as meaning that, when the legal requirements for a particular entity differed from GAAP, the legal requirements became GAAP for the entity. This interpretation is no longer viewed as sound. When GAAP and legal requirements conflict, governments should present their basic financial report in accordance with GAAP and, if the legal requirements differ materially from GAAP, the legally required reports can be published as supplemental data to the basic financial report or, if these differences are extreme, it may be preferable to publish a separate legal-basis report.

However, conflicts that arise between GAAP and legal provisions do not require maintaining two sets of accounting records. Rather, the accounting records typically would be maintained in accordance with the legal requirements but would include sufficient additional information to permit preparation of reports in accordance with GAAP.

(ii) Reporting Requirements   Under GASB Statement No. 34, the typical local government's set of basic financial statements consists of three components: (1) **Government-wide** financial statements; (2) **Fund** financial statements and (3) **Notes** to the financial statements. Governments will also have other supplementary information in addition to the basic financial statements themselves. An example of how the various elements of a local government's financial statement are related is shown in Exhibit 34.1.

The following table in Exhibit 34.2 summarizes the major features of the City and County of San Francisco's financial statements.

(f) GOVERNMENT-WIDE AND FUND ACCOUNTING SYSTEMS   Principle 2, fund accounting, is used by governments because of (1) legally binding restrictions that prohibit or seriously limit the use of much of a government's resources for other than the purposes for which the resources were obtained, and (2) the importance of reporting the accomplishment of various objectives for which the resources were entrusted to the government.

GASB Codification Section 1100.102 defines a fund for accounting purposes as

> A fiscal and accounting entity with a self-balancing set of accounts recording cash and other financial resources, together with all related liabilities and residual equities or balances, and changes therein, which are segregated for the purposes of carrying on specific activities or obtaining certain objectives in accordance with special regulations, restrictions, or limitations.

Thus a fund may include accounts for assets, liabilities, fund balance or net assets, revenues, expenditures, or expenses. Accounts may also exist for appropriations and encumbrances, depending on the budgeting system used.

		INTRODUCTORY SECTION		

Introductory Section

+

Management's Discussion and Analysis

	Government-wide Financial Statements	**Fund Financial Statements**		

		Governmental Funds	Proprietary Funds	Fiduciary Funds
CAFR Financial Section	Statement of net assets	Balance sheet	Statement of net assets	Statement of fiduciary net assets
		Statement of revenues, expenditures, and changes in fund balances	Statement of revenues, expenses, and changes in fund net assets	
	Statement of activities	Budgetary comparison statement	Statement of cash flows	Statement of changes in fiduciary net assets

Notes to the Financial Statements

Required Supplementary Information Other than MD&A

Information on individual non-major funds and other supplementary information that is not required

+

Statistical Section

STATISTICAL SECTION

EXHIBIT 34.1:   ORGANIZATION OF THE CITY AND COUNTY OF SAN FRANCISCO COMPREHENSIVE ANNUAL FINANCIAL REPORT

(*Source:* City and County of San Francisco, California, Comprehensive Annual Financial Report for the Year Ended June 30, 2006, pages 4 and 5)

A government should report separately on its most important, or "major," funds, including its general fund. A major fund is one whose revenues, expenditures/expenses, assets, or liabilities (excluding extraordinary items) are at least 10 percent of the corresponding totals for all governmental or enterprise funds and at least 5 percent of the aggregate amount for all governmental and enterprise funds. Any other fund may be reported as a major fund if the government's officials believe information about the fund is particularly important to the users of the statements. Other funds should be reported in the aggregate in a separate column. Internal service funds should be reported in the aggregate in a separate column on the proprietary fund statements. Separate fund financial statements should be presented for governmental and proprietary funds.

	Government-wide Statements	Fund Financial Statements		
		Governmental	Proprietary	Fiduciary
Scope	Entire entity (except fiduciary funds)	The day-to-day operating activities of the City for basic governmental services	The day-to-day operating activities of the City for business-type enterprises	Instances in which the City administers resources on behalf of others, such as employee benefits
Accounting basis and measurement focus	Accrual accounting and economic resources focus	Modified accrual accounting and current financial resources focus	Accrual accounting and economic resources focus	Accrual accounting and economic resources focus; except agency funds do not have measurement focus
Type of asset and liability information	All assets and liabilities, both financial and capital, short-term and long-term	Current assets and liabilities that come due during the year or soon thereafter	All assets and liabilities, both financial and capital, short-term and long-term	All assets held in a trustee or agency capacity for others
Type of inflow and outflow information	All revenues and expenses during year, regardless of when cash is received or paid	Revenues for which cash is received during the year or soon thereafter; expenditures when goods or services have been received and the related liability is due and payable	All revenues and expenses during year, regardless of when cash is received or paid	All additions and deductions during the year, regardless of when cash is received or paid

Exhibit 34.2: Summary of the Major Features of the City and County of San Francisco's Financial Statements

A government should present a summary reconciliation to the government-wide financial statements at the bottom of the fund financial statements or in a separate schedule. Fund balances for governmental funds should be segregated into reserved and unreserved categories. Proprietary fund net assets should be reported in the same categories required for the government-wide financial statements. Proprietary fund statements of net assets should distinguish between current and noncurrent assets and liabilities and should display restricted assets.

(g) TYPES AND NUMBER OF FUNDS   Because of the various nature of activities carried on by government, it is often important to be able to account for certain activities separately from others (i.e., when required by law). Principles 3 and 4 define seven basic fund types in which to account for various governmental activities. The purpose and operation of each fund type differs, and it is important to understand these differences and why they exist. Every fund maintained by a government should be classified into one of these three fund categories:

1. Governmental funds, emphasizing major funds:
    - The general fund
    - Special revenue funds
    - Capital projects funds
    - Debt service funds
    - Permanent funds
2. Proprietary funds:
    - Enterprise funds, emphasizing major funds
    - Internal service funds

3. Fiduciary funds and similar component units:
   ○ Pension and other employee benefit trust funds
   ○ Investment trust funds
   ○ Private-purpose trust funds
   ○ Agency funds

The general fund, special revenue funds, debt service funds, capital projects funds, and permanent funds are considered governmental funds since they record the transactions associated with the general services of a local governmental unit (i.e., police, public works, fire prevention) that are provided to all citizens and are supported primarily by general revenues. For these funds, the primary concerns, from the financial statement reader's point of view, are the types and amounts of resources that have been made available to the governmental unit and the uses to which they have been put.

The enterprise funds and internal services funds are considered proprietary funds because they account for activities for which the determination of operating income is important.

The trust and agency funds are considered fiduciary funds. There are basically three types of trust funds: pension (and other employee benefit) trust funds, investment trust funds and private-purpose trust funds that operate in a manner similar to proprietary funds, and agency funds that account for funds held by a government entity in an agent capacity. Agency funds consist of assets and liabilities only and do not involve the measurement of operations.

Although a government should establish and maintain those funds required by law and sound financial administration, it should set up only the minimum number of funds consistent with legal and operating requirements. The maintenance of unnecessary funds results in inflexibility, undue complexity, and inefficient financial administration. For instance, in the past, the proceeds of specific revenue sources or resources that financed specific activities as required by law or administrative regulation had to be accounted for in a special revenue fund. However, governmental resources restricted to purposes usually financed through the general fund should be accounted for in the general fund, provided that all legal requirements can be satisfied. Examples include state grants received by an entity for special education. If a separate fund is not legally required, the grant revenues and the grant-related expenditures should be accounted for in the fund for which they are to be used.

Another way to minimize funds is by accounting for debt service payments in the general fund and not establishing a separate debt service fund unless it is legally mandated or resources are actually being accumulated for future debt service payments (i.e., for term bonds or in sinking funds).

Furthermore, one or more identical accounts for separate funds should be combined in the accounting system, particularly for funds that are similar in nature or are in the same fund group. For example, the cash accounts for all special revenue funds may be combined, provided that the integrity of each fund is preserved through a distinct equity account for each fund.

(i) Governmental Funds

(A) GENERAL FUND

The general fund accounts for the revenues and expenditures not accounted for in other funds and finances most of the current normal functions of governmental units: general government, public safety, highways, sanitation and waste removal, health and welfare, culture, and recreation. It is usually the largest and most important accounting activity for state and local governments. Property taxes are often the principal source of general fund revenues, but substantial revenues may also be received from other financing sources.

increase in the government's debt burden, and the dependence on a higher rate of earnings on investments.

Quite often, a refunding bond is issued to replace or consolidate prior debt issues. Determining the appropriate accounting principles to apply to refunding bonds depends primarily on whether the bonds are enterprise fund obligations or general obligations. GASB Statement No. 7, "Advance Refundings Resulting in Defeasance of Debt," outlines the appropriate accounting and reporting principles. For the refunding of debt, the proceeds of the refunding issue become an "other financing source" of the fund receiving the proceeds of the refunding bond (oftentimes a debt service fund created to service the original issue or a capital projects fund). Since the proceeds are used to liquidate the original debt, an "other financing use" is also recorded in the debt service or capital projects fund in an amount equal to the remaining principal, interest, and other amounts due on the original debt.

If, as a result of the refunding, the liability to the bondholders is satisfied, the refunding is referred to as a *legal defeasance of debt* or *current refunding*. However, refundings often do not result in the immediate repayment of the debt; rather, assets are placed in a trust to be used to repay the debt as it matures. These refundings are called *advance refundings* or an *in-substance defeasance*. To qualify for an in-substance defeasance, the proceeds of the refunding bonds are placed in an irrevocable trust and invested in essentially risk-free securities, usually obligations of the U.S. Treasury or other government agencies, so that the risk-free securities, together with any premiums on the defeased debt and expenses of the refunding operation will be sufficient for the trust to pay off the debt to the bondholders when it becomes due. The accounting for an in-substance defeasance is identical to legal defeasances except that payment is made to a trustee rather than to bondholders. The trustee then pays principal and interest to the bondholders based on the maturity schedule of the bond. In addition, the recording of payments of proceeds to the trustee as another financing use is limited to the amount of proceeds.

Advance refundings of debt follow the accounting principles outlined in GASB Statement No. 23, "Accounting and Financial Reporting for Refundings of Debt Reported by Proprietary Activities." Statement No. 23 requires that the difference between the reacquisition price and the net carrying amount of the old debt be deferred and amortized as a component of interest expense over the remaining life of the old or the life of the new debt, whichever is shorter.

In addition, GASB Statement No. 7 requires the disclosure of a description of the refunding transaction; the cash flow gain or loss, which is the difference between the total cash outflow of the new debt (i.e., principal, interest, etc.) and the remaining cash outflow of the old debt; and the economic gain or loss, which is the difference between the present values of the cash flows of the new and old debt.

For advance refundings, each year after the defeasance, the footnotes to the financial statements should disclose the remaining amount of debt principal that the trustee has to pay to bondholders.

(D) Capital Projects Funds

The purpose of a capital projects fund is to account for the receipt and disbursement of resources used for the acquisition of major capital facilities other than those financed by enterprise funds. Capital projects are defined as outlays for major, permanent fixed assets having a relatively long life (e.g., buildings), as compared with those of limited life (e.g., office equipment). Capital projects are usually financed by bond proceeds, but they can also be financed from other resources, such as current revenues or grants from other governments.

Capital outlays financed entirely from the direct revenues of the general fund or a special revenue fund and not requiring long-term borrowing may be accounted for in the fund providing such resources rather than in a separate capital projects fund. Assets with a relatively short life—hence not capital projects—are usually financed from current revenues or by short-term obligations and are accounted for in the general or special revenue fund.

Accounting for Capital Projects Fund Transactions. Bonds are issued and capital projects are started under a multiyear capital program. In some instances, it is necessary to secure referendum approval to issue general obligation bonds. Obligations are then incurred and expenditures made according to an annual capital projects budget.

When a project is financed entirely from general obligation bond proceeds, the initial entry to be made in the capital projects fund when the bonds are sold is as follows:

Cash	$XXX
Other financing source—	
Proceeds of general obligation bonds	$XXX

Whereas the proceeds of the bonds are accounted for in the capital projects funds, the liability for the face amount of the bonds is recorded in the government-wide statement of net assets.

If bonds are sold at a premium (i.e., above par value), the premium increases the other financing sources. Often, the premium is transferred—by a debit to "other financing sources" and a credit to "cash"—to the debt service fund established to service the debt for the project. If the bonds are sold at a discount (i.e., below par value), the discount reduces the amount recorded as other financing sources in the capital projects fund. Bond issuance costs either paid out of available funds or withheld from the bond proceeds usually are accounted as debt service expenditures in the capital projects or debt service funds operating statement.

Bond Anticipation Notes (BANs). Governments sometimes issue BANs prior to the sale of bonds, planning to retire the notes with the proceeds of the bond issue to which the notes are related. The reasons would include

- The governmental unit wants to accelerate initiation of a project, and issuance of the long-term bonds will require more time than is required to issue BANs.
- The governmental unit does not want to undertake long-term financing until the project is complete and ready for use. Hence BANs are used to provide construction financing.
- The current and projected interest rates make it prudent to issue short-term notes first and to defer issuance of long-term bonds.
- The individual capital projects to be financed from the proceeds of the bond sale are so small as to make the sale of bonds to finance each project impracticable.

The cash proceeds and the liabilities resulting from the sale of BANs should be recorded in the capital projects fund as follows:

Cash	$XXX
Bond anticipation notes payable	$XXX

When the long-term bonds are sold, an "other financing source" should be recorded and the BANs payable debited in an amount equal to the portion of the BANs redeemed as follows:

Bond participation notes payable	$XXX
Other financing source	$XXX

If the BANs are not redeemed with long-term bond proceeds or other funds by the end of the year, and the governmental unit has both the intent and the ability (as those terms are defined in Statement of Financial Accounting Standards (SFAS) No. 6, "Classification of Short-Term Obligations Expected to Be Refinanced," pars. 10 and 11) to redeem the BANs with long-term debt, the BANs payable account should be debited and an "other financing source" should be credited. If the governmental unit does not have the intent or ability to redeem the BANs with long-term debt, it is appropriate to leave the liability in the capital projects fund. The ability to redeem the BANs could be demonstrated by a post–balance sheet issuance of long-term debt or the entering into of a long-term financing arrangement for the BANs.

Project Budgets.   When debt is issued to finance an entire capital project, it is usually done so at the beginning of the project in an amount equal to the total estimated project cost. Accordingly, a portion of the proceeds may remain unexpended over a considerable period of time. To the maximum extent possible, these excess proceeds should be invested in interest-bearing investments. However, consideration should be given to the federal arbitrage regulations that limit the amount of interest that can be earned from investing the proceeds of a tax-exempt bond issue. If certain limits are exceeded, the bond's tax-exempt status may be lost or severe penalties could be imposed on the issuer.

Project budgets are typically established for capital projects to control costs and to guard against cost overruns. All expenditures needed to place the project in readiness—that is, indirect as well as direct costs—should be recorded against this budget. The actual expenditures, however, will probably be either less or greater than the amounts authorized. Therefore, in the absence of any legal restrictions, any unspent balance should be transferred to the appropriate sources. If the project was financed only from bond proceeds, the transfer should be to the debt service fund from which the bond issue is to be repaid. If the resources were drawn from more than one source, such as bond proceeds and current revenues, the transfer should be split among the sources in proportion to their contributions. If the expenditures were greater than authorized and a deficit exists, sufficient funds must be transferred to liquidate any commitments.

As construction of the project is completed, the costs should be recorded in the capital account as Construction in Progress and then transferred to the final building account when construction is completed.

(E) PERMANENT FUNDS

Permanent funds should be used to report assets legally restricted so that only earnings, not principal, may be spent for the government's programs—that is, for the benefit of the government or its citizens.

(ii) Proprietary Funds

(A) ENTERPRISE FUNDS

Enterprise funds *may be* used to report any activity for which fees are charged to external users in exchange for goods or services. They are *required* to be used if *any one* of the following criteria is met in the context of the activity's principal revenue sources (insignificant activities, such as fees charged for frivolous small-claims suits, are excluded):

- The activity is financed with debt secured solely by a pledge of the net revenues from fees and charges of the activity. (This is met if the debt is secured in part by a portion of its own proceeds.)
- Laws or regulations require that the activity's costs of providing goods or services, including capital costs such as depreciation or debt service, be recovered by its fees and charges, not by taxes or similar revenues.
- The pricing policies of the activity result in fees and charges intended to recover the activity's costs, including capital costs such as depreciation or debt service.
- The primary focus of these criteria is on fees charged to external users.

Proprietary (enterprise) activities are frequently administered by departments of the general-purpose government—for example, a municipal water department or a state parks department. They can also be the exclusive function of a local special district, such as a water district, power authority, or bridge and tunnel authority.

User charges are one significant source of enterprise fund resources; revenue bond proceeds are another. Revenue bonds are long-term obligations, the principal and interest of which are paid from the earnings of the enterprise for which the bond proceeds were spent. The enterprise revenues may be pledged to the payment of the debt, and the physical properties may carry a mortgage that is to be liquidated in the event of default.

Revenue bond indentures usually also contain several requirements concerning the use of the bond proceeds, the computation and reporting of revenue bond coverage, and the establishment and use of restricted asset accounts for handling revenue bond debt service requirements. For instance, a revenue bond indenture may require the establishment of various bond accounts including a construction account, operations and maintenance account, current debt service account, future debt service account, and revenue and replacement account. This does not necessarily mean establishing individual accounting funds for each bond issue. Instead, the accounting and reporting requirements can be met through the use of various accounts within an accounting fund.

The revenue bond construction account normally represents cash and investments (including interest receivable) segregated by the bond indenture for construction. Construction liabilities payable from restricted assets should be reported as "contracts payable from restricted assets." If there are significant unspent debt proceeds at year-end, the portion of the debt attributable to the unspent proceeds should not be included in the calculation of amounts invested in capital assets, net of related debt. Instead, that portion of the debt should be included as the same net assets component as the unspent proceeds.

A revenue bond operations and maintenance account often is established pursuant to a bond indenture. Resources for this account are provided through bond proceeds and/or operating income or net income. This account generally accumulates assets equal to operating costs for one month. Once this account has been established, additional proceeds from future bond issues generally are necessary only to the extent the costs associated with these expanded operations are expected to increase. This account is normally balanced by a restricted net asset account for revenue bond operations and maintenance.

Bond indentures may also include a covenant requiring the establishment of a restricted account for the repayment of bond principal and interest. Resources for this account also are provided through bond proceeds and/or operating income or net income. Normally, assets accumulated for debt service payments (i.e., principal and interest) due within one year are classified in the revenue bond current debt service account. This account is at least partially associated with the bonds payable—current account and the accrued interest payable account. Any difference between the revenue bond current debt service account and related current bonds payable and accrued interest payable should be reported as restricted net assets. When accounts are restricted for debt service payments beyond the next 12 months, a revenue bond future debt service account should be established.

The final restricted account typically established pursuant to a covenant within a bond indenture is the revenue bond renewal and replacement account. Net income is often restricted for payments of unforeseen repairs and replacements of assets originally acquired with bond proceeds. Provided that liabilities have not been incurred for this purpose, the revenue bond renewal and replacement account is balanced by net assets restricted for revenue bond renewal and replacement.

The following general rule should be considered when determining the amount of restricted net assets to record: Unless otherwise required by the bond indenture, net assets should only be restricted for amounts of restricted assets in excess of related liabilities and the balance of restricted assets funded by bond proceeds.

Another restricted asset often found in enterprise funds for utility operations is the amount resulting from the deposits customers are required to make to ensure payment of their final charges and to protect the utility against damage to equipment located on the customer's property. These funds are not available for the financing of current operations and, generally, the amount, less the charges outstanding against the account, must be returned when the customer withdraws from the system. Also, these deposits may, depending on legal and policy requirements, draw interest at some stipulated rate.

In some instances, revenue bonds are also secured by the full faith and credit of the governmental unit. This additional security enables the bonds to obtain better acceptance in the securities market. If the bonds are to be serviced by the enterprise activity, the cash, liability, principal, and interest payments should be accounted for in the enterprise fund. Even if the bonds are secured only by full faith and credit and not by a revenue pledge but the intention is to use enterprise revenues to service the bonds, they should be accounted for as if they were revenue bonds. If, however, general obligation bond proceeds are used to finance the enterprise activity and there is no intention to service the bonds with enterprise fund resources, the amounts provided to the enterprise fund should be recorded as a transfer from the fund recording the proceeds of the bond—typically, the general fund.

Other sources of contributions also provide significant resources for enterprise activities. Such resources include capital contributions by other funds or other governmental bodies; capital contributions by customers or other members of the general public; the aforementioned proceeds of a bond issue to be repaid from general fund revenues, federal grants, or state grants; connection charges to users of utility services; payments by real estate developers for installing utility lines; and similar receipts.

Another resource is the support provided by or to other funds of the government. For instance, an enterprise fund will frequently use the services or commodities of a central facility operated as an internal service fund. Conversely, the general fund departments will use the services of an electric utility fund.

It is important to handle these relationships on a businesslike basis. All services rendered by an enterprise fund for other funds of the government should be billed at predetermined rates, and the enterprise should pay for all services received from other funds on the same basis that is utilized to determine charges for other users. The latter will often include payments in lieu of taxes to the general fund in amounts comparable to the taxes that would have been paid by the enterprise were it privately owned and operated, or an "administrative charge" if the enterprise does not have its own management capacity and instead uses management services provided by the general government. Unless this is done, the financial operations of a government-owned enterprise will be distorted, and valid comparisons of operating results with those for a similar privately owned enterprise cannot be made. However, other considerations, such as the amount of planned idle capacity, have an impact on the comparability of public and private enterprise funds.

Interfund transfers may also occur between an enterprise fund and governmental funds. Operating subsidy transfers from the general fund or special revenue fund are possible. There may also be transfers from an enterprise to finance general fund expenditures.

Finally, there are the nonoperating income and expenses, which are incidental to, or byproducts of, the enterprise's primary service function. Nonoperating income consists of such items as interest earnings, rent from nonoperating properties, intergovernmental revenues, and sale of excess supplies. Nonoperating expenses include items such as interest expense and fiscal agents' fees.

(B) INTERNAL SERVICE FUNDS

Internal service funds finance and account for special activities that are performed and commodities that are furnished by one department or agency of a governmental unit to other departments or agencies of that unit or to other governmental units on a cost-reimbursement basis. The services differ from those rendered to the public at large, which are accounted for in general, special revenue, or enterprise funds. Examples of activities in which internal service funds are established include central motor pools, duplication services, central purchasing and stores departments, and insurance and risk-management activities.

When an internal service fund is established, resources are typically obtained from contributions from other operating funds, such as the general fund or an enterprise fund, or from long-term advances from other funds that are to be repaid from operating income. The entry to be made when the fund is created varies depending on the source of the contributions.

The cost of services rendered and commodities furnished, including labor, depreciation on all capital assets used by the funds other than buildings financed from capital projects, and overhead, are charged to the departments served. These departments reimburse the internal service fund by recording expenditures against their budgeted appropriations. The operating objective of the fund is to recover costs incurred to provide the service, including depreciation. Accordingly, the operations of the fund should not result in any significant profit or loss. Whenever it uses the services of another fund, such as an enterprise fund, the fund pays for and records the costs just as if it had dealt with an outside organization.

Since exact overhead charges are usually not known when bills are prepared, the departments being served are usually billed for direct costs plus a uniform rate for their portion of estimated overhead. Any difference in actual overhead expenses may be charged or credited to the departments at fiscal year end or adjusted for in a subsequent year. At the end of each fiscal year, net income or loss must be determined. The excess of net billings to the department over costs is closed to the net assets account.

(iii) Fiduciary Funds   The purpose of fiduciary (trust and agency) funds is to account for assets held by a governmental unit in a trustee capacity or as an agent for other individuals, private organizations, or other governmental units.

Usually in existence for an extended period of time, trust funds deal with substantial vested interests and involve complex administrative problems. The government's records must provide adequate information to permit compliance with the terms of the trust as defined in the trust document, statutes, ordinances, or governing regulations.

(A) Pension (and other employee benefit) Trust Funds
In the pension (and other employee benefit) trust funds, the governments account for resources held for the future retirement and other postemployment benefits (defined benefit and defined contribution) benefit(s) of their employees. The resources of these funds are the members' contributions, contributions from the government employer, and earnings on investments in authorized securities. The expenses are the authorized retirement allowances and other benefits, refunds of contributions to members who resign prior to retirement, and administrative expenses. Professional actuaries make periodic actuarial studies of the retirement systems and compute the amounts that should be provided so that the benefits can be paid as required.

The proper accounting for pension trust funds has been on the GASB's agenda since its creation. The GASB initially allowed governments to choose from three different methods of accounting and financial reporting but required certain disclosures from all governments. The GASB has finally completed its consideration of pensions and other postemployment employee benefits (OBEB) and the current statements include: Statement No. 25, "Financial Reporting for Defined Benefit Pension Plans and Note Disclosures for Defined Contribution Plans," Statement No. 27, "Accounting for Pensions by State and Local Government Employers," Statement No. 43, "Financial Reporting for Postemployment Benefit Plans Other Than Pension Plans," Statement No. 45, "Accounting and Financial Reporting by Employers for Postemployment Benefits Other Than Pensions," and Statement No. 50, "Pension Disclosures—an Amendment of GASB Statements No. 25 and No. 27." Statements No. 25 and 43 address issues related to accounting by pension and other employee benefit plans along with pension and other employee benefit trust funds. Statements Nos. 27 and 45 address accounting and financial reporting for those employers who participate in a pension and other employee benefit plans.

Statements Nos. 25 and 43 describe two basic financial statements for pension (and other employee benefit) plans: the statement of plan net assets and the statement of changes in plan net assets. These two financial statements are designed to provide current information about plan assets and financial activities. Statements Nos. 25 (as amended by No. 50) and 43 have other requirements for note disclosure that include a brief plan description, a summary of significant accounting principles, and information about contributions, legally required reserves, investment concentrations, funded status of the plan as of the most recent actuarial valuation date, and the actuarial methods and significant assumptions used in the most recent actuarial valuation.

The accounting guidance is directed at employers which participate in a pension (and other employee benefit) plans and reflects two underlying principles. First, the pension or OPEB cost recognized should be related to the annual required contribution (ARC) as determined by an actuary for funding purposes. Second, the actuarial methods and assumptions used by employers should be consistent with those used by the plan in its separate reporting.

In implementing these basic principles, Statements Nos. 27 and 45 require the ARC to be recognized as pension or OPEB expense in government-wide financial statements and in the proprietary funds. Governmental funds will recognize pension expenditure to the extent that the ARC is expected to be liquidated with expendable available resources. If an employer does not contribute to the ARC (or has contributed in excess of the ARC), pension or OPEB expense/expenditure no longer equals the ARC. In these cases the ARC is adjusted to remove the effects of the actuarial adjustments included in the ARC and to reflect interest on previous under or over funding.

Although Statements Nos. 27 and 45 try to minimize the differences between accounting for pensions (and other employee benefits) and funding pensions (and other employee benefits), it does place certain limits or "parameters" on the actuary's modified calculation of the ARC. These parameters are consistent with parameters established for accounting for the plan itself in Statements Nos. 25 and 43. These parameters relate to the pension/OPEB obligation, actuarial assumptions, economic assumptions, actuarial cost method, actuarial valuation of assets, and amortization of unfunded actuarial accrued liability.

Statements Nos. 27 and 45 establish disclosure requirements that vary depending on whether the government merely participates in a pension (and other employee benefits) plan administered by another entity or includes a pension (and other employee benefits) trust fund(s). Disclosure requirements also vary for governments with a pension (and other employee benefits) trust fund based on whether the pension (and other employee benefits) plan issues separate publicly available financial statements. These disclosure requirements generally include a plan description, funding policy, pension cost components, actuarial valuation information, and trend data.

Resources accumulated for OPEB should be accounted for in a trust fund separate from resources accumulated for pension benefits.

(B) INVESTMENT TRUST FUNDS
Investment trust funds should be used by the sponsoring government to report the external part of investment pools, as required by GASB Statement No. 31, paragraph 18.

(C) PRIVATE-PURPOSE TRUST FUNDS
Private-purpose trust funds, such as one used to report escheat property, should be used to report all other trust arrangements under which principal and income benefit individuals, private organizations, or other governments.

(D) AGENCY FUNDS
Used by governments to handle cash resources held in an agent capacity, agency funds require relatively simple administration. The typical agency funds used by state and local governments include (1) tax collection funds, under which one local government collects a tax for an overlapping governmental unit and remits the amount collected less administrative charges to the recipient and (2) payroll withholdings, under which the government collects the deductions and periodically remits them in a lump sum to the appropriate recipient.

(iv) Special Assessment Activities   Special assessment activities pertain to (1) the financing and construction of certain public improvements, such as storm sewers, which are to be paid for wholly or partly from special assessments levied against the properties benefited by such improvements, or (2) the providing of services that are normally provided to the public as general governmental functions and that would otherwise be financed by the general fund or a special revenue fund. Those services may include street lighting, street cleaning, and snow

plowing. The payment by the property owners or taxpayers receiving the benefit distinguishes these activities from activities that benefit the entire community and are paid for from general revenues or general obligation bond proceeds. Sometimes, however, a special assessment bond, which is often used to finance the special assessment improvement, also carries the additional pledge of the full faith and credit of the governmental unit.

It should be emphasized that whereas GASB Statement No. 6 eliminated the requirement to report special assessment funds in an entity's basic financial statement, accounting for special assessment activities is still an important part of governmental accounting.

Capital improvement special assessment projects have two distinct and functionally different phases. The initial phase consists of financing and constructing the project. In most cases, this period is relatively short in duration, sometimes lasting only a few months, and rarely more than a year or two. The second phase, which may start at the same time as, during, or after the initial phase, consists of collecting the assessment principal and interest levied against the benefited properties and repaying the cost of financing the construction. The second phase is usually substantially longer than the first.

There are many ways of financing a capital improvement special assessment project. Assessments may be levied and collected immediately. Funds will then be available to pay construction costs, and it will not be necessary to issue special assessment bonds. Alternatively, a project may be constructed using the proceeds from short-term borrowing. When the project is complete and the exact cost is known, special assessment bonds are issued to provide the exact amount of money, and the short-term borrowings are repaid. A third—and perhaps the most common—financing alternative is for the government to levy a special assessment for the estimated cost of the improvement, issue bonds to provide the funds, construct the improvement using the bond proceeds, and then collect the assessments over a period of years, using the collections to service the bonds.

Five basic types of transactions are associated with a capital-project type special assessment:

1. Levying the special assessment
2. Issuing special assessment bonds
3. Constructing the capital project
4. Collecting the special assessment
5. Paying the bond principal and interest

Because the special assessment fund has been eliminated for financial reporting purpose, the transactions related to special assessment activities are typically reported in the same manner and on the same basis of accounting as any other capital improvement and financing transaction. Transactions of the construction phase of the project should generally be reported in a capital projects fund, and transactions of the debt service phase should be reported in a debt service fund, if one is required.

At the time of the levy, the governmental fund should recognize the special assessments receivable with the deferred revenue; the deferred revenue should be reduced as the assessments become measurable and available in the fund financial statements.

The entry for the retirement of special assessment bonds and for the construction of the special assessment project would follow the accounting principles outlined in the discussion on capital projects. The usual entries are made for expenditures and for encumbrances, if such a system exists. At the end of the year, the revenues and expenditures should be closed to the fund balance to reflect the balance that may be expended in future periods.

Although the accounting for special assessment construction activities is quite similar to other financing and construction activities, the major issue relating to special assessment activities involves the definition of special assessment debt. Special assessment debt is often defined as those long-term obligations, secured by a lien on the assessed properties, for which the primary source of repayment is the assessments levied against the benefiting properties.

However, the nature and composition of debt associated with special assessment–related capital improvements is not always consistent with this definition. Rather, it can vary significantly from one jurisdiction to another. Capital improvements involving special assessments may be financed by debt that is

- General obligation debt that is not secured by liens on assessed properties but nevertheless will be repaid in part by special assessment collections
- Special assessment debt that is secured by liens on assessed properties and is also backed by the full faith and credit of the government as additional security
- Special assessment debt that is secured by liens on assessed properties and is not backed by the full faith and credit of the government but is, however, fully or partially backed by some other type of general governmental commitment
- Special assessment debt that is secured by liens on assessed properties, is not backed by the full faith and credit of the government, and is not backed by any other type of general governmental commitment, the government not being liable under any circumstance for the repayment of this category of debt should the property owner default

In some cases special assessment debt is payable entirely by special assessment collections from the assessed property owners; in other cases the debt may be repaid partly from special assessment collections and partly from the general resources of the government, either because the government is a property owner benefiting from the improvements or because the government has agreed to finance part of the cost of the improvement as a public benefit. The portion of special assessment debt that will be repaid directly with governmental resources is, in essence, a general obligation of the government. If the government owns property that benefits from the improvements financed by special assessment debt as in item 4 in the preceding list, or if a public benefit assessment is made against the government, the government is obligated for the public benefit portion and the amount assessed against its property, even though it has no liability for the remainder of the debt issue.

Because the special assessment debt can have various characteristics, the extent of a government's liability for debt related to a special assessment capital improvement can also vary significantly. For example, the government may be primarily liable for the debt, as in the case of a general obligation issue; it may have no liability whatsoever for special assessment debt; or it may be obligated in some manner to provide a secondary source of funds for repayment of special assessment debt in the event of default by the assessed property owners. A government is obligated in some manner for special assessment debt if (1) it is legally obligated to assume all or part of the debt in the event of default or (2) the government may take certain actions to assume secondary liability for all or part of the debt—and the government takes, or has given indications that it will take, those actions.

Stated differently, the phrase "obligated in some manner" is intended to include all situations other than those in which (1) the government is prohibited (by constitution, charter, statute, ordinance, or contract) from assuming the debt in the event of default by the property owner or (2) the government is not legally liable for assuming the debt and makes no statement, or gives no indication, that it will, or may, honor the debt in the event of default.

Debt issued to finance capital projects that will be paid wholly or partly from special assessments against benefited property owners should be reported in one of the following three ways:

1. General obligation debt that will be repaid, in part, from special assessments should be reported like any other general obligation debt.
2. Special assessment debt for which the government is obligated in some manner should be reported in the capital projects fund, except for the portion, if any, that is a direct obligation of a proprietary fund, or that is expected to be repaid from operating revenues of a proprietary fund.
3. Special assessment debt for which the government is not obligated in any manner should not be displayed in the government's financial statements. However, if the government is liable for a portion of that debt (the public benefit portion, or as a property owner), that portion should be reported as previously stated.

(h) CAPITAL ASSETS REPORTING AND ACCOUNTING   The term *capital assets* includes land, improvements to land, easements, buildings, building improvements, vehicles, machinery, equipment, works of art and historical treasures, infrastructure, and all other tangible or intangible assets used in operations and that have initial useful lives beyond a single reporting period. Infrastructure assets are capital assets that are normally stationary and normally can be preserved for a significantly greater number of years than most other capital assets—for example, roads, bridges, tunnels, drainage systems, water and sewer systems, dams, and lighting systems. Buildings that are not ancillary parts of networks of infrastructure assets are not infrastructure assets.

Purchased capital assets should be reported at their acquisition costs, which should include ancillary charges needed to place the assets in their intended locations and conditions for use. Ancillary charges include costs directly attributable to asset acquisition, such as freight and transportation charges, site preparation costs, and professional fees. Donated capital assets should be reported at their fair values at their times of acquisition plus ancillary charges.

In general, capital assets should be depreciated. They should be reported net of accumulated depreciation in the statement of net assets, with accumulated depreciation reported on the face of the statement or in the notes. Capital assets not depreciated, such as land and infrastructure assets reported using the modified approach, discussed subsequently, should be reported separately if they are significant.

Capital assets may also be reported in greater detail, such as infrastructure, buildings and improvements, vehicles, machinery, and equipment. Capital assets should be depreciated over their useful lives based on their net costs less salvage values in a systematic and rational manner unless they are either inexhaustible, such as land and land improvements, or are infrastructure reported using the modified approach. Depreciation, reported in the statement of activities as discussed in the following text, may be calculated for (1) a class of assets, (2) a network of assets (all the assets that provide a particular kind of service for a government; a network of infrastructure assets may be only one infrastructure asset composed of many components—e.g., a dam composed of a concrete dam, a concrete spillway, and a series of locks), (3) a subsystem of a network (all assets that make up a similar portion or segment of a network of assets—e.g., interstate highways, state highways, and rural roads could each be a subsystem of a network of all the roads of a government), or (4) individual assets.

Eligible infrastructure assets, infrastructure assets that are part of a network or subsystem of a network, need not be depreciated but may be treated by a modified approach if both of the following are met:

1. The government manages them using an asset management system that has these characteristics:
   - It has an up-to-date inventory of eligible infrastructure assets.
   - It performs condition assessments of the eligible infrastructure assets and summarizes the results using a measurement scale. The assessments must be documented so they can be replicated—based on sufficiently understandable and complete measurement methods so that different measurers using the same methods would reach substantially similar results—performed by the government or by contract.
   - It estimates each year the annual cost to maintain and preserve the eligible infrastructure assets at the condition level established and disclosed by the government.
2. The government documents that the eligible infrastructure assets are being preserved approximately at or above a condition level established and documented by administrative or executive policy or by legislative action and documented by the government. Adequate documentation requires professional judgment and may vary within governments for different eligible infrastructure assets. Nevertheless, documentation should include
   - Complete condition assessments of eligible infrastructure assets performed consistently at least every three years. Statistical sampling may be used, and eligible infrastructure assets may be assessed on a cyclical basis. A complete assessment on a cyclical basis requires all or statistical samples of all eligible infrastructure assets in the network or subsystem to be assessed.
   - The three most recent complete condition assessments provide reasonable assurance that the eligible infrastructure assets are being preserved approximately at or above the condition level established and disclosed by the government. The condition level could be measured either by a condition index or as the percentage of a network of infrastructure assets in good or poor condition.

All expenditures other than for additions and improvements made for eligible infrastructure assets that meet the two requirements and are not depreciated should be reported as expense in the periods incurred. Additions and improvements increase the capacity or efficiency of infrastructure assets; expenditures for them should be capitalized. A change from depreciation to the modified approach should be reported as a change in an accounting estimate.

When and if the requirements to report capital assets by the modified approach are no longer met, they should be depreciated in subsequent periods. The change should be reported as a change in accounting estimate.

Governments should in general capitalize individual or collections of works of art, historical treasures, and similar assets at their acquisition costs or fair values at the dates of acquisition or donation (estimated if necessary). They are encouraged but not required to capitalize a collection and all additions to the collection, whether donated or purchased, that meets all three of the following conditions (but collections capitalized by June 30, 1999, should remain capitalized and additions to them should be capitalized regardless of whether they meet the conditions):

1. The collection is held for public exhibition, education, or research for public service, not financial gain.
2. The collection is protected, kept unencumbered, cared for, and preserved.
3. The collection is subject to an organizational policy that requires that the proceeds from sales of collection items are used to acquire other items for collections.

Governments that receive donations of works of art, historical treasures, and similar assets should report revenues in conformity with GASB Statement No. 33. Governments should report program expense equal to the revenue reported on donated assets added to noncapitalized collections.

Capitalized collections or individual items of works of art, historical treasures, and similar assets that are exhaustible, such as exhibits whose useful lives decrease because of display or educational or research use, should be depreciated over their estimated useful lives. Depreciation is not required for collections or individual items of works of art, historical treasures, and similar assets that are inexhaustible.

(i) Methods for Calculating Depreciation   Governments may use any established depreciation method. It may be based on the estimated useful life of a class of assets, a network of assets, a subsystem, a network, or individual assets. Estimated useful lives may be obtained from general guidelines obtained from professional or industry organizations, information for comparable assets of other governments, or internal information.

A government may use a composite method, applying one rate, to calculate depreciation—for example, for similar assets or dissimilar assets of the same class, such as all the roads and bridges of the government. Depreciation is determined as the product of the total cost times the rate. The rate can be determined based on a weighted average or an unweighted average estimate of the useful lives of the assets included. Alternatively, it may be based on condition assessment or experience with the useful lives of the group of assets. It is generally used throughout the life of the group of assets, but it should be recalculated if the composition of the assets or the estimate of average useful lives changes significantly.

(ii) Subsidiary Property Records   The maintenance of subsidiary property records aids in the control of fixed assets. The subsidiary records should contain such information as classification code, date of acquisition, name and address of vendor, unit charged with custody, location, cost, fund and account from which purchased, method of acquisition, estimated life, and repair and maintenance data.

(iii) Disposal or Retirement of Capital Assets   In the disposal or retirement of a capital asset the book value of the asset must be removed from the asset side and the gain or loss must be recorded in the statement of activities or the proprietary fund statements. If the asset is sold, the amount obtained in cash or by evidence of indebtedness should be recorded as another financing source in the appropriate governmental fund.

(iv) Impairment of Capital Assets   Governments should evaluate prominent events or changes in circumstances affecting capital assets to determine whether impairment of a capital asset has occurred. Indicators of impairment include physical damage, enactment or approval of laws or regulations or other changes in environmental factors, technological changes or evidence of obsolescence, changes in the manner or duration of use of a capital asset, and construction stoppage. A capital asset generally should be considered impaired if (1) the decline in service utility of the capital asset is large in magnitude and (2) the event or change in circumstance is outside the normal life cycle of the capital asset.

(i) REPORTING AND ACCOUNTING FOR LONG-TERM LIABILITIES   General long-term liabilities need to be clearly distinguished from fund long-term liabilities. General long-term liabilities are the unmatured principal of bonds, warrants, notes, or other forms of long-term general obligation indebtedness. They may arise from debt issuances, lease–purchase agreements, and other commitments that are not liabilities properly reported in governmental funds. Other general long-term liabilities include capital leases, operating judgments, pensions and other postemployment benefits, special termination benefits, and landfill closure and postclosure care liabilities that are not due.

General long-term liabilities should be reported in the governmental activities column in the government-wide statement of net assets, not in governmental funds.

Typically, the general long-term debt of a state or local government is secured by the general credit and revenue-raising powers of the government rather than by the assets acquired for specific fund resources. Furthermore, just as general capital assets do not represent financial resources available for appropriation and expenditure, general long-term liabilities do not require current appropriation and expenditure of a governmental fund's current financial resources. Thus, to include it as a governmental fund liability would be misleading for management control and accountability functions for the current period.

(j) MEASUREMENT FOCUS AND BASIS OF ACCOUNTING   The accounting and financial reporting treatment applied to the government-wide financial statements and the fund financial statements is determined by its measurement focus. The measurement focus refers to what is being expressed in reporting an entity's financial performance and position. A particular measurement focus is accomplished by considering not only which resources are measured but also when the effects of transactions or events involving those resources are recognized (the basis of accounting). This principle describes the measurement focus and basis of accounting used by governments.

(i) Measurement Focus   The government-wide and proprietary funds financial statements should be prepared using the economic resources measurement focus and the accrual basis of accounting. Assets, liabilities, revenues, expenses, and gains and losses that result from exchange transactions and exchange-like transactions should be reported when the transactions occur. (In an exchange-like transaction, the resources or services exchanged, though related, may not be quite equal or the direct benefits may not be exclusively for the parties to the transactions. Nevertheless, the transactions are similar enough to exchanges to justify treating them as exchanges.) Assets, liabilities, revenues, expenses, and gains and losses that result from nonexchange transactions should be reported as discussed further on in this chapter.

(ii) Basis of Accounting   The basis of accounting determines when revenues, expenditures, expenses, and transfers—along with the related assets and liabilities—are recognized in the accounts and reported in the financial statements. Specifically, it relates to the timing of the measurements made, regardless of the measurement focus. For example, whether depreciation is recognized depends on whether expenses or expenditures are being measured rather than on whether the cash or accrual basis is used.

CASH BASIS
Under the cash basis of accounting, revenues and transfers in are not recorded in the accounts until cash is received, and expenditures or expenses and transfers out are recorded only when cash is disbursed.

The cash basis is frequently encountered, but its use is not generally accepted for any governmental unit. With the cash basis, it is difficult to compare expenditures with services rendered, because the disbursements relating to those services may be made in the fiscal period following that in which the services occurred. Also, statements prepared on a cash basis do not show financial position and results of operations on a basis that is generally accepted.

ACCRUAL BASIS
Under the accrual basis of accounting, most transactions are recorded when they occur, regardless of when cash is received or disbursed. Items not measurable until cash is received or disbursed are accounted for at that time.

The accrual basis is considered a superior method of accounting for the economic resources of any organization because it results in accounting measurements that are based on the substance of transactions and events, rather than merely on the receipt or disbursement of cash.

MODIFIED ACCRUAL BASIS
As indicated previously, the financial flows of governments, such as taxes and grants, typically do not result from a direct exchange for goods or services and thus cannot be accrued based on the completion of the earnings process and an exchange taking place. Governments have thus devised the "susceptible to accrual" concept as the criterion for determining when inflows are accruable as revenue. A revenue is susceptible to accrual when it is both measurable and available to finance current operations. An amount is measurable when the precise amount is known because the transaction is completed or when it can be accurately estimated using past experience or other available information. An amount is available to finance operations when it is (1) physically available—that is, collectible within the current period or soon enough thereafter to be used to pay liabilities of the current period—and (2) legally available—that is, authorized for expenditure in the current fiscal period and not applicable to some future period.

On the expenditure side, a government's main concern, for governmental funds at least, is to match the financial resources used with the financial resources obtained. This measure of whether current-year revenues were sufficient to pay for current-year services is referred to as *interperiod equity*. A measure of interperiod equity shows whether current-year citizens received services but shifted part of the payment burden to future-year citizens or used up previously accumulated resources. Conversely, such a measure would show whether current-year revenues were not only sufficient to pay for current-year services but also increased accumulated net resources.

This adaptation of the accrual basis to the conditions surrounding government activities and financing has been given the term *modified accrual*. Modified accrual is currently used in all governmental fund types (i.e., the general fund, special revenue funds, etc.) where the intent is to determine the extent to which provided services have been financed by current resources.

In proprietary funds the objective is to determine net income, and the accounting should be essentially the same as commercial accounting. Hence, proprietary funds use the economic resources measurement focus and the accrual basis without the need for modification described above.

(iii) Revenue Transactions   The modified accrual basis of accounting is applied in practice for five different revenue transactions as follows:

1. Property taxes are recorded as revenue when the taxes are levied, provided that they apply to and are collected in the current period or soon enough thereafter to finance the current period's expenditures. The period after year-end generally should not exceed 60 days. The amount recorded as revenue should be net of estimated uncollectible taxes, abatements, discounts, and refunds. (Property taxes that are

measurable but not available—and hence not susceptible to accrual—should be deferred and recognized as revenue in the fiscal year they become available.)

2. Taxpayer-assessed income, gross receipts, and sales taxes should be recorded as revenues when susceptible to accrual.

3. Miscellaneous revenues such as fines and forfeits, athletic fees, and inspection charges are generally recognized when cash is received because they are usually not measurable and available until they are received.

4. Grants should be recorded when the government has an irrevocable right to the grant. If expenditure of funds is the prime factor for determining eligibility for the grant funds, revenue should be recognized when the expenditure is made.

5. Interest earned on special assessment levies may be accrued when due rather than when earned if it approximately offsets interest expenditures on special assessment indebtedness that is also recorded when due.

Escheat property, which consists of assets reverted to a governmental entity in the absence of legal claimants or heirs, should be reported in government-wide and fund financial statements generally as an asset in the governmental or proprietary fund to which the property ultimately escheats. If held for individuals, private organizations, or another government, it should be reported in a private-purpose trust fund or an agency fund, as appropriate (or in the governmental or proprietary fund in which escheat property is otherwise reported, with a corresponding liability).

Escheat revenue on escheat property reported in governmental or proprietary funds should be reduced and a governmental or proprietary fund liability reported to the extent that it is probable that escheat property will be reclaimed and paid to claimants. The liability should represent the best estimate of the amount ultimately expected to be reclaimed and paid, giving effect to such factors as previous and current trends and anticipated changes in those trends. The liability may differ from the amount specified in law to be held separately for payments to claimants.

Escheat-related transactions reported in the government-wide financial statements should be measured using the economic resources measurement focus and the accrual basis of accounting. Escheat transactions reported in private-purpose trust funds or in agency funds should be excluded from the government-wide financial statements.

(iv) Expenditure Transactions   Expenditure transactions under the modified accrual basis are treated as follows:

• If there is no explicit requirement to do otherwise, a governmental fund liability and expenditure should be accrued in the period in which the government incurs the liability. They include liabilities that normally are paid in a timely manner and in full from available financial resources, such as salaries, professional services, supplies, utilities, and travel. Unpaid, they represent claims against current financial resources and should be reported as governmental fund liabilities.

• Debt issue costs paid from debt proceeds, such as underwriter fees, should be reported as expenditures. Issue costs, such as attorneys' fees, rating agency fees, or bond insurance, paid from existing resources, should be reported as expenditures when liabilities for them are incurred.

• Inventory items may be considered expenditures either when purchased (the purchases method) or when used (the consumption method). Under either method significant amounts of inventory at the end of a fiscal year should be reported as an asset on the balance sheet.

- Expenditures for insurance and similar services extending over more than one accounting period need not be allocated between or among accounting periods, but they may be accounted for as expenditures of the period of acquisition.
- Interest expenditures on special assessment indebtedness may be recorded when due if they are approximately offset by interest earnings on special assessment levies that are also recorded when due.
- Compensated absences, claims and judgments, special termination benefits, landfill closure and postclosure care costs, and "other obligations" should be recorded as a governmental fund liability when they are **due** for payment in the current period.

(v) Reporting on Nonexchange Transactions   As with a nonreciprocal transaction discussed in APB Statement No. 4, in a nonexchange transaction, a government of any level other than the federal government gives or receives financial or capital resources, not including contributed services, without directly receiving or giving equal value in exchange. Such transactions are divided into four classes:

1. *Derived tax revenues.* These result from assessments imposed by governments on exchange transactions, such as personal and corporate income taxes and retail sales taxes. Some legislation enabling such a tax provides purpose restrictions, requirements that a particular source of tax be used for a specific purpose or purposes—for example, motor fuel taxes required to be used for road and street repairs.

2. *Imposed nonexchange revenues.* These result from assessments on nongovernmental entities, including individuals, other than assessments on exchange transactions, such as property taxes, fines, and penalties, or property forfeitures, such as seizures and escheats. Such a tax is imposed on an act committed or omitted by the payer, such as property ownership or the contravention of a law or a regulation that is not an exchange. Some enabling legislation provides purpose restrictions; some also provide time requirements, specification of the periods in which the resources must be used or when their use may begin.

3. *Government-mandated nonexchange transactions.* These occur when a government, including the federal government, at one level provides resources to a government at another level and provides purpose restrictions on the recipient government established in the provider's enabling legislation. Transactions other than cash or other advances are contingent on fulfillment of certain requirements, which may include time requirements, which are called *eligibility requirements.*

4. *Voluntary nonexchange transactions.* These result from legislative or contractual agreements but are not deemed an exchange (unfunded mandates are excluded, because they are not transactions), entered into willingly by two or more parties, at least one of which is a government, such as certain grants, certain entitlements, and donations by nongovernmental entities including individuals (private donations). Providers often establish purpose restrictions and eligibility requirements and require return of the resources if the purpose restrictions or the eligibility requirements are contravened after reporting of the transaction.

Labels such as "tax," "grant," "contribution," or "donation" do not necessarily indicate which of those classes nonexchange transactions belong to and therefore what principles should be applied. In addition, labels such as "fees," "charges," and "grants" do not always indicate whether exchange or nonexchange transactions are involved. Principles for reporting on nonexchange transactions depend on their substance, not merely their labels, and determining that requires analysis.

The following expense (or expenditure, for public colleges or universities) reporting principles for nonexchange transactions apply to both the accrual and the modified accrual basis, unless the transactions are not measurable or are not probable of collection. Such transactions that are not measurable should be disclosed.

Time requirements affect the timing of reporting of the transactions. The effect on the timing of reporting depends on whether a nonexchange transaction is an imposed nonexchange revenue transaction or a government-mandated or voluntary nonexchange transaction. Purpose restrictions do not affect the timing of reporting of the transactions. However, recipients should report resulting net assets, equity, or fund balance as restricted until the resources are used for the specified purpose or for as long as the provider requires the resources to be maintained intact, such as endowment principal.

Award programs commonly referred to as *reimbursement-type* or *expenditure-driven* grant programs may be either government mandated or voluntary nonexchange transactions. The provider stipulates an eligibility requirement that a recipient can qualify for resources only after incurring allowable costs under the provider's program. The provider has no liability and the recipient has no asset (receivable) until the recipient has met the eligibility requirements. Assets provided in advance should be reported as advances (assets) by providers and as deferred revenues (liabilities) by recipients until eligibility requirements have been met.

Assets should be reported from derived tax revenue transactions in the period in which the exchange transaction on which the tax is imposed occurs or in which the resources are received, whichever occurs first. Revenues net of estimated refunds and estimated uncollectible amounts should be reported in the period the assets are reported, provided that the underlying exchange transaction has occurred. Resources received in advance should be reported as deferred revenues (liabilities) until the period of the exchange.

Assets from imposed nonexchange revenue transactions should be reported in the period in which an enforceable legal claim to the assets arises or in which the assets are received, whichever occurs first. The date on which an enforceable legal claim to taxable property arises is generally specified in the enabling legislation, sometimes referred to as the *lien date*, though a lien is not formally placed on the property on that date. Others refer to it as the *assessment date*. (An enforceable legal claim by some governments arises in the period after the period for which the taxes are levied. Those governments should report assets in the same period they report revenues, as discussed next.)

Revenues from property taxes, net of estimated refunds and estimated uncollectible amounts, should be reported in the period for which the taxes are levied, even if the enforceable legal claim arises or the due date for payment occurs in a different period. All other imposed nonexchange revenues should be reported in the same period as the assets unless the enabling legislation includes time requirements. If it does, revenues should be reported in the period in which the resources are required to be used or in which use is first permitted. Resources received or reported as receivable before then should be reported as deferred revenues.

The following are the kinds of eligibility requirements for government-mandated and voluntary nonexchange transactions:

- The recipient and secondary recipients, if applicable, have the characteristics specified by the provider. For example, under a certain federal program, recipients are required to be states and secondary recipients are required to be school districts.

- Time requirements specified by enabling legislation or the provider have been met—that is, the period in which the resources are required to be sold, disbursed, or consumed or in which use is first permitted has begun, or the resources are being maintained intact, as specified by the provider.
- The provider offers resources on an "expenditure-driven" basis and the recipient has incurred allowable costs under the applicable program.
- The offer of resources by the provider in a voluntary nonexchange transaction is contingent on a specified action of the recipient—for example, to raise a specific amount of resources from third parties or to dedicate its own resources for a specified purpose, and that action has occurred.

Providers should report liabilities or decreases in assets and expenses from government-mandated or voluntary nonexchange transactions, and recipients should report receivables or decreases in liabilities and revenues, net of estimated uncollectible amounts, when all applicable eligibility requirements have been met (the need to complete purely routine requirements such as filing of claims for allowable costs under a reimbursement program or the filing of progress reports with the provider should not delay reporting of assets and revenues). Resources transmitted before the eligibility requirements are met should be reported as advances by the provider and as deferred revenue by recipients, except as indicated next for recipients of certain resources transmitted in advance. The exception does not cover transactions in which, for administrative or practical reasons, a government receives assets in the period immediately before the period the provider specifies as the one in which sale, disbursement, or consumption of resources is required or may begin.

A provider in some kinds of government-mandated and voluntary nonexchange transactions transmits assets stipulating that the resources cannot be sold, disbursed, or consumed until after a specified number of years have passed or a specific event has occurred, if ever. The recipient may nevertheless benefit from the resources in the interim—for example, by investing or exhibiting them. Examples are permanently nonexpendable additions to endowments and other trusts, term endowments, and contributions of works of art, historical treasures, and similar assets to capitalized collections. The recipient should report revenue when the resources are received if all eligibility requirements have been met. Resulting net assets, equity, or fund balance, should be reported as restricted as long as the provider's purpose restrictions or time requirements remain in effect.

If a provider in a government-mandated or voluntary nonexchange transaction does not specify time requirements, the entire award should be reported as a liability and an expense by the provider and as a receivable and revenue net of estimated uncollectible amounts by the recipients in the period in which all applicable eligibility requirements are met (applicable period). If the provider is a government, that period for both the provider and the recipients is the provider's fiscal year and begins on the first day of that year, and the entire award should be reported as of that date. But if the provider government has a biennial budgetary process, each year of the biennium should be treated as a separate applicable period. The provider and the recipients should then allocate one-half of the resources appropriated for the biennium to each applicable period, unless the provider specifies a different allocation.

Promises of assets including entities individuals voluntarily make to governments may include permanently nonexpendable additions to endowments and other trusts, term endowments, contributions of works of art, and similar assets to capitalized collections, or other kinds of capital or financial assets, with or without purpose restrictions or time requirements. Recipients of such promises should report receivables and revenue net of estimated uncollectible amounts when all eligibility requirements have been met if the promise is verifiable and the resources are measurable and probable of collection. If the promise involves a stipulation (time requirement) that the resources cannot be sold, disbursed, or consumed until after a specified number of years have passed or a specific event has occurred, if ever, the recipient does not meet the time requirement until the assets have been received.

After a nonexchange transaction has been reported in the financial statements, it may become apparent that (1) if the transaction was reported as a government-mandated or voluntary nonexchange transaction, the eligibility requirements are no longer met, or (2) the recipient will not comply with the purpose restrictions within the specified time limit. If it then is probable that the provider will not provide the resources or will require the return of all or part of the resources already provided, the recipient should report a decrease in assets or an increase in liabilities and an expense, and the provider should report a decrease in liabilities or an increase in assets and a revenue for the amount involved in the period in which the returned resources become available.

A government may collect derived tax revenue or imposed nonexchange revenue on behalf of another government, the recipient, that imposed the revenue source—for example, sales tax collected by a state, part of which is a local option sales tax. The recipient should be able to reasonably estimate the accrual-basis information needed to comply with the requirements previously stated for derived tax revenue or imposed nonexchange revenue. However, if a government shares in a portion of the revenue resulting from a tax imposed by another government, it may not be able to reasonably estimate the accrual-basis information nor obtain sufficient timely information from the other government needed to comply with the previously stated requirements for derived tax revenue or imposed nonexchange revenue. If it cannot, the recipient government should report revenue for a period in the amount of cash received during the period. Cash received afterward should also be reported as revenue of the period, less amounts reported as revenue in the previous period, if reliable information is consistently available to identify the amounts that apply to the current period.

Revenue from nonexchange transactions reported on the modified accrual basis should be reported as follows:

- Recipients should report derived tax revenue in the period in which the underlying exchange transaction has occurred and the resources are available.
- Recipients should report property taxes in conformity with NCGA Interpretation No. 3, as amended.
- Recipients should report other imposed nonexchange revenue in the period in which an enforceable legal claim has arisen and the resources are available.
- Recipients should report government-mandated nonexchange transactions and voluntary nonexchange transactions in the period in which all applicable eligibility requirements have been met and the resources are available.

(k) BUDGETING, BUDGETARY CONTROL, AND BUDGETARY REPORTING ACCOUNTING

(i) Types of Operating Budgets   Several types of annual operating budgets are used in contemporary public finance. Among the more common are the following:

- Line item budget
- Program budget
- Performance budget
- Zero-base budget

LINE ITEM BUDGETING

Listing the inputs for resources that each organizational unit requests for each line (or object) of expenditure is referred to as *line item budgeting*. This simple approach produces a budget that governing bodies and administrators can understand, based on their own experience. It provides for tight control over spending and is the most common local government budgeting approach, although this popularity is due primarily to tradition.

Line item budgeting is criticized because it emphasizes inputs rather than outputs, analyzes expenditures inadequately, and fragments activities among accounts that bear little relation to purposes of the government. However, all budgeting systems use objects for the buildup of costs and for execution of the budget.

Overcoming criticisms of a line item budgeting system can be accomplished by:

- Improving the budget structure to encompass all funds and organizational units in a manner that enables the total resources available to a particular organizational unit or responsibility center to be readily perceived
- Developing a level of detail for the object categories that permits adequate analysis of proposed expenditures and effective control over the actual expenditures
- Improving the presentation of historical data to stimulate the analysis of trends
- Providing a partial linking of outputs to the objects of expenditures

PROGRAM BUDGETING

Formulating expenditure requests on the basis of the services to be performed for the various programs the government provides is known as *program budgeting*. A program budget categorizes the major areas of citizen needs and the services for meeting such needs into programs. Goals and objectives are stated for each program, normally in relatively specific, quantified terms. The costs are estimated for the resources required (e.g., personnel and equipment) to accomplish the objective for each program. The governing body can then conduct a meaningful review of budget requests by adding or deleting programs or placing different emphasis on the various programs.

Program budgeting has existed for many years, but relatively few governments have adopted it, partly because line item budgeting is so familiar and comprehensible. Lack of acceptance also results from the difficulty of developing operationally useful program budgets that meet the governmental notion of accountability, that is, control of the number of employees and other expense items, rather than achievement of results in applying such resources.

The operational usefulness of program budgeting has also been questioned as a result of the complexity of the program structure, the vagueness of goals and objectives, the lack of organizational or individual responsibility for program funds that span several departments or agencies, and the inadequacy of accounting support to record direct and indirect program costs.

Nevertheless, program budgeting can be an extremely effective approach for a government willing to devote the effort. The steps that departments should take to implement the system are as follows:

- Identify programs and the reasons for their existence.
- Define the goals of programs.
- Define kinds and levels of services to be provided in light of budgetary guidelines (council- or CEO-furnished guidelines, e.g., budget priorities, budget assumptions, and budget constraints).

- Develop budget requests in terms of resources needed, based on the programs' purposes, the budgetary guidelines, the projected levels of services, and the previous years' expenditure levels for the programs.
- Submit budget requests for compilation, review, and approval.

PERFORMANCE BUDGETING

Formulating expenditure requests based on the work to be performed is the primary function of performance budgeting. It emphasizes the work or service performed, described in quantitative terms, by an organizational unit performing a given activity—for example, number of tons of waste collected by the Sanitation Department and case workload in the Department of Welfare. These performance data are used in the preparation of the annual budget as the basis for increasing or decreasing the number of personnel and the related operating expenses of the individual departments.

The development of a full-scale performance budget requires a strong budget staff, constructive participation at all levels, special accounting and reporting methods, and a substantial volume of processed statistical data. Primarily for these reasons, performance budgeting has been less widely used than line item budgeting.

The approach to developing a performance budgeting system is as follows:

- Decide on the extent to which functions and activities will be segmented into work units and services for formulation and execution of the budget.
- Define the functions in services performed by the government, and assemble them into a structure.
- Identify and assemble or develop workload and efficiency measures that relate to service categories.
- Estimate the total costs of the functions and services.
- Analyze resource needs for each service in terms of personnel, equipment, and so on.
- Formulate the first-year performance budget (for the first year, set the budget appropriations and controls at a higher level than the data indicate).
- Perform cost accounting for the functional budget category; initiate statistical reporting of the workload measures; match resources utilized to actual results.

ZERO-BASE BUDGETING

In the preparation of a budget, zero-base budgeting projects funding for services at several alternative levels, both lower and higher than the present level, and allocates funds to services based on rankings of these alternatives. It is an appropriate budgeting system for jurisdictions whose revenues are not sufficient for citizen demands and inflation-driven expenditure increases, where considerable doubt exists as to the necessity and effectiveness of existing programs and services, and where incremental budgeting processes have resulted in existing programs and their funding being taken as a given, with attention devoted to requests for new programs.

Zero-base budgeting can be used with any existing budgeting system, including line item, program, or performance budgeting. The budget format can remain unchanged.

The steps to implement zero-base budgeting are as follows:

- Define decision units—that is, activities that can be logically grouped for planning and providing each service.

- Analyze decision units to determine alternative service levels, determine the resources required to operate at alternative levels, and present this information in decision packages.
- Rank the decision packages in a priority order that reflects the perceived importance of a particular package to the community in relation to other packages.
- Present the budget to the governing body for a review of the ranking of the decision packages.

(ii) Budget Preparation   The specific procedures involved in the preparation of a budget for a governmental unit are usually prescribed by state statute, local charter, or ordinance. There are, however, certain basic steps:

- Preparation of the budget calendar
- Development of preliminary forecasts of available revenues, recurring expenditures, and new programs
- Formulation and promulgation of a statement of executive budget policy to the operating departments
- Preparation and distribution of budget instructions, budget forms, and related information
- Review of departmental budget requests and supporting work sheets
- Interviews with department heads for the purpose of adjusting or approving their requests in a tentative budget
- Final assembly of the tentative budget, including fixing of revenue estimates and the required tax levy
- Presentation of the tentative budget to the legislative body and the public
- Conduction of a public hearing, with advance legal notice
- Adoption of final budget by the legislative body

REVENUE AND EXPENDITURE ESTIMATES

The property tax has been the traditional basic source of revenue for local government. The amount to be budgeted and raised is determined by subtracting the estimated nonproperty taxes and other revenues, plus the reappropriated fund balance, from budgeted expenditures. This amount, divided by the assessed valuation of taxable property within the boundaries of the governmental unit, produces the required tax rate.

Many jurisdictions have legal ceilings on the property tax rates available for general operating purposes. Additionally, taxpayer initiatives have forced governments to seek new revenue sources. Accordingly, governmental units have turned increasingly to other types of revenue, such as sales taxes; business and nonbusiness license fees; charges for services; state-collected, locally shared taxes; and grants-in-aid from the federal and state governments. Department heads, however, ordinarily have little knowledge of revenue figures. As a result, the primary responsibility for estimating these revenues usually lies with the budget officer and the chief finance officer.

Most governmental units, as a safeguard against excessive accumulation of resources, require that any unappropriated amounts carried over from a previous year be included as a source of financing in the budget of that fund for the succeeding fiscal year. Most controlling laws or ordinances provide for inclusion of the estimated surplus (fund balance) at the end of the current year, although many require that the includable surplus be the balance at the close of the last completed fiscal year.

Departmental estimates of expenditures and supporting work programs or performance data generally are prepared by the individual departments, using forms provided by the central budget agency. Expenditures are customarily classified to conform to the standard account classification of the governmental unit and thus permit comparison with actual performance in the current and prior periods.

PERSONAL SERVICES

Generally, personal services are supported by detailed schedules of proposed salaries for individual full-time employees. Nonsalaried and temporary employees are usually paid on an hourly basis, and the budget requests are normally based on the estimated number of hours of work.

Estimates of materials and supplies and other services, ordinarily quite repetitive in nature, are most often based on current experience, plus an allowance, if justified, for rising costs. Capital outlay requests are based on demonstrated need for specific items of furniture or equipment by individual departments.

In recent years, governmental units, particularly at the county, state, and federal levels, have disbursed substantial sums annually that are unlike the usual current operating expenditures. These sums include welfare or public assistance payments, contributions to other governmental units, benefit payments, and special grants. They are properly classified as "other charges." Estimates of these charges are generally based on unit costs for assistance, legislative allotments, requests from outside agencies or governmental units, and specified calculations.

In addition to departmental expenditures, the budget officer must estimate certain nondepartmental or general governmental costs not allocated to any department or organizational unit. Examples include pension costs and retirement contributions, which are not normally allocated, election costs, insurance and surety bonds, and interest on tax notes.

Although most governments still operate under laws that require the budget to be balanced precisely, an increasing number permit a surplus or contingency provision in the expenditure section of the budget. This is usually included to provide a reserve to cover unforeseen expenditures during the budget year.

The expenditure budget may be approved by a board, a commission, or other governing body before presentation to the central budget-making authority.

PRESENTATION OF THE BUDGET

To present a comprehensive picture of the proposed fund operations for a budget year, a budget document is prepared that is likely to include a budget message, summary schedules and comparative statements, detailed revenue estimates, detailed expenditure estimates, and drafts of ordinances to be enacted by the legislative body.

The contents of a budget message should set forth concisely the salient features of the proposed budget of each fund and will generally include the following: (1) a total amount showing amounts of overall increase and decrease, (2) detailed amounts and explanations of the increases and decreases, and (3) a detailed statement of the current financial status of each fund for which a budget is submitted, together with recommendations for raising the funds needed to balance the budget of each fund. It should identify the relationship of the operating budget to the capital program and capital budget, which are submitted separately.

ADOPTION OF THE BUDGET

Most states adopt the budget by the enactment of one or more statutes. Many cities require the formality of an ordinance for the adoption of the budget. In other cases, the budget is adopted by resolution of the governing body.

APPROPRIATIONS

Because appropriations constitute maximum expenditure authorizations during the fiscal year, they cannot be exceeded legally unless subsequently amended by the legislative body (although some governments permit modifications up to a prescribed limit to be made by the executive branch). Unexpended or unencumbered appropriations may lapse at the end of a fiscal year or may continue as authority for subsequent period expenditures, depending on the applicable legal provisions.

It may be necessary for the legislative agency to adopt a separate appropriation resolution or ordinance, or the adoption of the budget may include the making of appropriations for the items of expenditure included therein. Provision for the required general property tax levy is usually made at this time, either by certifying the required tax rates to the governmental unit that will bill and collect the general property tax or by enacting a tax levy ordinance or resolution.

(iii) Budget Execution   The budget execution phase entails obtaining the revenues, operating the program, and expending the money as authorized. The accounts are usually structured on the same basis on which the budget was prepared. Many governments maintain budgetary control by integration of the budgetary accounts into the general and subsidiary ledger. The entry is as follows:

Estimated revenues	$XXX
Appropriations	$XXX

If estimated revenues exceed appropriations, a credit for the excess is made to "budgetary fund balance"; if they are less the appropriations, the difference is debited to "budgetary fund balance."

Individual sources of revenues are recognized in subsidiary revenue accounts. A typical revenue ledger report is illustrated in Exhibit 34.3. This format provides for the comparison, at any date, of actual and estimated revenues from each source.

To control expenditures effectively, the individual amounts making up the total appropriations are recorded in subsidiary expenditures accounts, generally called *appropriation ledgers*. Exhibit 34.4 presents an example of an appropriation ledger. It should be noted that this format provides for recording the budget appropriation and for applying expenditures and encumbrances (see the following text) relating to the particular classification against the amount appropriated at any date.

When the managerial control purposes of integrating the budgetary accounts into the general ledger have been served, the budgetary account balances are reversed in the process of closing the books at year-end. Budgetary accounting procedures thus have no effect on the financial position or results of operations of a governmental entity.

ENCUMBRANCES

An encumbrance, which is unique to governmental accounting, is the reservation of a portion of an applicable appropriation that is made because a contract has been signed or a purchase order issued. The encumbrance is usually recorded in the accounting system to prevent

NAME OF GOVERNMENTAL UNIT
BUDGET VERSUS ACTUAL REVENUE
BY REVENUE SOURCE
FOR ACCOUNTING PERIOD JUNE 30, 20XX
FUND TYPE: THE GENERAL FUND

	REVENUES	BUDGETED	ACTUAL	VARIANCE
015	Real & per. revenue recognized			
0110	Real & per. prop rev. recognized	$ 459,449,213	$ 460,004,317	$ (555,104)
	Revenue class total	459,449,213	460,004,317	(555,104)
020	Motor vehicle & other excise			
0121	M/V taxes—current year	16,000,000	22,727,905	(6,727,905)
0122	M/V taxes—prior 2007	0	2,886,605	(2,886,605)
0123	M/V taxes—2006	0	32,051	(32,051)
0124	M/V taxes—2005	0	45,378	(45,378)
0125	M/V taxes—2004	0	85,393	(85,393)
0126	M/V taxes—2003 and prior	0	2	(2)
0127	Boat excise—cur yr 2008	15,000	40,414	(25,414)
0128	Boat excise—2007	0	155	(155)
0131	M.V. lessor surcharge	200	60	139
	Revenue class total	16,015,200	25,817,963	(9,802,764)
025	Local excise taxes			
0129	Hotel/motel room excise	13,500,000	13,580,142	(80,142)
0130	Aircraft fuel excise	12,400,000	12,960,966	(560,966)
	Revenue class total	25,900,000	26,541,108	(641,108)
030	Departmental & other revenue			
0133	Penalties & int—prop. taxes	1,000,000	1,746,007	(746,007)
0134	Penalties & int.—M/V taxes	525,000	620,124	(95,124)
0135	Penalties & int.—sidewalk	0	115	(115)
0136	Penalties & interest/tax title	5,000,000	3,835,517	1,164,483
0138	Penalties & int./boat excise	0	3	(3)
3101	Data processing services	100	6,849	(6,749)
3103	Purchasing services	50,000	69,038	(19,038)
3104	Recording of legal instruments	150	291	(141)
3105	Registry division—fees	750,000	761,238	(11,238)
3107	City record/sale of publication	10,000	25,353	(15,353)
3108	Assessing fees	1,600	914	686
3109	Liens	400,000	373,410	26,590
3120	City clerk—fees	250,000	231,970	18,030
3130	Election—fees	12,000	10,633	1,367
3140	City council/sale of publication	200	310	(110)
3199	Other general services	35,000	18,691	16,309
3202	Police services	350,000	365,102	(15,102)
3211	Fire services	1,150,000	1,582,355	(432,355)
3221	Civil defense	40,000	161,835	(121,835)
3301	Parking facilities	3,350,000	3,775,810	(425,810)
	Revenue class total	$12,924,050	$13,585,565	$(661,515)

EXHIBIT 34.3: TYPICAL REVENUE LEDGER REPORT

NAME OF GOVERNMENTAL UNIT
BUDGET VERSUS ACTUAL EXPENDITURES
AND ENCUMBRANCES BY ACTIVITY
FOR ACCOUNTING PERIOD JUNE 30, 20XX
FUND TYPE: THE GENERAL FUND

EXPENDITURES		BUDGETED	ACTUAL [1]	VARIANCE
1100 Human services				
011-384-0384	Rent equity board	$1,330,977	$1,274,531	$56,446
011-387-0387	Elderly commission	2,534,005	2,289,549	244,456
011-398-0398	Physically handicapped comm	180,283	159,768	20,515
011-503-0503	Arts & humanities office	211,916	207,219	4,697
011-740-0741	Vet serv—veterans serv div	2,871,616	2,506,363	365,253
011-740-0742	Vet serv—veterans graves reg	158,270	146,392	11,878
011-150-1505	Jobs & community services	370,053	369,208	845
Activity total		7,657,120	6,953,030	704,090
1200 Public safety				
011-211-0211	Police department	116,850,000	117,145,704	(295,704)
011-221-0221	Fire department	80,594,068	79,587,423	1,006,645
011-222-0222	Arson commission	189,244	175,670	13,574
011-251-0251	Transportation—traffic div	13,755,915	13,707,890	48,025
011-252-0252	Licensing board	542,007	449,825	92,182
011-251-0253	Transportation—parking clerk	7,520,539	7,474,462	46,077
011-261-0260	Inspectional services dept	10,004,470	10,003,569	901
Activity total		229,456,243	228,544,543	911,700
1300 Public works				
011-311-0311	Public works department	64,900,000	60,281,837	4,618,163
011-331-0331	Snow removal	2,250,000	2,360,326	(110,326)
Activity total		67,150,000	62,642,163	4,507,837
1400 Property & development				
011-180-0180	RPD—general administration div	432,740	416,569	16,171
014-180-0183	Real property dept county	1,027,660	354,328	673,332
011-180-0184	RPD—buildings division	6,010,155	6,038,464	(28,309)
011-180-0185	RPD—property division	1,847,650	1,806,427	41,223
011-188-0186	PFD—code enforcement division	504,013	458,984	45,029
011-188-0187	PFD—administration division	4,677,365	4,697,167	(19,802)
011-188-0188	PFD—construction & repair div	3,063,637	2,808,266	255,371
Activity total		$17,563,220	$16,580,205	$983,015

[1] This example actual is presented as a non-GAAP budgetary basis that includes both expenditures plus encumbrances as a budgetary use of resources.

EXHIBIT 34.4:   TYPICAL APPROPRIATION LEDGER REPORT

overspending the appropriation. When the goods or services are received, the expenditure is recorded and the encumbrance is reversed. The entry to record an encumbrance is as follows:

Encumbrances	$XXX
Reserve for encumbrances	$XXX

The entries that are made when the goods or services are received are as follows:

Reserve for encumbrances	$XXX
Encumbrances	$XXX
Expenditures	$XXX
Vouchers payable	$XXX

Many governments report encumbrances that are not liquidated at year-end in the same way as expenditures because the encumbrances are another use of budgetary appropriations. The total amount of encumbrances not liquidated by year-end may be considered as a reservation of the fund balance for the subsequent year's expenditures, based on the encumbered appropriation authority carried over.

ALLOTMENTS

Another way to maintain budgetary control is to use an allotment system. With an allotment system, the annual budget appropriation is divided and allotted among the months or quarters in the fiscal year. A department is not permitted to spend more than its allotment during the period.

The International City Managers' Association lists the following four purposes of an allotment system:

1. To make sure that departments plan their spending so as to have sufficient funds to carry on their programs throughout the year, avoiding year-end deficiencies and special appropriations
2. To eliminate or reduce short-term tax anticipation borrowing by making possible more accurate forecast control of cash position throughout the fiscal year
3. To keep expenditures within the limits of revenues that are actually realized, avoiding an unbalanced budget in the operation of any fund as a whole
4. To give the chief administrator control over departmental expenditures commensurate with the administrative responsibility, allowing the administrator to effect economies in particular activities as changes in workload and improvements in methods occur

INTERIM REPORTS

The last element in the budget execution process is interim financial reports. These are prepared to provide department heads, senior management, and the governing body with the information needed to monitor and control operations, demonstrate compliance with legal and budgetary limitations, anticipate changes in financial resources and requirements due to events or developments that are unknown or could not be foreseen at the time the budget was initially developed, or take appropriate corrective action. Interim reports should be prepared frequently enough to permit early detection of variances between actual and planned operations, but not so frequently as to adversely affect practicality and economy. For most governmental units, interim reports on a monthly basis are necessary for optimum results. With smaller units, a bimonthly or quarterly basis may be sufficient. With sophisticated data-processing equipment, it may be possible to automatically generate the appropriate information daily.

Governmental units should prepare interim financial reports covering the following:

- Revenues
- Expenditures
- Cash projections
- Proprietary funds
- Capital projects
- Grant programs

The form and content of these reports should reflect the government's particular circumstances and conditions.

PROJECT BUDGETS

When debt is issued to finance an entire capital project, it is usually done so at the beginning of the project in an amount equal to the total estimated project cost. Accordingly, a portion of the proceeds may remain unexpended over a considerable period of time. To the maximum extent possible, these excess proceeds should be invested in interest-bearing investments. However, consideration should be given to the federal arbitrage regulations that limit the amount of interest that can be earned from investing the proceeds of a tax-exempt bond issue. If certain limits are exceeded, the bond's tax-exempt status may be lost or severe penalties could be imposed on the issuer.

Project budgets are typically established for capital projects to control costs and to guard against cost overruns. All expenditures needed to place the project in readiness—that is, indirect as well as direct costs, should be recorded against this budget. The actual expenditures, however, will probably be either less or greater than the amounts authorized. Therefore, in the absence of any legal restrictions, any unspent balance should be transferred to the appropriate sources. If the project was financed only from bond proceeds, the transfer should be to the debt service fund from which the bond issue is to be repaid. If the resources were drawn from more than one source, such as bond proceeds and current revenues, the transfer should be split among the sources in proportion to their contributions. If the expenditures were greater than authorized and a deficit exists, sufficient funds must be transferred to liquidate any commitments.

As construction of the project is completed, the costs should be recorded in the capital account as Construction in Progress and then transferred to the final building account when construction has been completed.

(iv) Proprietary Fund Budgeting   The nature of most operations financed and accounted for through proprietary funds is such that the demand for the goods or services largely determines the appropriate level of revenues and expenses. Increased demand causes a higher level of expenses to be incurred but also results in a higher level of revenues. Thus, as in commercial accounting, flexible budgets prepared for several levels of possible activity typically are better for planning, control, and evaluation purposes than are fixed budgets.

Accordingly, budgets are not typically adopted for proprietary funds. Furthermore, even when flexible budgets are adopted, they are viewed not as appropriations but as approved plans. The budgetary accounts are generally not integrated into the ledger accounts because it is considered unnecessary. Budgetary control and evaluation are achieved by comparing interim actual revenues and expenses with planned revenues and expenses at the actual level of activity for the period.

In some instances, fixed dollar budgets are adopted for proprietary funds either to meet local legal requirements or to control certain expenditures (e.g., capital outlay). In such cases, it may be appropriate to integrate budgetary accounts into the proprietary fund accounting system in a manner similar to that discussed for governmental funds.

(v) Capital Budget   Many governments also prepare a capital budget. A capital budget is a plan for capital expenditures to be incurred during a single budget year from funds subject to appropriation for projects scheduled under the capital program. The annual capital budget is adopted concurrently with the operating budgets of the governmental unit, being subject to a public hearing and the other usual legal procedures.

The capital budget should not be confused with a capital program or capital project budget. A capital program is a plan for capital expenditures to be incurred over a period of years, usually five or six years. The capital project budget represents the estimated amount to be expended on a specific project over the entire period of its construction. The capital budget authorizes the amounts to be expended on all projects during a single year. Controlling this amount is important for the proper use of available funds.

(vi) Budgetary Comparison Information   Under GASB Statement No. 34, the general fund's and the major special revenue funds' budgetary comparison schedules should present: (1) the original appropriated budgets; (2) the final appropriated budgets; and (3) actual inflows, outflows, and balances, stated on the governmental budgetary basis as discussed in NCGA Statement No. 1, paragraph 154. Separate columns may be provided comparing the original budget amounts with the actual amounts, the final budget amounts with the actual amounts, or both. The original budget is the first complete appropriated budget, which may be adjusted by reserves, transfers, allocations, supplementary appropriations, and other legally authorized legislative and executive changes made before the beginning of the reporting year. It also includes appropriation amounts automatically carried over from prior years by law. The final budget is the original budget adjusted by all legally authorized legislative and executive changes whenever signed into law or otherwise legally authorized. Governments may elect to report the budget comparison information in a budgetary comparison statement as part of the financial statements or as required supplementary disclosure as discussed in Section 34.4(m)(ii)(G) Required Supplementary Information (see Exhibit 34.5).

(l) CLASSIFICATION AND TERMINOLOGY   A common terminology and classification should be used consistently throughout the budget, the accounts, and the financial reports of each fund.

(i) Classification of Government Fund Revenues   Governmental fund revenues should be classified by fund and source. The major revenue source classifications are taxes, licenses and permits, intergovernmental revenues, charges for services, fines and forfeits, and miscellaneous. Governmental units often classify revenues by organizational units. This classification may be desirable for purposes of management control and accountability, as well as for auditing purposes, but it should supplement rather than supplant the classifications by fund and source.

(ii) Classification of Government Fund Expenditures   There are many ways to classify governmental fund expenditures in addition to the basic fund classification. Function, program, organizational unit, activity, character, and principal class of object are examples. Typically, expenditures are classified by character (current, intergovernmental, capital outlay, and/or debt service). Current expenditures are further classified by function and/or program.

	BUDGETED AMOUNTS		ACTUAL AMOUNTS (BUDGETARY BASIS) (SEE NOTE A)	VARIANCE WITH FINAL BUDGET POSITIVE (NEGATIVE)
	ORIGINAL	FINAL		
Budgetary fund balance, January 1	$3,528,750	$2,742,799	$2,742,799	$ —
Resources (inflows):				
Property taxes	52,017,833	51,853,018	51,173,436	(679,582)
Franchise taxes	4,546,209	4,528,750	4,055,505	(473,245)
Public service taxes	8,295,000	8,307,274	8,969,887	662,613
Licenses and permits	2,126,600	2,126,600	2,287,794	161,194
Fines and forfeitures	718,800	718,800	606,946	(111,854)
Charges for services	12,392,972	11,202,150	11,374,460	172,310
Grants	6,905,898	6,571,360	6,119,938	(451,422)
Sale of land	1,355,250	3,500,000	3,476,488	(23,512)
Miscellaneous	3,024,292	1,220,991	881,874	(339,117)
Interest received	1,015,945	550,000	552,325	2,325
Transfers from other funds	939,525	130,000	129,323	(677)
Amounts available for appropriation	96,867,074	93,451,742	92,370,775	(1,080,967)
Charges to appropriations (outflows)				
General government:				
Legal	665,275	663,677	632,719	30,958
Mayor, legislative, city manager	3,058,750	3,192,910	2,658,264	534,646
Finance and accounting	1,932,500	1,912,702	1,852,687	60,015
City clerk and elections	345,860	354,237	341,206	13,031
Employee relations	1,315,500	1,300,498	1,234,232	66,266
Planning and economic development	1,975,600	1,784,314	1,642,575	141,739
Public safety:				
Police	19,576,820	20,367,917	20,246,496	121,421
Fire department	9,565,280	9,559,967	9,559,967	—
Emergency medical services	2,323,171	2,470,127	2,459,866	10,261
Inspections	1,585,695	1,585,695	1,533,380	52,315
Public works:				
Public works administration	388,500	385,013	383,397	1,616
Street maintenance	2,152,750	2,233,362	2,233,362	—
Street lighting	762,750	759,832	759,832	—
Traffic operations	385,945	374,945	360,509	14,436
Mechanical maintenance	1,525,685	1,272,696	1,256,087	16,609
Engineering services:				
Engineering administration	1,170,650	1,158,023	1,158,023	—
Geographical information system	125,625	138,967	138,967	—
Health and sanitation:				
Garbage pickup	5,756,250	6,174,653	6,174,653	—
Cemetery:				
Personal services	425,000	425,000	422,562	2,438
Purchases of goods and services	299,500	299,500	283,743	15,757
Culture and recreation:				
Library	985,230	1,023,465	1,022,167	1,298
Parks and recreation	9,521,560	9,786,397	9,756,618	29,779
Community communications	552,350	558,208	510,361	47,847
Nondepartmental:				
Miscellaneous	—	259,817	259,817	—
Contingency	2,544,049	—	—	—
Transfers to other funds	2,970,256	2,163,759	2,163,759	—
Funding for school district	22,000,000	22,000,000	21,893,273	106,727
Total charges to appropriations	93,910,551	92,205,681	90,938,522	1,267,159
Budgetary fund balance, December 31	$2,956,523	$1,246,061	$1,432,253	$186,192

Exhibit 34.5: Budget-to-Actual Comparison Schedule for the General Fund in the Budget Document Format

(*Source:* Illustration G1 GASB Statement 34.)

- *Character classification*—reporting expenditures according to the physical period they are presumed to benefit. The major character classifications are: (1) current expenditures, which benefit the current fiscal period; (2) capital outlays, which are presumed to benefit both the present and future fiscal periods; and (3) debt service, which benefits prior fiscal periods as well as current and future periods. Intergovernmental expenditures is a fourth character classification that is used when one governmental unit makes expenditures to another governmental unit.
- *Function classification*—establishing groups of related activities that are aimed at accomplishing a major service or regulatory responsibility. Standard function classifications are as follows:
  - General government
  - Public safety
  - Health and welfare
  - Culture and recreation
  - Conservation of natural resources
  - Urban redevelopment and housing
  - Economic development and assistance
  - Education
  - Debt service
  - Miscellaneous
- *Program classification*—establishing groups of activities, operations, or organizational units that are directed at the attainment of specific purposes or objectives, for example, protection of property or improvement of transportation. Program classification is used by governmental units employing program budgeting.
- *Organizational unit classification*—grouping expenditures according to the governmental unit's organization structure. Organizational unit classification is essential to responsibility reporting.
- *Activity classification*—grouping expenditures according to the performance of specific activities. Activity classification is necessary for the determination of cost per unit of activity, which in turn is necessary for evaluation of economy and efficiency.
- *Object classification*—grouping expenditures according to the types of items purchased or services obtained—for example, personal services, supplies, other services, and charges. Object classifications are subdivisions of the character classification.

Excessively detailed object classifications should be avoided; they complicate the accounting procedure and are of limited use in financial management. The use of a few object classifications is sufficient in budget preparation; control emphasis should be on organization units, functions, programs, and activities rather than on the object of expenditures.

(iii) Classifications of Other Transactions   Certain transactions, although not revenues or expenditures of an individual fund, are increases or decreases in the net assets of an individual fund. These transactions are classified as other financing sources and uses and are reported in the operating statement separately from fund revenues and expenditures. The most common other financing sources and uses are

- *Proceeds of long-term debt issues.* Such proceeds (including leases) are not recorded as fund liabilities—for example, proceeds of bonds and notes expended through the capital project or debt service funds.

- *Transfers.* These are flows of assets such as cash or goods without equivalent flows of assets in return and without a requirement for repayment. They include payments in lieu of taxes that are not payments for, and are not reasonably equivalent in value to, services provided. They should be reported in governmental funds as other financing uses in the funds making transfers and as other financing sources in the funds receiving transfers. They should be reported in proprietary funds after nonoperating revenues and expenses.

Other interfund transactions are

- *Interfund loans and advances.* These are interfund loans, which are amounts provided with a requirement for repayment. They should be reported as interfund receivables and payables. They should not be reported as other financing sources or uses in the fund financial statements. If repayment is not expected within a reasonable time, the interfund balances should be reduced and the amount not expected to be repaid should be reported as a transfer from the fund that made the loan to the fund that received the loan.

  If the advance is long term in nature and the asset will not be available to finance current operations, a governmental fund balance reserve equal to the amount of the advance should be established.
- *Interfund services provided and used.* These are sales and purchases of goods and services between funds at prices that approximate their external exchange values. They should be reported as revenues in the seller funds and expenditures or expenses in purchases funds, except that when the general fund is used to account for risk-financing activity, interfund charges to other funds should be accounted for as reimbursements.

  Amounts should be accounted for as revenues in the recipient fund and as expenditures in the disbursing fund.
- *Interfund reimbursements.* These are repayments from the funds responsible for particular expenditures or expenses to the funds that initially paid for them. They should not be displayed in the financial statements.

(iv) Classifications of Proprietary Fund Revenues and Expenses   Proprietary fund revenues and expenses should be classified in essentially the same manner as those of similar business organizations, functions, or activities.

(v) Classification of Fund Equity   Fund equity is the difference between a fund's assets and its liabilities. The equity reported in the government-wide statement of net assets is called *net assets* and should be displayed in the following three categories:

- *Invested in capital assets, net of related debt*—this category consists of capital assets, including restricted capital assets, reduced by accumulated depreciation and by any outstanding debt incurred to acquire those assets.
- *Restricted net assets*—this category reports those net assets with restrictions on their use, either by external or internal factors.
- *Unrestricted net assets*—this category consists of all other net assets.

INVESTED IN CAPITAL ASSETS, NET OF RELATED DEBT

The amount of this component equals the amount of capital assets, including restricted capital assets, net of accumulated depreciation and less the outstanding balances of bonds, mortgages, notes, or other borrowings attributable to acquiring, constructing, or improving the assets. The portion of debt attributable to significant unspent debt proceeds should be included in the same net assets component as the unspent proceeds—for example, *restricted for capital projects.*

RESTRICTED NET ASSETS

Net assets should be reported as restricted if constraints on their use are either

1. Imposed externally, by creditors, grantors, contributors, or laws or regulations of other governments.
2. Imposed by law by constitutional provisions or enabling legislation that both authorizes the government to assess, levy, charge, or otherwise mandate receipt of resources from external providers and includes a legally enforceable requirement to use the resources for only the purposes stated in the legislation.

Permanent fund's principal amounts included in restricted net assets should be presented in two components—expendable and nonexpendable. Nonexpendable net assets are those required to be retained in perpetuity.

UNRESTRICTED NET ASSETS

Unrestricted net assets are other than net assets invested in capital assets, net of related debt, and other than restricted net assets.

Net assets are often *designated* by the management of the government if they do not consider them available for general operations. Such constraints are internal and can be removed or modified by the management. They are not restricted net assets.

The equity reported in the proprietary fund statement of net assets or balance sheet should be labeled either *net assets* or *fund equity,* using the three net asset components discussed for government-wide net assets.

An important amount in the fund equity account for governmental funds is the amount available for future appropriation and expenditure (i.e., unreserved and undesignated fund balance). The equity reported in the governmental fund balance sheets should be labeled *fund balances* and should be segregated into reserved and unreserved amounts. NCGA Statement 1 notes that fund balance reserves report the portions of the fund balances that are (1) legally segregated for a specific use or (2) not available for expenditure because the underlying asset is not available for current appropriation or expenditure. Reserves are not intended as valuation allowances but merely demonstrate the current unavailability of the subject assets to pay current expenditures. Reserves and designations are established by debiting unreserved, undesignated fund balance and crediting the reserve or designation. The reserve is not established by a charge to operations.

Designations of fund balance identify tentative plans for or restrictions on the future use of financial resources. Such designations should be supported by definitive plans and approved by either the government's CEO or the legislature. Examples of such designations include the earmarking of financial resources for capital projects and contingent liabilities. Management designations for the use of resources should not be reported in the statement of net assets but may be disclosed in notes to the financial statements.

GASB Statement No. 34 requires reserved fund balances of non-major governmental funds to be displayed in sufficient detail to disclose the purposes of the reservations, and requires unreserved fund balances of the non-major governmental funds to be displayed by fund type. Management designations of fund balances should be reported as part of unreserved fund balances and disclosed as separate line items or disclosed in the financial statement notes. In response, the GASB is currently working on developing new guidance on fund balance reporting and governmental fund type definitions to mitigate the diversity in practice as it relates to this issue.

The equity reported in the fiduciary fund statement of fiduciary net assets should be labeled *net assets* but does not require net assets to be categorized into the three components. GASB Statements No. 25, "Financial Reporting for Defined Benefit Pension Plans and Note Disclosures for Defined Contribution Plans;" No. 43, "Financial Reporting for Postemployment Benefit Plans Other Than Pension Plans;" and No. 31, "Accounting and Financial Reporting for Certain Investments and for External Investment Pools" contain specific disclosure requirements for these types of funds.

(m) FINANCIAL REPORTING   Prior to 1979, governments traditionally prepared external financial reports by preparing financial statements for every fund maintained by the government. This often resulted in lengthy financial reports. External financial reporting has evolved to require the presentation of financial statements on a more aggregated basis and the inclusion of legally separate entities that have special relationships. Principle 12 relates to financial reporting and is discussed in the following text.

(i) The Financial Reporting Entity   GASB Statement No. 14, "The Financial Reporting Entity," establishes standards for defining and reporting on the financial reporting entity.

The statement indicates that the financial reporting entity consists of (1) the Primary Government (PG) (2) organizations for which the PG is financially accountable, and (3) other organizations that, if omitted from the reporting entity, would cause the financial statements to be misleading.

The statement also outlines the basic criteria for including organizations in or excluding organizations from the reporting entity. All organizations for which the PG is *financially* accountable should be included in the reporting entity. Such organizations include

- The organizations that make up the PG's legal entity, and
- Component units—that is, organizations that are legally separate from the PG but
  - The PG's officials appoint a voting majority of the organization's governing board, and
  - Either the PG is able to impose its will on that organization or there is a potential for the organization to provide specific financial benefits to, or to impose specific financial burdens on, the PG.

A legally separate, tax-exempt organization should be reported as a component unit of a reporting entity if all of the following criteria are met:

- The economic resources received or held by the separate organization are entirely or almost entirely for the direct benefit of the PG, its component units, or its constituents.
- The PG (or its component units) is entitled to, or has the ability to otherwise access,[2] a majority of the economic resources received or held by the separate organization.

---

2.   Ability to otherwise access does not necessarily imply control over the other organization or its resources. It may be demonstrated in several ways. For example, the primary government or its component units historically may have received, directly or indirectly, a majority of

- The economic resources received or held by an individual organization that the specific PG (or its component units) is entitled to or has the ability to otherwise access, are significant to that PG.

Other organizations should be evaluated as potential component units if they are closely related to, or financially integrated[3] with, the PG. It is a matter of professional judgment to determine whether the nature and the significance of a potential component unit's relationship with the PG warrant inclusion in the reporting entity. Organizations not meeting the foregoing criteria are excluded from the reporting entity.

Reporting the inclusion of the various entities comprising the reporting entity can be done using one of two methods—blending or discrete presentation. Most component units should be included in the financial reporting entity by discrete presentation. Some component units, despite being legally separate entities, are so intertwined with the PG that, in substance, they are the same as the PG and should be "blended" with the transactions of the PG.

Certain other entities are not considered component units because the PG, while responsible for appointing the organization's board members, is not financially accountable. Such entities are considered related organizations. These related organizations as well as joint ventures and jointly governed organizations should be disclosed in the reporting entity's footnotes.

REPORTING COMPONENT UNITS

Discrete presentation of component unit financial information should be included in the statement of net assets and the statement of activities. However, information on component units that are fiduciary in nature should be included only in the fund financial statements, together with the PG's fiduciary funds. Information required by paragraph 51 of GASB Statement No. 14 about each major component unit can be given by

- Presenting each major component unit other than those that are fiduciary in nature in separate columns in the statements of net assets and activities,
- Including combining statements of major component units (with non-major component units aggregated in a single column) with the reporting entity's basic statements after the fund financial statements, or
- Presenting condensed financial statements in the notes.

The "aggregated total" component unit information, as discussed in paragraph 14 of GASB Statement No. 14, should be the entity totals derived from the component units' statements of net assets and activities. (Because component units that are engaged in only business-type activities are not required to prepare a statement of activities, this disclosure should be taken from the information provided in the component unit's statement of revenues, expenses, and changes in fund net assets.)

---

the economic resources provided by the organization; the organization may have previously received and honored requests to provide resources to the primary government; or the organization is a financially interrelated organization as defined by FASB Statement No. 136.
3. Financial integration may be exhibited and documented through the policies, practices, or organizational documents of either the primary government or the other organization. More than one column may be used to display components of a program revenue category. Governments may also provide more descriptive category headings to better explain the range of program revenues reported therein—for example, *operating grants, contributions, and restricted interest.*

If component unit information is presented in the notes, the following should be included:

- Condensed statement of net assets:
  - Total assets, distinguishing between capital assets and other assets. (Amounts receivable from the PG or from other component units should be reported separately.)
  - Total liabilities, distinguishing between long-term debt and other liabilities. (Amounts payable to the PG or to other component units should be reported separately.)
  - Total net assets, distinguishing between restricted, unrestricted, and amounts invested in capital assets net of related debt
- Condensed statement of activities:
  - Expenses by major functions and for depreciation expense if separately reported
  - Program revenues by type
  - Net program expense or revenue
  - Tax revenues
  - Other nontax general revenues
  - Contributions to endowments and permanent fund principal
  - Special and extraordinary items
  - Change in net assets
  - Beginning net assets
  - Ending net assets

The nature and amount of significant transactions with the PG and other component units should be reported in the notes for each component unit.

(ii) Basic Financial Statements   As discussed in Section 34.4(e)(ii) Reporting Requirements, the basic financial statements (BFS) include the financial statements of the governmental activities, the business-type activities, the aggregate discretely presented component units, each major fund, and the aggregate remaining fund information.

The two government-wide financial statements—the statement of net assets and the statement of activities—should report information about the reporting government without displaying individual funds or fund types. The statements should cover the PG and its component units, except for fiduciary funds of the PG and component units that are fiduciary in nature, which should be reported in the statements of fiduciary net assets and changes in fiduciary net assets.

The focus of the government-wide financial statements should be on the PG. The total PG and its discretely presented component units should be distinguished by separate rows and columns. A total column for the government entity and prior year information are optional.

Governmental and business-type activities of the PG should also be distinguished by separate rows and columns. (An activity need not be set out as a proprietary fund if it is not currently reported as such by the management of the government unless it is required to be reported as an enterprise fund, as discussed in Section 34.4(g)(ii)(A) Enterprise Funds.) Governmental and business-type activities are distinguished in general by their methods of financing. Governmental activities are generally financed by taxes, intergovernmental revenues, and other nonexchange-type revenues; they are generally reported in governmental funds and internal service funds. Business-type activities are financed in whole or in part by fees charged for goods or services; they are generally reported in enterprise funds.

These statements measure and report all financial and capital assets, liabilities, revenues, expenses, gains, and losses using the economic resources measurement focus and accrual basis of accounting.

Some amounts reported as interfund activity and balances in the funds should be eliminated or reclassified in aggregating information for the statement of net assets and the statement of activities.

Amounts reported in the funds as interfund receivables and payables should be eliminated in the governmental and business-type activities columns of the PG in the statement of net assets, except for the net residual amount due between the governmental and business-type activities, which should be reported as internal balances. (Amounts reported in the funds as receivable from or payable to fiduciary funds should be reported in the statement of net assets as receivable from and payable to external parties.) Internal balances should be eliminated in the total PG column.

The doubling-up effect of internal service fund activity should be eliminated in the statement of activities. Also, the effects of similar internal events, such as allocations of accounting staff salaries, which are, in effect, allocations of overhead expenses from one function to another or within a single function, should be eliminated so that the allocated expenses are reported by only the function to which they were allocated. (The effect of interfund services provided and used between functions should not be eliminated.)

(A) Statement of Net Assets
The statement of net assets should report all financial and capital resources and all liabilities, preferably in a format that displays *assets less liabilities equal net assets*, though the format *assets equal liabilities plus net assets* may be used. The difference between assets and liabilities should be reported as *net assets*, not *fund balance* or *equity*.

Governments are encouraged to report assets and liabilities in order of their relative liquidity (and subtotals of current assets and current liabilities may be provided). The liquidity of an asset depends on how readily it is expected to be converted to cash and whether restrictions limit the government's ability to use it. The liquidity of a liability depends on its maturity or on when cash is expected to be required to liquidate it. The liquidity of assets and liabilities may be determined by class, though individual assets or liabilities may be significantly more or less liquid than others in the same class, and some may have both current and long-term elements. Liabilities whose average maturities are more than one year should be reported by both the amount due within one year and the amount due in more than one year.

As discussed in Section 34.4(h)(v) Classification of Fund Equity, the three components of net assets are reported as (1) *invested in capital assets, net of related debt;* (2) *restricted,* distinguishing between major categories of restrictions; and (3) *unrestricted.*

Statement of Net Assets Format.   The City and County of San Francisco's statement of net assets at June 30, 2006 in Exhibit 34.6 illustrates the statement of net assets format.

(B) Statement of Activities
Some governments have a single function, program, activity, or component unit (together discussed as functions), as discussed subsequently. Most have more than one function. A government with more than one function should present a statement of activities that reports expenses by each function and revenues specifically pertaining to each function, arriving at net expense or net revenue by function. Net expense or net revenue is sometimes referred to as the *net cost* of a function or program and represents the total expenses of the function or program less its program revenues—that is, charges or fees and fines that derive directly from the function or program and grants and contributions that are restricted to the function or

program. That presentation indicates the financial burden (or benefit) each function places on the government's taxpayers and the extent to which each draws on the general revenues of the government or is self-financing. General revenues should be reported after expenses and revenues of the functions, together with contributions to term and permanent endowments, contributions to permanent fund principal, special and extraordinary items, and transfers reported separately, leading to change in net assets for the period.

CITY AND COUNTY OF SAN FRANCISCO
Statement of Net Assets

June 30, 2006
(In Thousands)

	Primary Government			Component Units	
	Governmental Activities	Business- Type Activities	Total	San Francisco Redevelopment Agency	Treasure Island Development Authority
ASSETS					
Current assets					
Deposits and investments City Treasury	$ 1,511, 936	$ 681,935	$ 2,193, 871	$ —	$ 1,268
Deposits and investments outside City Treasury	48,885	9,758	58,643	169,046	-
Receivables (net of allowance for uncollectible amounts of $84,334 for the primary government):					
Property taxes and penalities	42, 586	—	42,586	—	—
Other local taxes	168,457	—	168,457	—	—
Federal and state grants and subventions	154,086	57,707	211,793	—	—
Charges for services	22,194	194,800	216,994	—	—
Interest and other	16,132	43,787	59,919	7,641	4
Loans receivable	7,025	132	7,157	12	—
Capital lease receivable from primary government	—	—	—	14,460	—
Due from component unit	782	—	782	—	—
Inventories	—	53,051	53,051	—	—
Deferred charges and other assets	10,423	3,531	13,954	—	—
Restricted assets:					
Deposits and investments with City Treasury	—	54,218	54, 218	—	—
Deposits and investments outside City Treasury	—	45,306	45,306	78,413	—
Grants and other receivables	—	36	36	1,206	—
Total current assets	1,982,506	1,144,261	3,126,767	270,778	1,272
Noncurrent assets:					
Loans receivable (net of allowance for uncollectible amounts of $383,869 and $158, 166 for the primary government and component unit, respectively)	67,016	455	67,471	10,455	—
Advance to component unit	4,024	—	4,024	—	—
Capital lease receivable from primary government	—	—	—	175,636	—
Deferred charges and other assets	19,887	72,632	92,519	9,565	—
Restricted assets:					
Deposits and investments with City Treasury	—	617,925	617,925	—	—
Deposits and investments outside City Treasury	—	265,093	265,093	20,797	—
Grants and other receivables	—	61,670	61,670	—	—
Property held for resale	—	—	—	15,988	—
Capital assets:					
Land and other assets not being depreciated	504,527	1,208,435	1,712,962	119,965	—
Facilities, infrastructure, and equipment, net of depreciation	2,170,335	7,320,619	9,490,954	146,638	—
Total capital assets	2,674,862	8,529,054	11,203,916	266,603	—
Total noncurrent assets	2,765,789	9,546,829	12,312,618	499,044	—
Total Assets	$ 4,748,295	$ 10,691,090	$ 15,439,385	$ 769,822	$ 1,272

EXHIBIT 34.6: CITY AND COUNTY OF SAN FRANCISCO STATEMENT OF NET ASSETS (JUNE 30, 2006)

CITY AND COUNTY OF SAN FRANCISCO
Statement of Net Assets (Continued)
June 30, 2006
(In Thousands)

	Primary Government			Component Units	
	Governmental Activities	Business- Type Activities	Total	San Francisco Redevelopment Agency	Treasure Island Development Authority
LIABILITIES					
Current liabilities:					
Accounts payable	$ 178,765	$ 121,868	$ 300,633	$ 7,962	$ 3,207
Accrued payroll	64,377	46,498	110,875	—	—
Accrued vacation and sick leave pay	65,948	43,182	109,130	1,254	—
Accrued workers' compensation	41,803	35,466	77,269	—	—
Estimated claims payable	23,811	24,629	48,440	—	—
Bonds, loans, capital leases, and other payable	262,599	142,119	404,718	27,791	—
Capital lease payable to component unit	14,460	—	14,460	—	—
Accrued interest payable	7,764	18,472	26,236	27,207	—
Unearned grant and subvention revenues	2,421	—	2,421	—	—
Due to primary government	—	—	—	782	—
Internal balances	27,966	(27,966)	—	—	—
Deferred credits and other liabilities	125,111	91,061	216,172	750	664
Liabilities payable from restricted assets:					
Bonds, loans, capital leases, and other payables	—	17,393	17,393	—	—
Accrued interest payable	—	26,321	26,321	—	—
Other	—	38,331	38,331	—	—
Total current liabilities	815,025	577,374	1,392,399	65,746	3,871
Noncurrent liabilities:					
Accrued vacation and sick leave pay	66,576	36,381	102,957	1,553	—
Accrued workers' compensation	160,678	126,188	286,866	—	—
Estimated claims payable	45,666	53,154	98,820	—	—
Bonds, loans, capital leases, and other payables	1,690,096	5,438,803	7,128,899	700,942	—
Advance from primary government	—	—	—	4,024	—
Capital lease payable to component unit	175,636	—	175,636	—	—
Accrued interest payable	—	—	—	63,839	—
Deferred credits and other liabilities	—	46,757	46,757	6,117	—
Total noncurrent liabilities	2,138,652	5,701,283	7,839,935	776,475	—
Total liabilities	2,953,677	6,278,657	9,232,334	842,221	3,871
NET ASSETS					
Invested in capital assets, net of related debt	1,438,010	3,438,397	4,876,407	67,463	—
Restricted for:					
Reserve for rainy day	121,976	—	121,976	—	—
Debt service	53,076	256,055	309,131	54,821	—
Capital projects	10,589	148,957	159,546	—	—
Community development	71,207	—	71,207	—	—
Transportation Authority activities	23,727	—	23,727	—	—
Grants and other purposes	148,071	32,354	180,425	15,988	—
Unrestricted (deficit)	(72,038)	536,670	464,632	(210,671)	(2,599)
Total net assets (deficit)	$1,794,618	$4,412,433	$6,207,051	$(72,399)	$(2,599)

EXHIBIT 34.6: (CONTINUED)

At a minimum, the statement of activities should present

- Activities accounted for in governmental funds by function, as discussed in NCGA Statement No. 1, paragraph 112, to coincide with the level of detail required in the governmental fund statement of revenues, expenditures, and changes in fund balances.
- Activities accounted for in enterprise funds by different identifiable activities. An activity is identifiable if it has a specific revenue stream and related expenses and gains and losses that are accounted for separately.

Expenses.   All expenses should be reported by function other than special or extraordinary items, defined subsequently. At a minimum, direct expenses, those clearly identifiable with a particular function, should be presented. In addition, some or all indirect expenses of the functions may be reported by function, in columns separate from the direct expenses. A column reporting the total of direct and indirect expenses by function may also be presented. Governments that charge functions for centralized expenses need not identify and eliminate such charges. The fact that they are included in direct expenses should be disclosed in the summary of significant accounting policies.

Depreciation expense on capital assets specifically identifiable with functions should be included in their direct expenses. Depreciation expense on shared capital assets should be assigned ratably to the direct expense of the functions benefiting. Depreciation expense on capital assets that serve all functions, such as city hall, need not be included in the direct expense of the functions but may be reported as a separate line in the statement of activities or as part of the general government function. A government that reports unallocated depreciation on a separate line should state on the face of the statement of activities that this item does not include direct depreciation expenses of the various functions.

Depreciation expense for general infrastructure assets should be reported as a direct expense of the function that the government normally associates with capital outlays for and maintenance of infrastructure assets or on a separate line in the statement of activities.

Interest on long-term liabilities should generally be reported as an indirect expense on a separate line in the statement of activities, clearly indicating that it excludes direct interest expenses, if any, reported in other functions. The amount excluded should be disclosed on the face of the statement or in the notes. However, interest should be included in direct expense on borrowings essential to the creation or continuing existence of a program (e.g., a new, highly leveraged program in its early stages) if excluding it would be misleading.

Revenues.   A government obtains revenue essentially from four sources:

1. Entities that buy, use, or directly benefit from the goods or services of programs, including the citizens of the government or others
2. Entities outside the citizens of the government, including other governments, nongovernmental entities, or persons
3. The government's taxpayers, regardless of whether they benefit from particular programs
4. The government itself—for example, from investing

Type 1 is always a program revenue. Type 2 is a program revenue if restricted to specific programs. If unrestricted, type 2 is a general revenue. Type 3 is always a general revenue, even if restricted to specific programs. Type 4 is usually a general revenue.

Program revenues reduce the net cost of program function required to be financed by general revenue. They should be reported separately in three categories:[4] (1) charges for services, (2) program-specific operating grants and contributions, and (3) program-specific capital grants and contributions. For identifying the function to which a program revenue pertains, the

---

4.   More than one column may be used to display components of a program revenue category. Governments may also provide more descriptive category headings to better explain the range of program revenues reported therein—for example, *operating grants, contributions, and restricted interest.*

determining factor for charges for services is which function generates[5] the revenue. For grants and contributions, the determining factor is the function to which the revenues are restricted.

All other revenues are general revenues, including all taxes and all nontax revenues that do not meet the criteria to be reported as program revenues. General revenues should be reported after total net expense of the government's functions.

The following should be reported separately at the bottom of the statement of activities in the same manner as general revenues, to arrive at the all-inclusive change in net assets for the reporting period:

- Contributions to term and permanent endowments
- Contributions to permanent fund principal
- Special and extraordinary items (discussed in the following text)
- Transfers between governmental and business-type activities

Other financing sources and uses include face amount of long-term debt, issuance premium or discount, certain payments to escrow agents for bond refundings, transfers, and sales of capital assets (unless the sale meets the criteria for reporting as a special item).

Special and Extraordinary Items. Special items, significant events within the control of management that are either unusual or infrequent as defined in APB Opinion No. 30, should be reported separately at the bottom of the statement of activities. Extraordinary items, significant events that are both unusual and infrequent, should also be reported separately at the bottom of the statement of activities.

Statement of Activities Format. The City and County of San Francisco's statement of activities for the year ended June 30, 2006 illustrates the statement of activities format (see Exhibit 34.7).

(C) BASIC FINANCIAL STATEMENTS—FUND FINANCIAL STATEMENTS
Governmental Fund Balance Statement Format. Exhibit 34.8 presents the balance sheet presentation of the City and County of San Francisco's General Fund, the only major governmental fund of the City and County of San Francisco. Non-major funds are aggregated in an "Other" column. Note: the City and County of San Francisco's financial statements include optional partial or summarized prior year comparative information.

(D) REQUIRED RECONCILIATION TO GOVERNMENT-WIDE STATEMENTS
The amount of net assets reported for a PG in the government-wide statement of net assets usually will differ from the aggregate amount of equity reported in its fund financial position statements, because the fund statements are prepared using the funds flow measurement focus and modified accrual method (see discussion at Section 34.4(j), Measurement Focus and Basis of Accounting). There will also be differences between the changes in net assets reported in the various activity statements.

A government should present a summary reconciliation to the government-wide financial statements at the bottom of the fund financial statements or in a schedule. Brief explanations

---

5.   It may sometimes be difficult or impractical to identify a specific function that generates a program revenue. For example, in many jurisdictions fines could be attributed to a public safety or a judicial function. If the source of a program revenue is not clear, the government should adopt a classification policy for assigning those revenues and apply it consistently.

CITY AND COUNTY OF SAN FRANCISCO
Statement of Activities
Year Ended June 30, 2006
(In Thousands)

| | | Program Revenues | | | Primary Government | | | Component Units | |
| | | | | | | | | Net (Expense) Revenue and Changes in Net Assets | |
Functions/Programs	Expenses	Charges for Services	Operating Grants and Contributions	Capital Grants and Contributions	Governmental Activities	Business-Type Activities	Total	San Francisco Redevelopment Agency	Treasure Island Development Authority
Primary government:									
Government activities:									
Public protection	$ 780,642	$ 51,874	$ 103,358	$ —	$ (625,410)	$—	$ (625,410)	$ —	$ —
Public works, transportation and commerce	272,397	113,861	30,223	37,411	(90,902)	—	(90,902)	—	—
Human welfare and neighborhood development	858,396	29,181	437,381	150	(391,684)	—	(391,684)	—	—
Community health	478,844	52,183	278,218	—	(148,443)	—	(148,443)	—	—
Culture and recreation	244,423	64,720	3,144	210,768	34,209	—	34,209	—	—
General administration and finance	167,490	55,799	2,400	—	(109,291)	—	(109,291)	—	—
General City responsibilities	49,054	31,647	5,195	—	(12,212)	—	(12,212)	—	—
Unallocated interest on long-term debt	94,923	—	—	—	(94,923)	—	(94,923)		
Total governmental activities	2,946,169	399,265	859,919	248,329	(1,438,656)	—	(1,438,656)		
Business-type activities:									
Airport	633,102	455,342	—	48,544	—	(129,216)	(129,216)	—	—
Transportation	695,593	210,692	122,057	58,399	—	(304,445)	(304,445)	—	—
Port	55,329	58,588	—	3,460	—	6,719	6,719	—	—
Water	213,584	201,833	—	—	—	(11,751)	(11,751)	—	—
Power	119,146	149,500	—	—	—	30,354	30,354	—	—
Hospitals	646,149	472,327	66,585	—	—	(107,237)	(107,237)	—	—
Sewer	160,701	164,703	30	—	—	4,032	4,032	—	—
Market	1,035	1,503	—	—	—	468	468	—	—
Total Business-type activities	2,524,639	1,714,488	188,672	110,403	—	(511,076)	(511,076)	—	—
Total primary government	$5,470,808	$2,113,753	$1,048,591	$ 358,732	(1,438,656)	(511,076)	(1,949,732)		

Component units									
San Francisco Redevelopment Agency	$142,493	$25,345	$13,912	$—				(103,236)	—
Treasure Island Development Authority	9,188	8,208	—	—				—	(980)
Total component units	$151,661	$33,553	$13,912	$—				(103,236)	(980)

General Revenues:						
Taxes:						
Property taxes		1,016,220	—	1,106,220	65,826	—
Business taxes		323,153	—	323,153	—	—
Other local taxes		595,664	—	595,664	5,549	—
Interest and investment income		71,129	53,161	124,290	10,751	56
Other		56,022	272,873	328,895	9,722	527
Transfers—internal activities of primary goverment		(329,996)	329,996	—	—	—
Total general revenues and transfers		1,732,192	656,030	2,388,222	91,848	583
Changes in net assets		293,536	144,954	438,490	(11,388)	(397)
Net assets (deficit)—beginning		1,501,082	4,267,479	5,768,561	(61,011)	(2,202)
Net assets (deficit)—ending		$1,794,618	$4,412,433	$6,207,051	$(72,399)	$(2,599)

EXHIBIT 34.7: CITY AND COUNTY OF SAN FRANCISCO STATEMENT OF ACTIVITIES (YEAR ENDED JUNE 30, 2006)

presented on the face of the statements often are sufficient. However, if aggregated information in the reconciliation obscures the nature of the individual elements of a particular reconciling item, a more detailed explanation should be provided in the notes to financial statements.

Exhibit 34.9 presents the reconciliation of the governmental funds balance sheet to the statement of net assets of the City and County of San Francisco. This reconciliation provides

CITY AND COUNTY OF SAN FRANCISCO
Balance Sheet
Governmental Funds
June 30, 2006
(with comparative financial information as of June 30, 2005)
(In Thousands)

	General Fund		Other Governmental Funds		Total Governmental Funds	
	2006	2005	2006	2005	2006	2005
ASSETS						
Deposits and investments with City Treasury	$ 443,102	$ 314,607	$ 1,060,891	$ 915,547	$ 1,503,993	$ 1,230,154
Deposits and investments outside City Treasury	1,465	355	22,287	45,745	23,752	46,100
Receivables:						
Property taxes and penalities	34,157	26,141	8,429	6,890	42,586	33,031
Other local taxes	154,505	148,744	13,952	12,788	168,457	161,532
Federal and state grants and subventions	63,843	61,412	90,243	89,559	154,086	150,971
Charges for services	17,117	7,416	5,077	6,832	22,194	14,248
Interest and other	6,184	4,406	9,035	3,726	15,219	8,132
Due from other funds	30,859	29,743	3,960	12,303	34,819	42,046
Due from component unit	3,848	2,416	958	959	4,806	3,375
Loans receivable (net of allowance for uncollectible amount of $383,869 in 2006; $165,336 in 2005)	—	1,174	74,041	241,728	74,041	242,902
Deferred charges and other Assets	7,243	6,797	1,729	1,570	8,972	8,367
Total assets	$762,323	$603,211	$1,290,602	$1,337,647	$2,052,925	$1,940,858
LIABILITIES AND FUND BALANCES						
Liabilities:						
Accounts payable	$ 84,710	$ 82,524	$ 88,151	$ 53,335	$ 172,861	$ 135,859
Accrued payroll	51,792	39,729	10,982	8,812	62,774	48,541
Deferred tax, grant, and subvention revenues	33,473	26,880	30,442	19,371	63,915	46,251
Due to other funds	821	1,857	61,964	77,614	62,785	79,471
Agency obligations	—	—	—	40	—	40
Deferred credits and other liabilities	130,251	144,541	94,755	267,899	225,006	412,440
Bonds, loans, capital leases, and other payables	—	—	150,000	150,000	150,000	150,000
Total liabilities	301,047	295,531	436,294	577,071	737,341	872,602
Fund balances:						
Reserved for rainy day	121,976	48,139	—	—	121,976	48,139
Reserved for assets not available for appropriation	10,710	9,031	20,202	17,683	30,912	26,714
Reserved for debt service	—	—	57,429	45,540	57,429	45,540
Reserved for encumbrances	38,159	57,762	423,120	97,920	461,279	155,682
Reserved for appropriation carryforward	124,009	36,198	294,340	549,571	418,349	585,769
Reserved for subsequent years' budgets	27,451	22,351	8,004	8,004	35,455	30,356
Unreserved (deficit), reported in:						
General fund	138,971	134,199	—	—	138,971	134,199
Special revenue funds	—	—	35,243	30,809	35,243	30,809
Capital project funds	—	—	13,662	7,193	13,662	7,193
Permanent fund	—	—	2,308	3,856	2,308	3,856
Total fund balances	461,276	307,680	854,308	760,576	1,315,584	1,068,256
Total liabilities and fund balances	$762,323	$603,211	$1,290,602	$1,337,647	$2,052,925	$1,940,858

Exhibit 34.8: City and County of San Francisco Balance Sheet Governmental Funds

summarized explanations that do not describe the nature of the individual elements of these reconciling items. As a result, the City and County of San Francisco provides a more detailed explanation in the notes to financial statements.

Reconciling items between the Governmental Funds Balance Sheets and the Government-Wide Statement of Net Assets include the effects of

- Reporting capital assets at their acquisition cost and depreciating them instead of reporting capital acquisitions as expenditures when incurred.
- Adding general long-term liabilities not due and payable in the current period.
- Reducing deferred revenue for amounts not available to pay current-period expenditures.
- Adding internal service fund net asset balances.

CITY AND COUNTY OF SAN FRANCISCO
Reconciliation of the Governmental Funds Balance Sheet
to the Statement of Net Assets
June 30, 2006

(In Thousands)

Fund balances—total governmental funds	$ 1,315,584
Amounts reported for governmental activities in the statement of net assets are different because:	
Capital assets used in governmental activities are not financial resources and, therefore, are not reported in the funds.	2,670,387
Bond issue costs are not financial resources and, therefore, are not reported in the funds.	14,338
Long-term liabilities, including bonds payable, are not due and payable in the current period and therefore are not reported in the funds.	(2,161,461)
Interest on long-term debt is not accrued in the funds, but rather is recognized as an expenditure when due.	(6,459)
Because the focus of governmental funds is on short-term financing, some assets will not be available to pay for current period expenditures. Those assets are offset by deferred revenue in the funds.	164.015
Internal service funds are used by management to charge the costs of capital lease financing, fleet management, printing and mailing services, and information systems to individual funds. The assets and liabilities of internal service funds are included in governmental activities in the statement of net assets.	(201,786)
Net assets of governmental activities	$1,794,618

Exhibit 34.9: City and County of San Francisco Reconciliation of the Governmental Funds Balance Sheet to the Statement of Net Assets (June 30, 2006)

Reconciling items between the Governmental Funds Statement of Revenues, Expenditures and Changes in Fund Balances and the Government-Wide Statement of Activities include the effects of

- Reporting revenues on the accrual basis.
- Reporting annual depreciation expense instead of expenditures for capital outlays.
- Reporting long-term debt proceeds in the statement of net assets as liabilities instead of other financing sources.
- Reporting debt principal payments in the statement of net assets as reductions of liabilities instead of expenditures.
- Reporting other expenses on the accrual basis.
- Adding the net revenue or subtracting the expense of internal service funds.

For enterprise funds, (1) total enterprise fund net assets should be reconciled to the net assets of business-type activities (however, since both are on the accrual basis, there often are no differences) and (2) the total change in enterprise fund net assets should be reconciled to the change in net assets of business-type activities, provided there are differences that require reconciliation.

(E) Reporting Internal Service Fund Balances
Internal service funds are reported as proprietary funds. Nevertheless, their activities, financing goods and services for other funds, are usually more governmental than business type.

Therefore, internal service fund asset and liability balances not eliminated should normally be reported in the governmental activities column of the statement of net assets. However, if enterprise funds are the predominant or only participants in an internal service fund, that fund's residual assets and liabilities should be reported in the business-type activities column.

(F) DISCLOSURE REQUIREMENTS
Information essential to fair presentation in the financial statements that cannot be displayed on the faces of the statements should be presented in the notes to the financial statements, which should focus on the PG—its governmental activities, business-type activities, major funds, and non-major funds in the aggregate. Information about the government's discretely presented component units should be presented as discussed in GASB Statement No. 14, paragraph 63.

General Disclosure Requirements. Governments should provide the following added disclosures to the extent applicable in their summaries of significant accounting policies:

- A description of the government-wide financial statements, indicating that fiduciary funds and component units that are fiduciary in nature are not included
- The measurement focus and basis of accounting used in the government-wide statements
- The policy for eliminating internal activity in the statement of activities
- The policy for applying FASB pronouncements issued after November 30, 1989, to business-type activities and to enterprise funds of the PG
- The policy for capitalizing assets and for estimating their useful lives (A government that uses the modified approach for reporting eligible infrastructure assets should describe the approach.)
- A description of the kinds of transactions included in program revenues
- A description of the policy for allocating indirect expenses to functions in the statement of activities
- The government's policy for defining operating and nonoperating revenues of proprietary funds
- The government's policy on whether to first use restricted or unrestricted resources when an expense is incurred for purposes for which both restricted and unrestricted net assets are available

Required Note Disclosures about Cash and Investments. A government is subject to numerous GASB disclosures about cash and investments. The following are among the required disclosures:

- Description of how investments are valued, including the methods and significant assumptions used to estimate the fair value of investments
- The types of investments authorized by legal or contractual provisions
- The types of investments made during the period but not owned as of the balance-sheet date
- By type of investment, the investments' carrying amounts and fair values at year-end
- The custodial credit risk for uncollateralized deposits with financial institutions and investment securities that are uninsured and unregistered
- The credit and interest rate risks related to investments in debt instruments

- Terms of investments with fair values that are highly sensitive to changes in interest rates
- The concentration of credit risk for amount invested in a separate issuer (except investments held in or guaranteed by the U.S. government) when that amount is at least 5 percent of total investments
- The foreign currency risk of its investments denominated in a foreign currency
- Details about derivative instruments that are not reported at fair value
- The assignment of investment income between funds
- Specific information related to investment appreciation and income available for spending on donor-restricted endowments

Required Note Disclosures about Capital Assets and Long-Term Liabilities.   Details should be disclosed in the notes about capital assets and long-term liabilities of the PG, divided into their major classes and between those associated with governmental activities and those associated with business-type activities. Capital assets not being depreciated should be disclosed separately. The following information should be disclosed about major classes of capital assets:

- Beginning- and end-of-year balances, with accumulated depreciation presented separately from acquisition cost
- Capital acquisitions
- Sales or other dispositions
- Current depreciation expense, including the amounts charged to each of the functions in the statement of activities

Collections of works of art, historical treasures, and similar assets not capitalized should be described, and the reasons they are not capitalized should be given. Disclosures, as previously stated, should be given for collections capitalized.

The following information should be disclosed about long-term debt and other long-term liabilities, such as compensated absences, claims, and judgments:

- Beginning- and end-of-year balances
- Increases and decreases, presented separately
- The portions of each due within one year
- The governmental funds that typically have been used to liquidate other long-term liabilities

Debt service to maturity separated by principal and interest for each of the succeeding five fiscal years and in at least five-year increments thereafter for all outstanding debt should be disclosed. Interest on variable-rate debt should be calculated using the rate in effect at the financial statement date and the terms that the interest rates change for variable-rate debt should also be disclosed.

Whether to make similar disclosures about capital assets and long-term liabilities of discretely presented component units is a matter of professional judgment, depending on each individual component unit's significance to the total of all discretely presented component units and the component unit's relationship with the PG.

(G) REQUIRED SUPPLEMENTARY INFORMATION

Management Discussion and Analysis. A management discussion and analysis (MD&A) is an overview and analysis of the government's financial statements. It should provide an objective and easily readable analysis of the government's financial activities based on facts, decisions, or conditions of which management is aware as of the date of the auditor's report. It should discuss the current-year results and compare them with the results of the prior year, including positive and negative aspects.

MD&A requirements are general to encourage effective reporting of only the most relevant information and to avoid boilerplate discussion. The information presented should be confined to the following eight items, including additional details pertaining to those items:

1. A brief discussion of the basic financial statements, including the relationships of the statements to each other and the significant differences in the information they provide. Analyses should be provided that help users understand why measurements and results reported in fund financial statements either reinforce information in government-wide statements or provide additional information.

2. Condensed financial information derived from government-wide financial statements comparing the current year to the prior year. Governments should present the information needed to support their analysis of financial position and results of operations.

3. An analysis of the government's overall financial position and results of operations, addressing both governmental and business-type activities as reported in the government-wide financial statements, to help users assess whether the financial position has improved or deteriorated as a result of the year's operations.

4. An analysis of balances and transactions of the individual funds, including the reasons for significant changes in fund balances or fund net assets and whether restrictions, commitments, or other limitations significantly affect the availability of fund resources for future use.

5. An analysis of significant variations between original and final budget amounts and between final budget amounts and actual budget results for the general fund or its equivalent, including any known reasons for such of those variations that are expected to have a significant effect on future services or liquidity.

6. A description of significant capital-asset and long-term debt activity during the year, including a discussion of commitments for capital expenditures, changes in credit ratings, and debt limitations that may affect financing of planned facilities or services.

7. A discussion by governments that use the modified approach to report some or all of their infrastructure assets.

8. A description of facts, decisions, or conditions of which management is aware at the date of the independent auditor's report that are expected to significantly affect financial position or results of operations—revenues, expenses, and other changes in net assets.

In addition to the information required to be presented as Required Supplementary Information (RSI) by GASB Statement Nos. 10, 25, 27, 43, 45 and other RSI required to be presented by GASB Statement No. 34 includes MD&A, budgetary comparison schedules for governmental funds, and information about infrastructure assets reported using the modified approach.

Budgetary Comparison Information.   Under GASB Statement No. 34, budgetary comparison schedules should present (1) the original appropriated budgets; (2) the final appropriated budgets; and (3) actual inflows, outflows, and balances, stated on the governmental budgetary basis as discussed in NCGA Statement No. 1, paragraph 154.

Information in a separate schedule or in notes to RSI should be provided that reconciles budgetary information to GAAP information. Notes to RSI should disclose excesses of expenditures over appropriations in individual funds presented in the budgetary comparison, as discussed in NCGA Interpretation No. 6, paragraph 4, as amended by GASB Statement No. 37. (If the budgetary comparison information is included in the basic statements, these disclosures should be in the notes to the financial statements rather than as notes to RSI.)

Modified Approach for Reporting Infrastructure.   A government with eligible infrastructure assets (for subsystems, if any) reported using the modified approach should present as RSI these schedules derived from the asset management systems:

- The assessed condition, based on assessments performed at least every three years, for at least the three most recent complete condition assessments, indicating the dates of the assessments
- The estimated annual amount calculated at the beginning of the year to maintain and preserve the assets at or above the condition level established and disclosed by the government compared with the amounts actually reported as expense for each of the past five reporting periods

The following should be disclosed with the schedules:

- The basis for the condition measurement and the measurement scale used to assess and report condition. For example, a basis could be distresses in pavement surfaces. A scale could range from zero for a failed pavement to 100 for pavement in perfect condition.
- The condition level at which the government intends to preserve its eligible infrastructure assets reported using the modified approach.
- Factors that significantly affect trends in the information reported in the schedules, including any changes in the basis for the condition measurement, the measurement scale, or the condition measurement methods used. Also to be disclosed is an estimate of the effect of a change in the condition level at which the government intends to preserve eligible infrastructure assets of the estimated annual amount to maintain and preserve the assets for the current period.

A government that has asset management systems for infrastructure assets that gather the information required under this subsection but do not use the modified approach are encouraged to disclose it as supplement information.

(iii) Comprehensive Annual Financial Report (CAFR)   Even though the GASB encourages each governmental entity to prepare a CAFR, the basic financial statement constitutes fair presentation of financial position and the respective changes in financial position and cash flows, where applicable in accordance with GAAP and could be opined on as such by an independent auditor. The statements would be suitable for inclusion in an official statement for a securities offering and for widespread distribution to users requiring less detailed information about the governmental unit's finances than is contained in the CAFR.

The CAFR differs from the BFS in the level of detail and the quantity of data presented. The additional data are *not* necessary for fair presentation of financial position or results of operation in accordance with GAAP, but they are useful and informative for certain readers of a government's financial report. Furthermore, the CAFR may be the vehicle for providing the necessary information for fulfilling the legal and other disclosure requirements of higher levels of government, bondholders, and similar groups. It is also useful in demonstrating management's stewardship responsibilities, since alongside the comparative budgets it presents in more detail the use of the available resources.

The recommended contents of the general-purpose government's CAFR include the following:

- *Introductory section*:
  - Title page. Contains the title "Comprehensive Annual Financial Report," the name of the governmental unit, the period of time covered, and the names of the principal government officials. Component units that issue separate statements should indicate the PG of which it is a component.
  - A title such as "City Hospital, a Component Unit of City, Any State" is recommended.
  - Table of contents. Identifies the presence and location of each item included in the report.
  - Transmittal letter. From the government's chief finance officer (or CEO), other information that is not included in the management's discussion and analysis that provides basic information about the government and how it operates along with other information useful in assessing the government's economic condition. The letter may include, for example, changes in financial policies; discussion of internal controls; significant elements of financial management; budget procedures and current budget; and a preview of the significant developments or changes contemplated in the coming year including economic conditions, outlook, and major initiatives.
- *Financial section*:
  - Independent auditor's report.
  - Basic financial statements. Includes all required financial statements and related notes as previously described.
  - Required supplementary information. Included when disclosure is required by the GASB.
  - Combining financial statements. Used when a governmental unit has more than one fund of a given type.
  - Individual fund financial statements and schedules. Used when this information is not provided in a separate column in a combining statement or it is desirable to present a level of detail that would be excessive for the BFS or the combining statements. Examples are detail comparisons to budgets that cannot be reflected on the combining statements, comparative data for prior years, or a demonstration of an individual fund's compliance with legal provisions.
  - Schedules necessary to demonstrate compliance. Included when such are required by state law or by a bond covenant.
  - Other schedules desired by the government. Used for reporting particular kinds of information that are spread throughout the numerous financial statements and that can be brought together and presented in greater detail than in the individual

statements, or that show the details of a specific amount or amounts presented in the BFS, the combining statements, or the individual fund financial statements.

- *Statistical section*:
  - ○ Statistical tables cover a period of several years and contain data drawn from more than just the accounting records. Their purpose is to present social, economic, and financial trends, and the fiscal capacity of the governmental unit. The following titles indicate recommended statistical tables for a local general-purpose government's CAFR:
  - ○ Net Assets by Components—Last Ten Fiscal Years
  - ○ Changes in Net Assets—Last Ten Fiscal Years
  - ○ Governmental Activities Tax Revenue by Source—Last Ten Fiscal Years
  - ○ Changes in Fund Balances of Governmental Funds—Last Ten Fiscal Years
  - ○ General Governmental Tax Revenues by Source—Last Ten Fiscal Years
  - ○ Assessed Value and Estimated Actual Value of Taxable Property—Last Ten Fiscal Years
  - ○ Property Tax Rates—Direct and Overlapping Governments—Last Ten Fiscal Years
  - ○ Principal Taxpayers—Current Fiscal Year and Nine Years Ago
  - ○ Property Tax Levies and Collections—Last Ten Fiscal Years
  - ○ Ratios of Outstanding Debt by Type—Last Ten Fiscal Years
  - ○ Direct and Overlapping Governmental Activities Debt
  - ○ Legal Debt Margin Information Last Ten Fiscal Years
  - ○ Pledged-Revenue Coverage Last Ten Fiscal Years
  - ○ Demographic and Economic Statistics—Last Ten Fiscal Years
  - ○ Principal Employers—Current Fiscal Year and Nine Years Ago
  - ○ Full-time Equivalent City Government Employees by Function—Last Ten Fiscal Years
  - ○ Operating Indicators by Function—Last Ten Fiscal Years
  - ○ Capital Asset Statistics by Function—Last Ten Fiscal Years
- *Single Audit section*:
  Although it is not a required part of a CAFR, some governments include in a separate section the information, including auditor's reports, required by the Single Audit Act Amendments of 1996.

(iv) Certificate of Achievement Program   Governmental units may submit their CAFRs to the GFOA (180 North Michigan Avenue, Chicago, IL 60601) for evaluation in accordance with the standards of financial reporting established by the GASB and the GFOA. If the report substantially adheres to these standards, the government is awarded a Certificate of Achievement for Excellence in Financial Reporting. The certificate is valid for only one year. It may be reproduced in the government's annual report and should be included in the subsequent year's CAFR. Annually, the GFOA publishes a list of the governments that hold valid certificates.

Many governments endeavor to obtain the certificate. They realize that credit rating agencies and others familiar with governmental accounting and financial reporting recognize that governments holding a certificate typically maintain complete financial records and effectively report their financial information to permit detailed analyses to be performed. This characteristic can improve the government's bond rating.

(v) Popular Reports   Governments also prepare popular reports to communicate with persons who are neither interested in a complete set of financial statements or able to review them. Popular reports are also called *condensed summary data.*

There are three types of popular reports. The first is an aggregation of the data from the financial statements that disregards the distinction among fund types and the different bases of accounting and presents the data as if all the assets, liabilities, equities, revenues, and expenditures (expenses) pertained not to the fund types but to the government as a whole. This results in a presentation similar to that made by corporations and their subsidiaries. In such cases, the government usually eliminates significant interfund transactions before arriving at totals.

The second approach is to visually present the entity's financial information—for example, by using pie charts or bar graphs. A common presentation is to present one pie to show the composition of revenue by cutting the pie into slices with each slice representing a major revenue source. The size of the slice would reflect the magnitude of the respective revenue source. Similar pie charts can be used to show the major categories of expenditures, the major categories of assets, and the major categories of liabilities.

The third approach is to issue consolidated government-wide financial statements. Such a consolidated approach replaces the funds and government-wide financial statements by a single "fund" that is used to report the financial position and results of operations of the entire oversight unit or reporting entity. Intra-governmental transactions are eliminated in the consolidation process, and a single basis of accounting (normally accrual) is used for all transactions.

Consolidated financial statements typically include a balance sheet and an operating statement. Because the accrual basis of accounting is normally used, capital assets are reported and depreciated. In addition, long-term obligations are reported.

34.5 BASIC FINANCIAL STATEMENTS REQUIRED FOR SPECIAL-PURPOSE GOVERNMENTS

Special-purpose governments are legally separate entities that are component units or other stand-alone governments, which are legally separate government organizations that (1) do not have separately elected governing bodies and (2) are not component units, plus joint ventures, jointly governed organizations, and pools.

A special-purpose government that is engaged in more than one governmental program or that has both governmental and business-type activities should meet the reporting requirements for governments that are not special-purpose governments. A special-purpose government is engaged in more than one governmental program if it budgets, manages, or accounts for its activities as multiple programs, such as a school district that provides regular instruction, special instruction, vocational education, and adult education.

(a) REPORTING BY SPECIAL-PURPOSE GOVERNMENTS ENGAGED IN GOVERNMENTAL ACTIVITIES   A special-purpose government engaged in a single governmental activity, such as some cemetery districts, levee districts, assessment districts, and drainage districts, may combine its government-wide financial statements and its fund financial statements in a columnar format that reconciles line items of fund financial information to government-wide information in a separate column on the face of the financial statements rather than at the bottom of the statements or in an accompanying schedule. Otherwise, the special-purpose government may present separate government-wide and fund financial statements and may present its government-wide statement of activities in a different format. For example, it may be

presented in a single column that reports expenses first followed by revenues by major sources. The difference, net revenue or expense, should be followed by contributions to permanent and term endowments, special and extraordinary items, transfers, and beginning and ending net assets.

(b) REPORTING BY SPECIAL-PURPOSE GOVERNMENTS ENGAGED ONLY IN BUSINESS-TYPE ACTIVITIES   A government engaged in only business-type activities should present only the financial statement required for enterprise funds, as follows:

- MD&A
- Enterprise fund financial statements:
  - Statement of net assets or balance sheet
  - Statement of revenues, expenses, and changes in fund net assets
  - Statement of cash flows
  - Notes to financial statements
- Applicable RSI other than MD&A

(c) REPORTING BY SPECIAL-PURPOSE GOVERNMENTS ENGAGED ONLY IN FIDUCIARY ACTIVITIES   A special-purpose government engaged in only fiduciary activities should present only the financial statement required for fiduciary funds, as follows:

- MD&A
- Statement of fiduciary net assets
- Statement of changes in fiduciary net assets
- Notes to financial statements

A Public Employees Retirement System (PERS) is a special-purpose government that administers one or more defined benefit pension plans and may also administer other kinds of employee benefit plans, such as defined contribution, deferred compensation, and postemployment health care plans. One that administers more than one defined benefit pension plan or postemployment health care plan should present combining financial statements for all such plans and, if applicable, required schedules for each plan. (A PERS that administers one or more agent multiple-employer plans applies these requirement at the aggregate plan level.) It should (1) present a separate column for each plan on the statement of fiduciary net assets and the statement of changes in fiduciary net assets or (2) present combining statements for the plans as part of the basic financial statements.

34.6 ACCOUNTING PRINCIPLES AND PRACTICES—PUBLIC COLLEGES AND UNIVERSITIES

Public colleges and universities should apply the principles discussed in this chapter. The primary guidance for public colleges and universities is GASB Statement No. 35, Basic Financial Statements—and Management's Discussion and Analysis—for Public Colleges and Universities.

34.7 AUDITS OF GOVERNMENTAL UNITS

Audits of governmental units with financial statements can be performed in accordance with

- Generally accepted auditing standards (GAAS)
- *Government Auditing Standards* (the "Yellow Book")

- The Single Audit Act Amendments of 1996 and Office of Management and Budget (OMB) Circular A-133

When performing an audit in accordance with GAAS, the guidance contained in the *AICPA Professional Standards* is followed. This is the same guidance followed by auditors when auditing the financial statement of commercial entities and typically results in the issuance of an opinion of the financial statements and perhaps a management letter. *Government Auditing Standards,* also known as the *Yellow Book* (U.S. Comptroller General, rev. 2007), establishes the concept of an expanded scope audit that includes both financial and compliance features. According to the Yellow Book, a financial audit can help determine whether

- The financial statements of an audited entity present fairly the financial position and the results of financial operations in accordance with GAAP.
- The entity has complied with laws and regulations that may have a material effect on the financial statements.

The Yellow Book incorporates the AICPA Professional Standards previously mentioned and sets forth additional standards and requirements, including the following six:

1. A review is to be made of compliance with applicable laws and regulations, as set forth in federal audit guides and other applicable reference sources.
2. The auditor reports on the entity's compliance with laws, regulations, contracts, and grant agreements and shall also include material instances of noncompliance and instances or indications of noncompliance or fraud found during or in connection with the audit.
3. The auditors shall report on their consideration of the entity's internal control over financial reporting as part of the financial audit.
   They shall identify as a minimum:
   a. Scope of auditor's work in obtaining an understanding of the internal control over financial reporting.
   b. The significant deficiencies including separate identification of material weaknesses identified as a result of the auditor's work.
4. Auditors performing government audits are required to obtain 80 hours of continuing education that directly enhance the auditor's professional proficiency to perform audits and/or attestation engagements every two years, of which 24 hours should be directly related to government. At least 20 of the 80 hours should be completed in each year of the two-year period.
5. Audit organizations performing government audits are required to establish an internal quality control system and participate in an external quality control review program.
6. The auditor communicates certain information related to the conduct of the audit to the audit committee or to the individuals with whom they have contracted for the audit.

(a) THE SINGLE AUDIT ACT AMENDMENTS OF 1996   Many state and local governments are required to obtain a periodic audit of the federal funds they receive, usually once a year. The audits are normally performed by an independent certified public accountant (CPA) or public accountant, or, in some states, by the government's internal audit personnel. A few jurisdictions have an independently elected or appointed auditor who conducts the audit. Single audits are conducted in accordance with GAAS, *Government Auditing Standards,* and the Single Audit Amendments Act of 1996 and its implementing regulation OMB Circular A-133, including its Compliance Supplement. These requirements have been updated for fiscal years beginning on or after July 1, 1997, by the Single Audit Amendments Act of 1996 (the Act).

The objectives of the Act are

- To improve the financial management of state and local governments with respect to federal financial assistance programs through improved auditing
- To establish uniform requirements for audits of federal financial assistance provided to state and local governments
- To promote the efficient and effective use of audit resources
- To ensure that federal departments and agencies, to the maximum extent practicable, rely on and use audit work performed pursuant to the requirements of the Single Audit Act

Though the single audit builds on the annual financial statement audit currently required by most state and larger local governments, it places substantial additional emphasis on the consideration and testing of internal controls and the testing of compliance with laws and regulations.

The Single Audit Act and OMB Circular A-133 require the auditor to determine whether

- The financial statements of the government, department, agency, or establishment present fairly its financial position and the results of operations in conformity with GAAP.
- The organization has internal and other control structures to provide reasonable assurance that it is managing federal financial assistance programs in compliance with applicable laws and regulations.
- The organization has complied with laws and regulations that may have a material effect on its financial statements and on each major federal financial assistance program.

Non-federal entities that expend $500,000 or more in a year in federal awards are subject to a single audit unless they elect (if qualified) to have a program-specific audit conducted. If less than $500,000 is expended, the entity is exempt from federal audit requirements for that year, but records must be retained for review or audit, by, for example, the General Accountability Office (GAO).

The Single Audit Act provides auditors with guidance on the focus of the audit by defining a level of audit work based on the concept of "major" federal programs. OMB Circular A-133 §___.520 provides specific guidance on how to determine what are major federal programs and outlines the three steps required in identifying "major" federal programs. These three steps are as follows:

1. Identify "Type A" and "Type B" programs. For most small and medium-sized governments, a Type A program is defined as the larger of $300,000 or 3 percent of the total federal *expenditures* for all federal programs. For larger governments whose total federal expenditures exceed $100 million, a major federal financial assistance program based on a sliding scale. All programs that are not categorized as a Type A program are "Type B" programs.
2. Identify "Low Risk Type A" programs by assessing all Type A programs. Typically, a Low Risk Type A program must have been audited as a "major" program within the last two years and must have no audit findings as defined in §___.510(a). All

Type A programs which are not low risk are high risk and must be audited as a major program.

3. Identify "High Risk Type B" programs if there are one or more Low Risk Type A programs identified. Auditors have two options in assessing risks in Type B programs:

   ○ *Option one.* Complete a risk assessment for **all** Type B programs that are greater than the Type B floor amount, then classify as major programs one-half of the Type B programs greater than the floor amount identified as high risk with a cap in the number of major programs at the number of Low Risk Type A programs.

   ○ *Option two.* Complete a risk assessment for *some* of the Type B programs that are greater than the Type B floor amount until the same number high-risk Type B programs are greater than or equal to the number of Low Risk Type A programs.

If a federal grantor agency formally designates a program to be major, this program must also be audited in addition to the major programs identified in previous steps.

The Single Audit Act and OMB Circular A-133 require the auditor to issue the following reports:

- A report on the audit of the basic financial statements of the entity as a whole, or the department, agency, or establishment covered by the audit
- A report on compliance and internal control based on an audit of the basic financial statements
- A report on compliance and internal control over compliance applicable to each major federal award program

In a Single Audit, the report on the audit of the basic financial statements is typically expanded to include an opinion on the fair presentation of the supplementary schedule of expenditures of federal awards in relation to the audited financial statements.

(b) OTHER CONSIDERATIONS   Most government officials and auditors of governmental units realize that a good audit should furnish more than an opinion on the financial statements. Other services a governmental auditor can provide are pinpointing the key information upon which decisions should be based and contributing to the presentation of this information in a manner that facilitates decision making; uncovering deficiencies in the accounting system and providing suggestions for improving the efficiency and effectiveness of the system; and obtaining and presenting information useful for marketing securities.

Obtaining a qualified auditor, particularly one who can provide the additional services described above, requires that the selection be based on qualifications and experience, and not solely cost. The National Intergovernmental Audit Forum, in its handbook *How to Avoid a Substandard Audit: Suggestions for Procuring an Audit*, indicates that

> Public entities should never select auditors without considering five basic elements of an effective audit procurement process:
>
> planning (determining what needs to be done and when),
> fostering competition by soliciting proposals (writing a clear and direct solicitation document and disseminating it widely),

technically evaluating proposals and qualifications (authorizing a committee of knowledgeable persons to evaluate the ability of prospective auditors to effectively carry out the audit),

preparing a written agreement (documenting the expectations of both the entity and the auditor), and

monitoring the auditor's performance (periodically reviewing the progress of that performance).

This *handbook* provides detailed information about the five elements of procurement previously listed as well as the use of audit committees in a government environment, along with other useful information about the auditor procurement process.

(i) Governmental Rotation of Auditors   The automatic rotation of auditors after a given number of years is a common practice in many governments; however, it is not always beneficial. Many governments have followed this policy, believing that they will (1) receive a fresh outlook from the audit, (2) spread the work among several firms, and (3) encourage lower fees. What the Government Accountability Office (GAO) found in its November 2003 *Required Study on the Potential Effects of Mandatory Audit Firm Rotation* is that mandatory audit firm rotation may not be the most efficient way to strengthen auditor independence and improve auditing quality considering the additional financial costs and the loss of institutional knowledge. Automatic rotation may be harmful in that it could deprive the government of the extensive knowledge of the entity developed by the current auditor. It may also impair auditing effectiveness, given that a new auditor may need to spend considerable time learning the government's system. The government may actually incur more cost since its personnel will need to spend time explaining the organization, systems, and data to the new auditors, and the new auditors will need to spend valuable time reviewing information that is already part of the previous auditor's workpapers. Although a government should continuously monitor its auditor's performance to ensure that the service obtained is commensurate with the cost, the entity should normally change auditors only because of dissatisfaction with services and not for the sake of receiving a lower fee.

(ii) Audit Committees   In recent years, governments have started establishing audit committees similar to those in the private sector. Some appropriate tasks for a local government's audit committee include the following:

- Reviewing significant financial information for reliability, timeliness, clarity, appropriateness of disclosure, and compliance with GAAP and legal requirements
- Ascertaining that internal controls are appropriately designed and functioning effectively
- Evaluating independent audit firms and selecting one for approval by the appropriate body
- Overseeing the scope and performance of the independent audit function
- Ensuring that the auditors' recommendations for improvements in internal controls and operating methods receive management's attention and are implemented on a timely basis
- Providing an effective communications link between the auditors and the full governing board

The primary benefit of an audit committee is in assisting the full governing board to fulfill its responsibilities for the presentation of financial information about the governmental unit. There are also secondary benefits: The other parties involved in the issuance of financial information—management and independent and internal auditors—can perform their roles more effectively if an audit committee is involved in the process. Finally, there are advantages for the government's constituencies—in particular, the taxpayers and bondholders.

34.8 CONCLUDING REMARKS

Governmental accounting and reporting is changing and expanding at an increasing rapid rate. Coupling this with public accountability issues, the federal government's pressure for increased audit quality, and the penalties for substandard audit performance results in increasing levels of audit risk. Government audits, often considered low-risk engagements by many, are quickly becoming areas of extremely high risk. Auditing professionals need to recognize the risk associated with government engagements now and in the future before incurring severe penalties or embarrassment. The technical issues involved in government auditing are on a par with those in the commercial environment, but auditors have much less experience and less technical guidance to fall back on.

Dealing with these technical issues requires well-trained, highly motivated individuals and can no longer be left to less experienced members of the audit team. Dealing with the *real* issues governments are facing (e.g., infrastructure, terrorism, prison overcrowding, drugs, etc.) requires even more from the individuals in the profession. Like it or not, government accounting and reporting is being thrust into the spotlight and will be scrutinized by a multitude of individuals and groups. It is imperative that individuals in the industry realize this fact and begin now to prepare for the future.

34.9 SOURCES AND SUGGESTED REFERENCES

American Institute of Certified Public Accountants, "AICPA Audit and Accounting Guide: State and Local Governments." AICPA, New York, 2007.

_____, "AICPA Audit and Accounting Guide: Government Auditing Standards and Circular A-133 Audits." AICPA, New York, 2007.

_____, "AICPA Professional Standards." AICPA, New York, 2007.

City and County of San Francisco, California, "Comprehensive Annual Financial Report For the Year Ended June 30, 2006," 2006.

Financial Accounting Standards Board, "Classification of Short-Term Obligations Expected to Be Refinanced," Statement of Financial Accounting Standards No. 6. FASB, Stamford, CT, 1975.

_____, "Accounting for Leases," Statement of Financial Accounting Standards Board No. 13. FASB, Stamford, CT, 1975.

_____, "Objectives of Financial Reporting by Nonbusiness Organizations," Statement of Financial Accounting Concepts No. 4. FASB, Stamford, CT, 1980.

General Accounting Office, "Government Auditing Standards, July 2007 Revision." GAO, Washington, DC, 2003.

_____, "Required Study on the Potential Effects of Mandatory Audit Firm Rotation", GAO, Washington, DC, 2003.

Governmental Accounting Standards Board, "Basic Financial Statements—and Management's Discussion and Analysis—for State and Local Governments." GASB Statement No. 34. GASB, Norwalk, CT, 1999.

_____, "Codification of Governmental Accounting and Financial Reporting Standards." GASB, Norwalk, CT, 2007.

Government Finance Officers Association, "Governmental Accounting, Auditing and Financial Reporting." GFOA, Chicago, IL, 2005. (Study guide available)

Ives, Martin "The Governmental Accounting Standards Board: Factors Influencing Its Operation and Initial Technical Agenda". *Government Accounting Journal*, Spring 2002, v49 (1), 22–27.

Mead, Dean Michael, "What You Should Know About Your Local Government's Finances." GASB, Norwalk, CT, 2007.

Office of Management and Budget, "Circular No. A-133, Audits of States, Local Governments, and Non-Profit Organizations, June 27, 2003 Revision." Office of Management and Budget, Washington, DC, 2003.

APPENDIX 34.1: PRONOUNCEMENTS ON STATE AND LOCAL GOVERNMENT ACCOUNTING

	Government Accounting Standard Board	Effective Date
Statement No. 1	Authoritative Status of NCGA Pronouncements and AICPA Industry Audit Guide	On issuance (7/84)
Statement No. 2	Financial Reporting of Deferred Compensation Plans Adopted under the Provisions of Internal Revenue Code Section 457	Superseded by GASB Statement No. 32
Statement No. 3	Deposits with Financial Institutions, Investments (including Repurchase Agreements), and Reverse Repurchase Agreements	Financial statements for periods ending after 2/15/86
Statement No. 4	Applicability of FASB Statement No. 87, "Employers' Accounting for Pensions," to State and Local Governmental Employers	Superseded by GASB Statement No. 27
Statement No. 5	Disclosure of Pension Information by Public Employee Retirement Systems and State and Local Governmental Employers	Financial reports issued for fiscal years beginning after 12/15/86
Statement No. 6	Accounting and Financial Reporting for Special Assessments	Financial statements for periods beginning after 6/15/87
Statement No. 7	Advance Refundings Resulting in Defeasance of Debt	Fiscal periods beginning after 12/15/86
Statement No. 8	Applicability of FASB Statement No. 93, "Recognition of Depreciation by Not-for-Profit Organizations," to Certain State and Local Governmental Entities	Superseded by GASB Statement No. 35
Statement No. 9	Reporting Cash Flows of Proprietary and Nonexpendable Trust Funds and Governmental Entries that Use Proprietary Fund Accounting	Fiscal periods beginning after 12/15/89
Statement No. 10	Accounting and Financial Reporting for Risk Financing and Related Insurance Issues	Pools—Fiscal periods beginning after 6/15/90
		Other—Fiscal periods beginning after 6/15/93

(Continued)

APPENDIX 34.1 *(Continued)*

Government Accounting Standard Board		Effective Date
Statement No. 11	Measurement Focus and Basis of Accounting—Governmental Fund Operating Statements	Fiscal periods beginning after 6/15/94
Statement No. 12	Disclosure of Information on Postemployment Benefits Other than Pension Benefits by State and Local Governmental Employers	Fiscal periods beginning after 6/15/90
Statement No. 13	Accounting for Operating Leases with Scheduled Rent Increases	Leases with terms beginning after 6/30/90
Statement No. 14	The Financial Reporting Entity	Fiscal periods beginning after 12/15/92
Statement No. 15	Governmental College and University Accounting and Financial Reporting Models	Superseded by GASB Statement No. 35
Statement No. 16	Accounting for Compensated Absences	Fiscal periods beginning after June 15, 1993
Statement No. 17	Measurement Focus and Basis of Accounting—Governmental Fund Operating Statements: Amendment of Effective Dates of GASB Statement No. 11 and Related Statements	Immediately
Statement No. 18	Accounting for Municipal Solid Waste Landfill Closure and Post-closure Care Costs	Fiscal periods beginning after June 15, 1993
Statement No. 19	Governmental College and University Omnibus Statement–an Amendment of GASB Statements No. 10 and 15	Superseded by GASB Statement No. 35
Statement No. 20	Accounting and Financial Reporting for Proprietary Funds and Other Governmental Entities That Use Proprietary Fund Accounting	Fiscal periods beginning after December 15, 1993
Statement No. 21	Accounting for Escheat Property	Fiscal periods beginning after June 15, 1994
Statement No. 22	Accounting for Taxpayer-Assessed Tax Revenues in Governmental Funds	Superseded by GASB Statement No. 33
Statement No. 23	Accounting and Financial Reporting for Refundings of Debt Reported by Proprietary Activities	Fiscal periods beginning after June 15, 1994

	Government Accounting Standard Board	Effective Date
Statement No. 24	Accounting and Financial Reporting for Certain Grants and Other Financial Assistance	Fiscal periods beginning after June 15, 1995
Statement No. 25	Financial Reporting for Defined Benefit Pension Plans and Note Disclosures for Defined Contribution Plans	Fiscal periods beginning after June 15, 1996, Statement No. 26 must be implemented simultaneously
Statement No. 26	Financial Reporting for Postemployment Healthcare Plans Administered by Defined Benefit Pension Plans	Fiscal periods beginning after June 15, 1996, Statement No. 25 must be implemented simultaneously
Statement No. 27	Accounting for Pensions by State and Local Governmental Employers	Fiscal periods beginning after June 15, 1997
Statement No. 28	Accounting and Financial Reporting for Securities Lending Transactions	Fiscal periods beginning after December 15, 1995
Statement No. 29	The Use of Not-for-Profit Accounting and Financial Reporting Principles by Governmental Entities	Fiscal periods beginning after December 15, 1995
Statement No. 30	Risk Financing Omnibus	Fiscal periods beginning after June 15, 1996
Statement No. 31	Accounting and Financial Reporting for Certain Investments and for External Investment Pools	Fiscal periods beginning after June 15, 1997
Statement No. 32	Accounting and Financial Reporting for Internal Revenue Code Section 457 Deferred Compensation Plans	Earlier of fiscal periods beginning after December 31, 1998, or amendment of the IRC Section 457 Plan
Statement No. 33	Accounting and Financial Reporting for Nonexchange Transactions	Periods beginning after June 15, 2000
Statement No. 34	Basic Financial Statements—and Management's Discussion and Analysis—for State and Local Governments	[6]

(Continued)

---

6.   In three phases, based on total annual revenue in the first fiscal year ending after June 15, 1999; Phase 1 - governments with total annual revenues of $100 million or more, fiscal periods beginning after June 15, 2001; Phase 2 - governments with total annual revenues of $10 or more but less than $100 million, fiscal periods beginning after June 15, 2002; Phase 3 - governments with total annual revenues of less than $10 million, fiscal periods beginning after June 15, 2003.

APPENDIX 34.1 *(Continued)*

Government Accounting Standard Board		Effective Date
Statement No. 35	Basic Financial Statements—and Management's Discussion and Analysis—for Public Colleges and Universities: Amendment of GASB Statement No. 34	[7]
Statement No. 36	Recipient Reporting for Certain Shared Nonexchange Revenues: Amendment of GASB Statement No. 33	Simultaneously with Statement No. 33
Statement No. 37	Basic Financial Statements—and Management's Discussion and Analysis—for State and Local Governments: Omnibus	[8]
Statement No. 38	Certain Financial Statement Note Disclosures and Discussion and Analysis—for State and Local Governments	[9]
Statement No. 39	Determining Whether Certain Organizations Are Component Units	Periods beginning after June 15, 2003
Statement No. 40	Deposit and Investment Risk Disclosures—An Amendment of GASB Statement No. 3	Periods beginning after June 15, 2004
Statement No. 41	Budgetary Comparison Schedules—Perspective Differences—An Amendment of GASB Statement No. 34	Simultaneously with Statement 34
Statement No. 42	Accounting and Financial Reporting for Impairment of Capital Assets and for Insurance Recoveries	Periods beginning after December 15, 2004

---

7. Public institutions that are components of another reporting entity should implement the Statement no later than the same year as their primary government. For public institutions that are not components of another reporting entity, this Statement is effective in the three phases indicated in the preceding footnote.
8. Simultaneously with Statement No. 34. For governments that implemented Statement No. 34 before Statement No. 37 was issued, Statement No. 37 is effective for periods beginning after June 15, 2000.
9. In three phases, based on total annual revenue in the first fiscal year ending after June 15, 1999: Phase 1 - governments with total annual revenues of $100 million or more, fiscal periods beginning after June 15, 2001; Phase 2 - governments with total annual revenues of $10 million or more but less than $100 million, fiscal periods beginning after June 15, 2002; Phase 3 - governments with total annual revenues of less than $10 million, fiscal periods beginning after June 15, 2003.

Government Accounting Standard Board		Effective Date
Statement No. 43	Financial Reporting for Postemployment Benefit Plans Other Than Pension Plans	Effective in three phases based on a government's total annual revenues in the first fiscal year ending after June 15, 1999: for periods beginning after December 15, 2005, 2006, and 2007
Statement No. 44	Economic Condition Reporting—The Statistical Section—An Amendment of NCGA Statement 1	Statistical sections prepared for periods beginning after June 15, 2005
Statement No. 45	Accounting and Financial Reporting by Employers for Postemployment Benefits Other Than Pensions	Effective in three phases based on a government's total annual revenues in the first fiscal year ending after June 15, 1999: for periods beginning after December 15, 2006, 2007, and 2008
Statement No. 46	Net Assets Restricted by Enabling Legislation—An Amendment of GASB Statement No. 34	Periods beginning after June 15, 2005
Statement No. 47	Accounting for Termination Benefits	For termination benefits provided through an existing defined benefit OPEB plan, the provisions of this Statement should be implemented simultaneously with the requirements of Statement 45. For all other termination benefits, this Statement is effective for financial statements for periods beginning after June 15, 2005.
Statement No. 48	Sales and Pledges of Receivables and Future Revenues and Intra-Entity Transfers of Assets and Future Revenues	Periods beginning after December 15, 2006
Statement No. 49	Accounting and Financial Reporting for Pollution Remediation Obligations	Periods beginning after December 15, 2007

(Continued)

APPENDIX 34.1 *(Continued)*

Government Accounting Standard Board		Effective Date
Statement No. 50	Pension Disclosures—an amendment of GASB Statements No. 25 and No. 27	Periods beginning after June 15, 2007, except for requirements related to the use of the entry age actuarial cost method for the purpose of reporting a surrogate funded status and funding progress of plans that use the aggregate actuarial cost method, which are effective for periods for which the financial statements and RSI contain information resulting from actuarial valuations as of June 15, 2007, or later.
Statement No. 51	Accounting and Financial Reporting for Intangible Assets	Periods beginning after June 15, 2009
Statement No. 52	Land and Other Real Estate Held as Investments by Endowments	Periods beginning after June 15, 2008
Interpretation No. 1	Demand Bonds Issued by State and Local Governmental Entities	Fiscal periods ending after June 15, 1985
Interpretation No. 2	Disclosure of Conduit Debt Obligations	Fiscal periods beginning after December 15, 1995
Interpretation No. 3	Financial Reporting for Reverse Repurchase Agreements	Fiscal periods beginning after December 15, 1995
Interpretation No. 4	Accounting and Financial Reporting for Capitalization Contributions to Public Entity Risk Pools	Fiscal periods beginning after June 15, 1996
Interpretation No. 5	Property Tax Revenue Recognition in Governmental Funds	Fiscal periods beginning after June 15, 2000
Interpretation No. 6	Recognition and Measurement of Certain Liabilities and Expenditures in Governmental Fund Financial Statements: an Interpretation of NCGA Statements 1, 4, and 5, NCGA Interpretation 8, and GASB Statement Nos. 10, 16, and 18	Simultaneously with Statement No. 34
Technical Bulletin No. 84–1	Purpose and Scope of GASB Technical Bulletins and Procedures for Issuance	None

	Government Accounting Standard Board	Effective Date
Technical Bulletin No. 2003–1	Disclosure Requirements for Derivatives Not Reported at Fair Value on the Statement of Net Assets	Financial statements issued after June 15, 2003
Technical Bulletin No. 2004–1	Tobacco Settlement Recognition and Financial Reporting Entity Issues	June 15, 2004
Technical Bulletin No. 2004–2	Recognition of Pension and Other Postemployment Benefit Expenditures/ Expense and Liabilities by Cost-Sharing Employers	Pension transactions: for financial statements for periods ending after December 15, 2004. OPEB transactions: applied simultaneously with the requirements of Statement 45
Technical Bulletin No. 2006–1	Accounting and Financial Reporting by Employers and OPEB Plans for Payments from the Federal Government Pursuant to the Retiree Drug Subsidy Provisions of Medicare Part D	On issuance (6/06) except for the portions of answers pertaining specifically to measurement, recognition, or required supplementary information requirements of Statement No. 43 or Statement No. 45. Those provisions should be applied simultaneously with the implementation of Statement 43 or Statement 45.
Concepts Statement No. 1	Objectives of Financial Reporting	None
Concepts Statement No. 2	Reporting Service Efforts and Accomplishments	None
Concepts Statement No. 3	Communication Methods in General Purpose External Financial Reports That Contain Basic Financial Statements	None
Concepts Statement No. 4	Elements of Financial Statements	None

	National Council On Government Accounting	Effective Date
Statement 1	Governmental Accounting and Financial Reporting Principles	Fiscal years ending after 6/30/80
Statement 2	Grant, Entitlement, and Shared Revenue Accounting by State and Local Governments	Fiscal years ending after 6/30/80
Statement 3	Defining the Governmental Reporting Entity	Issued 12/81; superseded by GASB Statement No. 14
Statement 4	Accounting and Financial Reporting Principles for Claims and Judgments and Compensated Absences	Fiscal years beginning after 12/31/82; 20 extended indefinitely by NCGAS 11
Statement 5	Accounting and Financial Reporting Principles for Lease Agreements of State and Local Governments	Fiscal years beginning after 6/30/83
Interpretation 1	GAAFR and the AICPA Audit Guide (Superseded)	Issued 4/86; superseded by NCGAS 1
Interpretation 2	Segment Information for Enterprise Funds	Issued 6/80; superseded by GASB Statement No. 34
Interpretation 3	Revenue Recognition—Property Taxes	Fiscal years beginning after 9/30/81
Interpretation 4	Accounting and Financial Reporting for Public Employee Retirement Systems and Pension Trust Funds (Superseded)	Fiscal years beginning after 6/15/82; superseded by NCGAS 6 and repealed by NCGAI 8
Interpretation 5	Authoritative Status of Governmental Accounting, Auditing, and Financial Reporting	Issued 3/82; superseded by GASB Statement No. 34
Interpretation 6	Notes to the Financial Statements Disclosure	Prospectively for fiscal years beginning after 12/31/82
Interpretation 7	Clarification as to the Application of the Criteria in NCGA Statement, "Defining the Governmental Reporting Entity"	Issued 9/83; superseded by GASB Statement No. 14
Interpretation 8	Certain Pension Matters	Fiscal years ending after 12/31/83
Interpretation 9	Certain Fund Classifications and Balance Sheet Accounts	Fiscal years ending after 6/30/84
Interpretation 10	State and Local Government Budgetary Reporting	Fiscal years ending after 6/30/84
Interpretation 11	Claim and Judgment Transactions for Governmental Funds	Issued 4/84; superseded by GASB Statement No. 10

CHAPTER 50

COST-VOLUME-REVENUE ANALYSIS FOR NONPROFIT ORGANIZATIONS[1] (NEW)

Jae K. Shim, PhD
California State University, Long Beach

---

1. This entire chapter also appeared in the 2006 Cumulative Supplement to the *Accountants' Handbook*, Tenth Edition.

Managers of nonprofit organizations generally are not skilled in financial matters. They often are preoccupied with welfare objectives and ignore operations efficiency and operating cost controls. There are nine questions that nonprofit financial managers should address in connection with an organization's financial condition and activity:

1. Do we have a profit or a loss?
2. Do we have sufficient reserves?
3. Are we liquid?
4. Do we have strong internal controls?
5. Are we operating efficiently?
6. Are we meeting our budget goals?
7. Are our programs financially healthy?
8. Are we competing successfully?
9. Is our prioritizing of programs and activities reasonable?

By definition, the goal of a nonprofit entity is *not* to earn a profit. Its objective is to render as much suitable service as possible while using the least amount of human and physical services as possible. Ideally, breaking even should be the goal of a nonprofit organization. Breaking even occurs when revenues equal costs. If the nonprofit generates a surplus, it may not receive the same amount from the funding agency as last year. On the other hand, by operating at a deficit, the nonprofit may become insolvent or unable to perform the maximum amount of services. Chances are the nonprofit may not be able to borrow money from the bank as not-for-profit entities often have a weak financial stance. However, one thing is clear—over the long run, nonprofit entities cannot sustain persistent deficits unless they have large reserves. Even with large reserves, a nonprofit may have to operate below potential. This means the benefit of the nonprofit will not be maximized.

This chapter deals with many planning issues surrounding nonprofit organizations. Cost-volume-revenue (CVR) analysis, together with cost behavior information, helps nonprofit managers perform many useful planning analyses. CVR analysis deals with how revenue and costs change with a change in the service level. More specifically, it looks at the effects on revenues from changes in such factors as variable costs, fixed costs, prices, service level, and mix of services offered. By studying the relationships of costs, service volume, and revenue, nonprofit management is better able to cope with many planning decisions.

Break-even analysis, a branch of CVR analysis, determines the break-even service level. The break-even point (the financial crossover point at which revenues exactly match costs) does not show up in financial reports, but nonprofit financial managers find it an extremely useful measurement in numerous ways. It reveals which programs are self-supporting and which are subsidized.

50.1   QUESTIONS ANSWERED BY CVR ANALYSIS

CVR analysis tries to answer four questions:

1. What service level (or which units of service) is required to break even?
2. How would changes in price, variable costs, fixed costs, and service volume affect a surplus?
3. How do changes in program levels and mix affect aggregate surplus/deficit?
4. What alternative break-even strategies are available?

50.2 ANALYSIS OF REVENUES

Revenues for nonprofit entities are typically classified into the following categories:

- Grants from governments
- Grants from private sources
- Cost reimbursements and sales
- Membership dues
- Public contributions received directly or indirectly
- Donations and pledges
- Legacies, bequests, and memorials
- Program fees
- Other revenue, such as investment income (e.g., interest, dividends)

For managerial purposes, however, each type of revenue is grouped into its fixed and variable parts. Fixed revenues are those that remain unchanged regardless of the level of service. Examples are gifts, grants, and contracts. As an example, in a university setting, donations, gifts, and grants have no relationship to the number of students enrolled. In contrast to fixed revenues, variable revenues are the ones that vary in proportion to the volume of activity. Examples include cost reimbursements and membership fees. Continuing the example of a university setting, the total amount of tuition and fees received varies as the number of students enrolled increases or decreases. Different nonprofit entities may have different sources of revenue: variable revenue only, fixed revenue only, or a combination of both. In this chapter, we discuss all three cases in analyzing break-even and CVR applications.

50.3 ANALYSIS OF COST BEHAVIOR

For external reporting purposes, costs are classified by managerial function such as payroll, occupancy, office, and so on, as well as by programs and supporting services. See Exhibit 50.1 for a model functional classification.

For managerial purposes (i.e., planning, control, and decision making), further classification of costs is desirable. One classification is by behavior. Depending on how they react or respond to changes in the level of activity, costs may be viewed as variable or fixed. This classification assumes a known high and low volume of service activity called the *relative range of activity*. The relevant range is the volume zone within which the behavior of variable costs, fixed costs, and prices can be predicted with reasonable accuracy. The relevant range falls between the planned highest and lowest service level for the nonprofit. Within this level of normal activity the behavior of variable costs, fixed costs, and prices can be predicted with reasonable accuracy. Typical activity measures are summarized in Exhibit 50.2.

(a) VARIABLE COSTS Total variable costs change as the volume or level of activity changes. Examples of variable costs include supplies, hourly wages, printing and publications, and postage and shipping.

(b) FIXED COSTS Total fixed costs do not change regardless of the volume or level of activity. Examples include property tax, yearly salaries, accounting and consulting fees, and depreciation. Exhibit 50.3 shows the fixed-variable breakdown of IRS Form 990 functional expenses.

IRS FORM 990 LINE #	FUNCTIONAL EXPENSE CATEGORY
26	Salaries and wages
27	Pension plan contributions
28	Other employee benefits
29	Payroll taxes
30	Professional fundraising fees
31	Accounting fees
32	Legal fees
33	Supplies
34	Telephone
35	Postage and shipping
36	Occupancy
37	Equipment rental and maintenance
38	Printing and publications
39	Travel
40	Conferences, conventions, meetings
41	Interest
42	Depreciation, depletion, etc.
43	Other expenses (itemize)

EXHIBIT 50.1:   IRS FORM 990 PART II—STATEMENT OF FUNCTIONAL EXPENSES

Nonprofit Types	Units of Service
Hospital or Healthcare	Bed days, patient contact hours, patient days, service hours
Educational	Number of student enrollments, class size, FTE (full-time equivalent) hours
Social Clubs	Number of members served

EXHIBIT 50.2:   MEASURES OF THE SERVICE LEVEL

(c) TYPES OF FIXED COSTS: PROGRAM-SPECIFIC OR COMMON   Fixed costs of nonprofit entities are subdivided into two groups: (1) direct or program-specific fixed costs and (2) common costs. Direct or program-specific fixed costs are those that can be directly identified with individual programs. These costs are avoidable or escapable if the program is dropped. Examples include the salaries of those staff members whose services can be used only in a given program and depreciation of equipment used exclusively for the program. Common fixed costs continue even if an individual program has been discontinued. Examples include depreciation of the building and property taxes.

IRS FORM 990 LINE	EXPENSE CATEGORY
Fixed Costs	
26	Salaries and wages (not hourly employees)
27	Pension plan
28	Other benefits
29	Payroll taxes
30	Fund-raising fees
31	Accounting fees
32	Legal fees
36	Occupancy
37	Equipment rental/maintenance
41	Interest
42	Depreciation
43	Other
Variable Costs	
33	Supplies
34	Telephone
35	Postage and shipping
38	Printing and publications
39	Travel
40	Conferences, meetings
43	Other

EXHIBIT 50.3: FIXED-VARIABLE BREAKDOWN OF IRS FORM 990 FUNCTIONAL EXPENSES

50.4 CVR ANALYSIS WITH VARIABLE REVENUE ONLY

For accurate CVR analysis, a distinction must be made between variable costs and fixed costs. In order to compute the break-even point and perform various CVR analyses, the following concepts are important.

(a) CONTRIBUTION MARGIN (CM) The contribution margin is the amount by which total revenue (R) exceeds the variable costs (VC) of the service. It is the amount of money available to cover fixed costs (FC) and to generate surplus. This is symbolically expressed as:

$$CM = R - VC \tag{1}$$

(b) UNIT CM The unit CM is the amount by which the unit price (p) exceeds the unit variable cost (v). This is symbolically expressed as:

$$\text{unit } CM = p - v$$

(c) CM RATIO The CM ratio is the contribution margin as a percentage of revenue:

$$CM \text{ ratio} = CM/R = (R - VC)/R = 1 - (VC/R) \tag{2}$$

or

$$\text{Unit CM} = (p - v)/p = 1 - (v/p) \tag{3}$$

Note: Once you know the contribution margin ratio, then the variable cost ratio is 1–CM ratio. Similarly, if you know the variable cost ratio (VC/R), the contribution margin ratio is (1–VC ratio).

EXAMPLE 50.1

The Los Altos Community Hospital has the following data. This information will be used to illustrate the various concepts of contribution margin and contribution margin ratio:

Average revenue per day	=	$	250
Variable costs per patient day	=	$	50
Total fixed costs	=	$650,000	
Expected number of patient days	=	4,000	

	Total	Per unit	Percentage
Revenue (4,000 days)	$1,000,000	$250	100%
Less: Variable costs (4,000 days)	200,000	50	20
Contribution margin	$ 800,000	$200	80%
Less: Fixed costs (annual)	650,000		
Net income	$ 150,000		

Note that unit CM = p − v = $250 − $50 = $200 and CM ratio = unit CM/p = $200/$250 = .8 = 80%

50.5 BREAK-EVEN ANALYSIS

The break-even point represents the level of revenue that equals the total of the variable and fixed costs for a given volume of output service at a particular capacity use rate. Other things being equal, the lower the break-even point, the higher the surplus and the less the operating risk. The break-even point also provides nonprofit managers with insights into surplus/deficit planning. To develop the formula for the break-even units of service, we set:

$$R = TC \text{ (total costs)} \tag{4}$$

$$R = VC + FC \tag{5}$$

$$px = vx + FC \tag{6}$$

Solving for x yields the following formula for break-even sales volume:

$$x = \frac{FC}{(p - v)} = \frac{\text{Fixed Costs}}{\text{Unit CM}}$$

or

$$\text{Break-even point in dollars (R)} = \frac{\text{Fixed Costs}}{\text{CM Ratio}}$$

EXAMPLE 50.2

Using the same data given in Example 50.1, the number of break-even patient days and break-even dollars are computed as follows:

Break-even point in units   = FC/unit CM   = \$650,000/\$200 = 3,250 patient days

Break-even point in dollars = FC/CM Ratio = \$650,000/0.8   = \$812,500

Or, alternatively,

Break-even point in dollars = 3,250 patient days × \$250 revenue per patient
= 3,250 × \$250 = \$812,500

The hospital therefore needs 3,250 patient days or \$812,500 dollars of revenue to break even.

(a) GRAPHICAL APPROACH IN A SPREADSHEET FORMAT   The graphical approach to obtaining the break-even point is based on the so-called break-even (B-E) chart as shown in Exhibit 50.4. Revenue, variable costs, and fixed costs are plotted on the vertical axis while service volume, x, is plotted on the horizontal axis. The break-even point is the point where the total revenue line intersects the total cost line. The chart can report surplus potentials over a wide range of activity and therefore can be used as a tool for discussion and presentation.

The surplus-volume (S-V) chart, as shown in Exhibit 50.5, focuses on how surplus varies with changes in volume. Surplus is plotted on the vertical axis while units of output are shown on the horizontal axis. The S-V chart provides a quick condensed comparison of how alternatives related to pricing, variable costs, or fixed costs may affect surplus (or deficit) as volume changes. The S-V chart can be easily constructed from the B-E chart. Note that the slope of the chart is the unit CM.

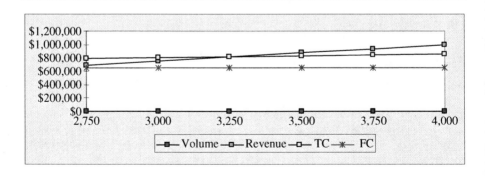

EXHIBIT 50.4:   BREAK-EVEN (B-E) CHART—VARIABLE REVENUE

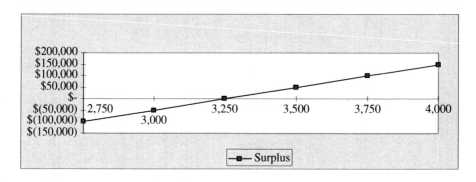

$200,000
$150,000
$100,000
$50,000
$-
$(50,000) 2,750
$(100,000)
$(150,000)
3,000
3,250
3,500
3,750
4,000

—■— Surplus

EXHIBIT 50.5: SURPLUS-VOLUME (S-V) CHART—VARIABLE REVENUE

(b) DETERMINATION OF TARGET SURPLUS VOLUME   Cost-Volume-Revenue (CVR) analysis can be used to determine the activity levels necessary to attain a target surplus (TS). Once the break-even level of activity has been computed, it is useful to determine the level of activity necessary to create a desired surplus. At the break-even point, all fixed costs have been covered.

Therefore, any additional revenue above the break-even level increases the surplus. To calculate the level of service needed to obtain our target surplus, we only need to expand our break-even formula—that is, expand the numerator of the break-even formula to include the amount of desired surplus in addition to fixed costs. In other words, to achieve our desired increase in surplus, not only fixed costs must be recovered but also the desired increase in surplus.

By expanding the break-even formula to obtain the level of activity for a desired target surplus, the formula becomes:

$$\text{Target income surplus level} = \frac{\text{Fixed Costs} + \text{Target Surplus}}{\text{Unit CM}} \qquad (7)$$

EXAMPLE 50.3
Using the same data given in Example 50.1, assume the hospital wishes to accumulate a surplus of $250,000 per year. Then the target surplus service level would be: $$\frac{\text{Fixed Costs} + \text{Target Surplus}}{\text{Unit CM}} = \frac{\$650,000 + \$250,000}{\$200} = 4,500 \text{ patient days}$$

(c) MARGIN OF SAFETY   The margin of safety is a measure of difference between the actual level of service and the break-even level of service. It is expressed as a percentage of expected service level. The margin of safety determines how far the estimated or expected level of service can decline and have the nonprofit still be profitable.

$$\text{Margin of safety} = \frac{\text{Expected Level} - \text{Break-Even Level}}{\text{Expected Level}}$$

The margin of safety is used as a measure of operating risk. The larger the ratio, the safer the situation since there is less risk of reaching the break-even point.

EXAMPLE 50.4

Assume Los Altos Hospital projects 4,000 patient days with a break-even level of 3,250. The projected margin of safety is:

$$\frac{4,000 - 3,250}{4,000} = 18.75\%$$

This means that the hospital's revenue can drop 18.75% before it suffers a deficit.

EXAMPLE 50.5

A nonprofit college offers a program in management for executives. The program has been experiencing financial difficulties. The dean of the school wants to know how many participants are needed to break even. Operating data for the most recent year are shown as follows.

Tuition per participant	= $ 7,000	
Variable expense per participant	= $ 4,000	
Total fixed expenses	= $150,000	
Tuition revenue (40 participants @$7,000)		$280,000
Less variable expenses (@$4,000)		160,000
Contribution margin		$120,000
Less: Fixed expenses		150,000
Operating deficit		$ (30,000)

The break-even calculation is:

$$\$150,000/(\$7,000 - \$4,000) = 50 \text{ participants}$$

EXAMPLE 50.6

In Example 50.5, the dean of the school is convinced that the class size can be increased to more economic levels without lowering the quality. He is prepared to spend $15,000 per year in additional promotional and other support expenses. The promotional and other support expenses are additional fixed costs. If he spends the $15,000 on promotional expenses, the dean wants to know the new break-even number of participants and how many participants are needed to generate a surplus of $30,000.

If that is the case, the formula to calculate the new break-even point is

$$(\$150,000 + \$15,000)/\$3,000 = 55 \text{ participants to break even}$$

The formula to calculate the number of participants necessary to generate a target surplus of $30,000 is

$$[(\$150,000 + \$15,000) + \$30,000]/\$3,000 = 65 \text{ participants}$$

(d) SOME APPLICATIONS OF CVR ANALYSIS AND WHAT-IF ANALYSIS   The concepts of contribution margin and the contribution income statement have many applications in surplus/deficit planning and short-term decision making. Many "what-if" scenarios can be evaluated using these concepts as planning tools, especially utilizing a spreadsheet program. Some applications are illustrated in Example 50.7 using the same data as in Example 50.1.

EXAMPLE 50.7

Assume that the Los Altos Community Hospital in Example 50.1 expects revenues to go up by $250,000 for the next period. How much will surplus increase?

Using the CM concepts, we can quickly compute the impact of a change in the service level on surplus or deficit. The formula for computing the impact is

Change in surplus = Dollar change in revenue × CM ratio

Thus:

Increase in surplus = $250,000 × 80% = $200,000

Therefore, the income will go up by $200,000, assuming there is no change in fixed costs. If we are given a change in service units (e.g., patient days) instead of dollars, then the formula becomes:

Change in surplus = Change in units × Unit CM.

EXAMPLE 50.8

Assume the Los Altos Community Hospital in Example 50.1 expects patient days to go up by 500 units. How much will surplus increase? From Example 50.1, the hospital's unit CM is $200. Again, assuming there is no change in fixed costs, the surplus will increase by $100,000, computed as follows:

500 additional patient days × $200 CM per day = $100,000

EXAMPLE 50.9

Referring back to Example 50.5, another alternative under consideration is to hold the present program without any change in the regular campus facilities instead of in rented outside facilities that are better located. If adopted, this proposal will reduce fixed costs by $60,000. The variable costs will decrease by $100 per participant. Is the move to campus facilities advisable if it leads to a decline in the number of participants by 5?

	Present		Proposed
S(40 × $7,000)	$280,000	(35 × $7,000)	245,000
VC(40 × $4,000)	160,000	(35 × $3,900)	136,500
CM	$120,000		$108,500
FC	150,000		90,000
Surplus	$(30,000)		$18,500

The answer is yes, since the move will turn into a surplus.

50.6 CVR ANALYSIS WITH FIXED REVENUE ONLY

In many nonprofit activities, the objectives are not as clear-cut as the objective of profit in commercial business. Furthermore, the relationship between revenue and volume for a non-profit organization (NPO) is not nearly as well established as is the revenue–volume relationship in business. For example, some NPOs may have only one source of revenue, which is a lump-sum appropriation. This source does not change with changes in volume. Let FR be fixed revenue, or lump-sum appropriation. At break-even,

$$FR = VC + FC$$

$$FR = vx + FC$$

$$x = (FR - FC)\, v$$

$$\text{or break-even units} = \frac{\text{Fixed revenue} - \text{Fixed costs}}{\text{Unit variable cost}}$$

EXAMPLE 50.10

A social service agency has a government budget appropriation of $750,000. The agency's main mission is to assist handicapped people who are unable to seek or hold jobs. On the average, the agency supplements each individual's income by $6,000 annually. The agency's fixed costs are $150,000. The agency CEO wishes to know how many people could be served in a given year. The break-even point can be computed as follows:

$$\text{Break-even units} = \frac{\text{Fixed revenue} - \text{Fixed costs}}{\text{Unit variable cost}} = \frac{750,000 - \$150,000}{\$6,000} = 100$$

The number of people that could be served in a given year is 100.

Exhibits 50.6 and 50.7 display the B-E and S-V charts for this situation.

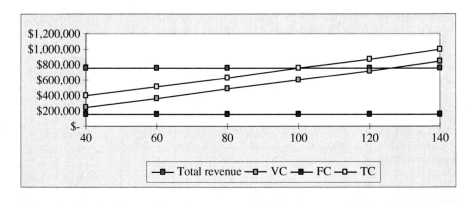

EXHIBIT 50.6:   BREAK-EVEN (B-E) CHART—FIXED REVENUE

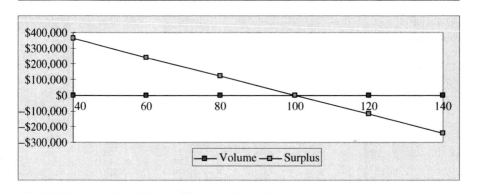

Nonprofits with a lump-sum appropriation have little incentive to increase their level of service. Doing so would either increase a deficit or reduce a surplus (see Exhibit 50.7). Either of these alternatives more than likely would result in a poorer performance evaluation for the program.

EXAMPLE 50.11

In Example 50.10, assume that the CEO is concerned that the total budget for the year will be reduced by 10 percent to a new amount of 90 percent ($750,000) = $675,000.
The new break-even point is:

$$\text{Break-even units} = \frac{\text{Fixed revenue} - \text{Fixed costs}}{\text{Unit variable cost}} = \frac{\$675,000 - \$150,000}{\$6,000} = 88 \text{ (rounded)}$$

The CEO's options facing budget cuts can be any one or a combination of three ways: (1) cut the service level as computed previously, (2) reduce the variable cost (the supplement per person), and (3) seek to cut down on the total fixed costs.

50.7   CVR ANALYSIS WITH VARIABLE AND FIXED REVENUES

Many NPOs derive two types of revenue: fixed and variable. A lump-sum appropriation may exist to subsidize the activity, and a fee for services may also exist (e.g., state-supported colleges and universities). There are two cases in this situation, however.

Case 1: Lump-sum appropriation is less than total fixed costs; fee for service is greater than unit variable cost of service.

Note that $R = FR + px$.

At break-even, $FR + px = vx + FC$, where $FR < FC$ and $p > v$.

$$x = \frac{FC - FR}{pv}$$

$$\text{or break-even units} = \frac{\text{Fixed costs} - \text{Fixed revenue}}{\text{Unit CM}}$$

Case 2: Lump-sum appropriation is higher than total fixed costs; fee is lower than unit variable cost (subsidized activity) resulting in negative unit CM.

$$\text{Note that } R = FR + px$$

$$\text{At break-even, } FR + px = vx + FC, \text{ where } FR > FC \text{ and } p < v$$

$$x = \frac{FR - FC}{vp}$$

$$\text{or break-even units} = \frac{\text{Fixed revenue} - \text{Fixed costs}}{-\text{Unit CM}}$$

In this situation, the fixed revenue covers more than the actual fixed costs. However, the variable costs for service are already more than the nonprofit can charge. In this scenario the number of units that can be served is limited. There is a heavily subsidized unit with a small fee for service to discourage unnecessary use but still making the service available at low cost. This type of appropriate and unit pricing can be used for essential services such as community health services or mass transit.

Example 50.12

ACM, Inc., a mental rehabilitation provider, has the following:

- $1,200,000 lump-sum annual budget appropriation to help rehabilitate mentally ill clients
- Monthly charge per patient for board and care = $600
- Monthly variable cost for rehabilitation activity per patient = $700
- Yearly fixed cost = $800,000

The agency manager wishes to know how many clients can be served.

$$\text{Break-even number of patients} = \frac{\text{Fixed revenue} - \text{Fixed costs}}{-\text{Unit CM}} = \frac{1,200,000 - \$800,000}{-(\$600 - \$700)}$$

$$= \frac{\$400,000}{-(-\$10)} = \frac{\$400,000}{\$100} = 4,000 \text{ per year}$$

The number of patients that can be served is 4,000 per year.

Exhibits 50.8 and 50.9 display the B-E and S-V charts for variable and fixed revenue.

Note that at the level of service greater than B-E service (i.e., 4,000 units), the service is overused or underpriced (or both) (see Exhibit 50.9). We will investigate two "what-if" scenarios.

EXAMPLE 50.13

Using the same data as in Example 50.12, suppose the manager of the agency is concerned that the total budget for the coming year will be cut by 10 percent to a new amount of $1,080,000. All other things remain unchanged. The manager wants to know how this budget cut affects the next year's service level. Using the formula yields

$$\text{Break-even number of patients} = \frac{\text{Fixed revenue} - \text{Fixed costs}}{-\text{Unit CM}} = \frac{\$1,080,000 - \$800,000}{-(\$600 - \$700)}$$

$$= \frac{\$280,000}{-(-\$10)} = 2,800 \text{ Clients per year}$$

The service level will be cut from 4,000 clients to 2,800 clients.

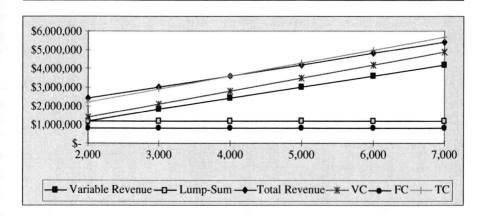

EXHIBIT 50.8:   BREAK-EVEN (B-E) CHART—VARIABLE AND FIXED REVENUE (CASE 2)

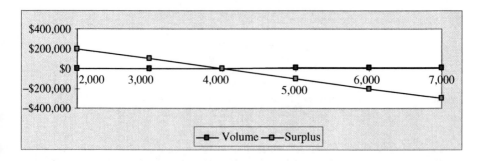

EXHIBIT 50.9:   SURPLUS-VOLUME (S-V) CHART—VARIABLE AND FIXED REVENUE (CASE 2)

EXAMPLE 50.14

In Example 50.13, suppose that the manager does not reduce the number of clients served despite a budget cut of 10 percent. All other things remain unchanged. How much more does the manager have to charge clients for board and care?

Let v = board and care charge per year and x = 4,000 = number of clients served.

The following formula can be used to make this determination:

$$R = \$1,080,000 + 4,000p$$

$$VC + FC = \$700(4,000) + \$800,000$$

$$R + VC + FC$$

$$\$1,080,000 + 4,000p = \$700(4,000) + \$800,000$$

$$4,000p = \$2,800,000 + \$800,000 - 1,080,000$$

$$4,000p = \$2,520,000$$

$$p = \$630$$

Thus, the monthly board and care charge must be increased to $630.

50.8 PROGRAM MIX ANALYSIS

Previously, our main concern was to determine program-specific break-even volume. However, most nonprofit organizations are involved in multiservice, multiprogram activities. One major concern is how to plan aggregate break-even volume, surplus, and deficits. Break-even and Cost-Volume-Revenue analysis requires additional computations and assumptions when an organization offers more than one program. In multiprogram organizations, program mix is an important factor in calculating an overall break-even point. Different rates and different variable costs result in different unit CMs. As a result, break-even points and Cost-Volume-Revenue relationships vary with the relative proportions of the programs offered.

By defining the product as a package, the multiprogram problem is converted into a single-program problem. The first step is to determine the number of packages that need to be served to break even. The following example illustrates a multiprogram, multiservice situation.

EXAMPLE 50.15 (SHEET 1 OF 2)

The Cypress Counseling Services is a nonprofit agency offering two programs: psychological counseling (PC) and alcohol addiction control (AAC). The agency charges individual clients an average of $10 per hour of counseling provided under the PC program. The local Chamber of Commerce reimburses the nonprofit organizations at the rate of $20 per hour of direct service provided under the AAC. The nonprofit organization believes that this billing variable rate is low enough to be affordable for most clients and also high enough to derive clients' commitment to the program objectives. Costs of administering the two programs are given as follows:

	PC	AAC
Variable costs	$ 4.6	$ 11.5
Direct fixed costs	$120,000	$180,000

EXAMPLE 50.15 (SHEET 2 OF 2)

Other fixed costs are common to the two programs, including general, administrative, and fundraising costs of $255,100 per year. The projected surplus for the coming year, segmented by programs, follows.

	PC	AAC	TOTAL
Revenue	$500,000	$800,000	$1,300,000
Program mix in hours	(50,000)	(40,000)	
Less: VC	(230,000)	(460,000)	(690,000)
Contribution margin	$270,000	$340,000	$ 610,000
Less: Direct FC	(120,000)	(180,000)	(300,000)
Program margin	$150,000	$160,000	$ 310,000
Less: Common FC			(255,100)
Surplus			$ 54,900

First, based on program-specific data on the rates, the variable costs, and the program mix, we can compute the package (aggregate) value as follows:

PROGRAM	P	V	UNIT CM	MIX*	PACKAGE CM
PC	$10`	$4.6	$5.4	5	$27
AAC	20	11.5	8.5	4	34
Package total					$61

*The mix ratio is 5:4 (50,000 hours for PC and 40,000 hours for AAC).

We know that the total fixed costs for the agency are $555,100. Thus, the package (aggregate) break-even point is:

$$\$555,100/\$61 = 9,100 \text{ packages}$$

The company must provide 45,500 hours of PC (5 × 9,100) and 36,400 hours of AAC (4 × 9,100) to avoid a deficit. To prove,

	PC	AAC	TOTAL
Revenue	$ 455,000(a)	$ 728,000(b)	$1,183,000
Program mix in hours	(45,500)	(36,400)	
Less: VC	(209,300)(c)	(418,600)(d)	(627,900)
Contribution margin	$ 245,700	$ 309,400	$ 555,100
Less: Direct FC	(120,000)	(180,000)	(300,000)
Program margin	$ 125,700	$ 129,400	$ 255,100
Less: Common FC			(255,100)
Surplus			$ 0

(a) 45,500 × $10   (c) 45,500 × $4.60
(b) 36,400 × $20   (d) 36,400 × $11.50

EXAMPLE 50.16

Assume in Example 50.15 that 56,000 hours of PC services are budgeted for the next period. The nonprofit organization wants to know how many hours of AAC services are necessary during that period to avoid an overall deficit. The answer is 29,729 hours, shown as follows:

INPUT DATA	PC	AAC
Rates	$ 10	$ 20
Units of service (Hours)	56,000	29,729
Variable cost per unit	$ 4.6	$ 11.5

CONTRIBUTION STATEMENT OF SURPLUS OR DEFICIT

	PC	AAC	TOTAL
Revenue	$560,000	$594,588	$1,154,588
Less: Variable costs	257,600	341,888	599,488
Contribution margin	$302,400	$252,700	$ 555,100
Less: Direct fixed costs	120,000	180,000	300,000
Program margin	$182,400	$72,700	$ 255,100
Less: Common fixed costs			255,100
Surplus			$ (0)

50.9 MANAGEMENT OPTIONS

Cost-Volume-Revenue analysis is useful as a frame of reference, as a vehicle for expressing overall managerial performance, and as a planning device via break-even techniques and what-if scenarios. Using CVR, many planning decisions, such as adding or dropping a service, outsourcing, answering special requests, and changing budget limits can be made on a sounder basis.

In many practical situations, management will have to resort to a combination of approaches to reverse a deficit, including

- Selected changes in volume of activity
- Planned savings in fixed costs at all levels
- Some savings in variable costs
- Additional fund drives or grant seeking
- Upward adjustments in pricing
- Cost reimbursement contracts

All of these must be mixed to form a feasible planning package. Many nonprofit managers fail to develop such analytical approaches to the economics of their operations. Further, the accounting system is not designed to provide the information needed to investigate Cost-Volume-Revenue relations.

50.10 REFERENCES AND SUGGESTED READINGS

Shim, Jae K., *Cost Accounting for Managers: A Managerial Emphasis,* 6th ed. (California: Delta Publishing, 2006).

Siegel, Joel and Shim, Jae K., *Barron's Accounting Handbook* (New York: Barron's, 2005).

INDEX